The John Dewey Lecture

The John Dewey Lecture has been delivered annually since 1958 under the sponsorship of the John Dewey Society. The intention of the series is to provide a setting where able thinkers from various sectors of our intellectual life can direct their most searching thoughts to problems that involve the relation of education to culture. Arrangements for the presentation of the Lecture and its publication by Teachers College Press are under the direction of Daniel Tanner, Chairperson.

RECENT TITLES IN THE SERIES

Learning Power:
Organizing for Education and Justice
Jeannie Oakes and John Rogers
with Martin Lipton

Cultural Miseducation:
In Search of a Democratic Solution
Jane Roland Martin

John Dewey and the Philosopher's Task
Philip W. Jackson

In Praise of Education
John I. Goodlad

Cultural Politics and Education
Michael W. Apple

Education for Intelligent Belief or Unbelief
Nel Noddings

The Dialectic of Freedom
Maxine Greene

Learning Power

Organizing for
Education and Justice

JEANNIE OAKES and JOHN ROGERS

with

MARTIN LIPTON

Teachers College
Columbia University
New York and London

Published by Teachers College Press, 1234 Amsterdam Avenue, New York, NY 10027

All photos by Martin Lipton.

Library of Congress Cataloging-in-Publication Data

Oakes, Jeannie.
    Learning power : social inquiry, grassroots organizing, and educational justice / Jeannie Oakes & John Rogers, with Martin Lipton
        p.   cm. — (The John Dewey lecture)
    Includes bibliographical references and index.
    ISBN-13: 978-0-8077-4703-2 (cloth : alk. paper)
    ISBN-13: 978-0-8077-4702-5 (pbk. : alk. paper)
    ISBN-10: 0-8077-4703-3 (cloth : alk. paper)
    ISBN-10: 0-8077-4702-5 (pbk. : alk. paper)
        1. Educational equalization—United States.   2. Social justice—Study and teaching—United States.   I. Rogers, John, 1961 Aug. 20–   II. Lipton, Martin, 1942–   III. Title.   IV. John Dewey lecture (Teachers College Press)
    LC213.2.O25   2006
    378.2'6—dc22   2005055977

ISBN-13:   ISBN-10:
978-0-8077-4702-5 (paper)   0-8077-4702-5 (paper)
978-0-8077-4703-2 (cloth)   0-8077-4703-3 (cloth)

Printed on acid-free paper
Manufactured in the United States of America

13   12   11   10   09   08   07   06   8   7   6   5   4   3   2   1

Contents

Acknowledgments

WE OWE an enormous debt of gratitude to many colleagues, students, community partners, and funders who, over the past several years, have contributed to and supported the thinking, activities, and research that we share in this book. Our research group at UCLA's Institute for Democracy, Education, and Access (IDEA) has been pivotal, providing us a community with which to explore the connections among research, activism, and educational justice. An extraordinary team of faculty, staff, postdoctoral fellows, Ph.D. students, and undergraduates has brought together theoretical frameworks, created social design experiments, and carried out the daily work of programmatic activities, data collection, and analyses that ground our writing.

Our UCLA faculty colleagues Ernest Morrell, Danny Solórzano, Megan Franke, and Gary Blasi have been particularly influential on our thinking and the projects we describe in this book. Ernest and Danny have provided us with a model and vision of what it means to engage young people in critical research; Megan has helped us see the powerful connections between learning theory and social justice; and Gary has served as our bridge between the worlds of law, schooling, and grassroots organizing.

Several of IDEA's postdoctoral scholars and Ph.D. students have conducted their own research as part of our projects, and we have drawn heavily on their work. The dissertation research of Tony Collatos and Susan Auerbach was essential to our understanding of the Futures Project, reported in Chapter 4, as were extraordinarily helpful studies by Marisa Saunders, Irene Serna, Makeba Jones, and Susan Yonezawa. The dissertation research of Karina Otoya and postdoctoral research of Jeff Duncan-Andrade contributed enormously to the critical inquiry and research with teachers that we describe in Chapter 5. Michelle Renee's dissertation research broadened and deepened our understanding of grassroots organizing for education equity, which we describe in Chapter 6. Laila Hasan's groundbreaking efforts to enact and study radical forms of parent engagement underlie our discussion of parent activism in Chapter 7. Julie Flapan and Rocio Cordoba have worked alongside us and Gary Blasi on the Educational Justice Collaborative Project described in Chapter 8, infusing the initiative with an energetic combination of scholarship, relationship building, and communications savvy. This project has been sustained through the invaluable research of Ph.D. students Noah DeLissovoy, Joanna Goode, Jamy Stillman, Veronica Terriquez, and Siomara Valladares.

UCLA undergraduates Magaly Zapien, Yvonne Ballesteros, Maribel Santiago, Nancy Sanchez, Jessie Castro, and Cinthya Felix have supported each of our projects in a variety of ways, including providing us with inspiring daily reminders of the remarkable intellectual and social contributions that result when young people of color have access to high-quality schooling.

IDEA colleagues Jerchel Anderson, Jared Planas, Nery Orellana, Solange Belcher, Claude Potts, Christine Senteno, and Claudia Viscarra-Barton provided the administrative, technical, and communications infrastructure on which all of the projects depend. Other IDEA researchers—Karen Hunter Quartz, Jane Margolis, Jennifer Jellison Holme, and David Silver—helped to create a wonderful intellectual environment that keeps issues of democracy and justice at the core of our work.

Several IDEA colleagues also helped with preparation of the manuscript. Carolyn Castelli, Michelle Renee, Siomara Valladeres, and Lauren Wells were stalwart in their editing, fact checking, and hunting down of references. Their good cheer enlivened us all.

We have also been very fortunate to have colleagues and friends outside of UCLA whose scholarship has made us think and rethink our work. Among these are Kevin Welner, Amy Stuart Wells, Jennifer Gong, Bud Mehan, Joe Kahne, Dennis Shirley, Mark Warren, Jean Anyon, Andy Hargreaves, Norm Fruchter, Kavitha Mediratta, Pauline Lipman, Linda Darling-Hammond, and Pedro Noguera, to name just a few.

None of this work would have been possible without generous funders. Over the years, our IDEA projects have been supported by the Atlantic Philanthropies, the Ford Foundation, the Bill and Melinda Gates Foundation, the John Randolph Haynes and Dora Haynes Foundation, the William and Flora Hewlett Foundation, Lumina Foundation, the Rockefeller Foundation, the Charles Stewart Mott Foundation, Edison International, and the Stuart Foundation. The University of California's All Campus Consortium of Research on Diversity and UCLA's Chancellor also provided essential support along the way. Of course, none of them should be held responsible for the ideas we express here, only for helping us create them.

Our families have sustained our work and lifted our spirits. Sharla Fett offers daily encouragement and the inspiring model of her own writing. Ella and Jacob Rogers-Fett provide an instant energy boost and a constant reminder of the power of learning. The Oakes/Lipton grandchildren and their parents add much-needed hugs, bits of wisdom, and very funny stories.

Finally, we must express our enormous appreciation to the wonderful people who have partnered with our IDEA team in the work we describe here. Many are named in the book, though some we cannot acknowledge by name because we have promised confidentiality. The students in Futures continue to amaze us with their intellectual development and with their unflagging commitment to their communities and to social justice. To a person, they have become wonderful young adults. The teachers we have worked with inspire us with their commitment to young people and the power of learning—even as they daily confront poor school conditions and undemocratic school policies. The members of Parent U-Turn have surpassed our wildest imagining about what is possible when parents arm themselves with knowledge and power. Doing so, they have reinvigorated our democratic commitments. Lastly, we must thank the civil rights attorneys, community organizers, and hundreds of young people and adults engaged in the advocacy and grassroots groups that participate in the Educational Justice Collaborative. That they have trusted us to share their hard work, struggles, and commitment to a more decent world is a high and humbling honor. We hope we have done them justice.

Prologue

Learning Power

Los Angeles Times

Wednesday, May 21, 2003

Schools See 'an Awakening' of Student Activism

By Erika Hayasaki,
Los Angeles Times Staff Writer

Roosevelt High School's newly appointed principal, Cecilia Quemada, had barely been on the job for a month when a group of student activists approached her with a list of requests last October.

The teenagers, who are members of an organization called Youth Organizing Communities, spoke passionately about improving education for the 5,100 students who attend the severely overcrowded campus on Los Angeles' Eastside. The school is notorious for low test scores, and in 2001 it was one of 13 schools in California, and 10 in Los Angeles Unified, targeted for reform by the state.

The students wanted more information on college preparatory courses and graduation requirements, improved academic counseling and culturally relevant social studies classes emphasizing the history of Latinos, who make up the majority of the student body.

"The administration was making all of these rules we had to follow, but we didn't really know what was going on," said Rene Martinez, 16, a Roosevelt student. "It wasn't fair, so we decided we had to do something about it."

Quemada had been charged with the task of revitalizing the campus, after the controversial decision by the state and district to remove the previous principal, Henry Ronquillo. She was put off, at first, by the students' collective determination.

"I was really uneasy about it," she said. "That whole activism thing, you know, that can work in reverse sometimes."

Quemada didn't want to be pushed around, but she also didn't want to ignore the concerns of students. So she met with them and eventually agreed to some of their ideas. Within a few months, some of the students' wishes were met.

The school's tardy room was closed after the group complained that it was a waste of instructional time for students. Instead, tardy students remain in class

1

and receive alternative punishment, such as after-school detention, as well as counseling.

Quemada agreed to add two Mexican American studies classes to the course list, hire three more guidance counselors and include mandatory counseling about graduation course requirements during homeroom.

"Here was a group that wanted to be in the loop, and I thought, 'Why not make something positive out of that?'" Quemada said.

Youth Organizing Communities, which has more than 50 student members at Roosevelt, formed three years ago as an outgrowth of a statewide movement against Proposition 21, a measure that allowed prosecutors to decide whether juveniles ages 14 to 17 who are charged with murder or sex crimes should be tried as adults. Proposition 21 passed in March 2000, but the Los Angeles students who participated in the statewide movement wanted to take their activism back to their campuses.

The student organization is sponsored and funded by Inner City Struggle, an East Los Angeles community action organization supported by private and public grants and donations. Youth Organizing Communities started its second chapter at Garfield High School recently.

Youth Organizing Communities is one of a handful of youth activist organizations in Los Angeles that have emerged over the last several years to advocate for better conditions in their schools. For example, South Central Youth Empowered Through Action, a similar coalition of students, has been seeking more Advanced Placement courses on such campuses as Fremont, Locke and Manual Arts.

The Eastside students meet three to four times a week during lunch, after school or on weekends, either on campus or at Inner City Struggle's one-room office on Whittier Boulevard.

They discuss problems in their schools such as unsafe learning environments, too few bathrooms, overcrowding and not enough books. They also receive tutoring and mentoring from college counselors who volunteer their time.

"This provides a safe place for you to come and voice your opinion and know you can make a change," said Nancy Meza, 15, a Garfield student.

One of the group's recent campaigns was called Educational Justice Week, which took place in February. Students took to campuses to talk to their classmates about economic and educational inequality, and to make them aware of the classes required for high school graduation and college admittance.

The students involved are "working with the administration to create policies that support students. And that's a large step forward," said Lester Garcia, 20, who helped form the group when he was a student at Roosevelt and who now, while attending Cal State Long Beach, is the youth organizer for Inner City Struggle.

Many teachers at Roosevelt say they are impressed by the hard work of the students.

Aldo Parral, a history teacher at the school, said students involved with the group are "more confident and empowered, whereas, in the past, they let the system overrun them."

The group's advisor, Javier Cid, also a history teacher, said the group "is more than just a club, it's a movement, an awakening."

Los Angeles Unified school board member Jose Huizar and state Sen. Gil Cedillo (D–Los Angeles) recently sponsored a community fund-raiser for Inner City Struggle and Youth Organizing Communities, raising $5,000.

"I was very impressed with their knowledge of the educational system, and their real identifications of the inequities in our school system," Huizar said. "I found them advocating for some of the very same issues I was advocating for on the board of education."

Now, group members say they want to see similar improvements at Garfield, Wilson and Lincoln high schools.[1]

ROOSEVELT HIGH SCHOOL history teacher Javier Cid got it exactly right: InnerCity Struggle (ICS) "is more than just a club, it's a movement, an awakening." ICS is about learning and about power. Its members believe both are necessary to bring high-quality schooling to their working-class Latino neighborhood.

Maria Brenes, a lead organizer at ICS, knows about the relationship between learning and power. A graduate of the University of California Berkeley and Harvard, Brenes was barred as a youth from her school on the American side of the California–Mexico border. Only a grassroots campaign and lawsuit secured her admission. This incident politicized her and gave her a new understanding of "education as a vehicle for social change" and of the "possibilities of education building the leadership capacity of young people of color to be community change agents." For Brenes, "it is essential that students learn the necessary conceptual and practical skills to create community and justice."[2] That learning, and those skills, add up to power for change.

Under the tutelage of Maria Brenes and other leaders, ICS youth Rene Martinez, Nancy Meza, and now more than 300 other student members at three high schools are *learning power* as they seek to remedy the problems that afflict their schools. And they are learning power in multiple ways.

First, the young people of ICS are *learning about power* in American society and about where and with whom the power over their education and futures resides. In their meetings on campus and at the ICS office, youth learn to construct "power maps"—a tried-and-true strategy of social movement organizations. They identify who has the power to grant or deny their demands as they campaign for better schools. Depending on the particular issue (more college prep classes, more counselors, a new school building, an end to military recruitment on their campus, etc.), the power map might include teachers, district and city officials, corporate leaders, state and federal elected policymakers, and more. The students place the power holders on a continuum according to how likely each is to say "yes" or "no." The students trace the relationships among the power holders and, in turn, their relationships with other individuals and groups that could influence them. ICS members try to figure out how sympathetic these potentially influential "allies" might be by examining their public statements and prior actions.

The young people of ICS are exploring the *power of learning*. They produce knowledge and use it to effect change. They use participatory research to identify and understand causes of the most pressing problems facing students at their schools. For example, in the spring of 2002, ICS members at Roosevelt High School surveyed the views of 754 of their classmates regarding school discipline policies, culturally relevant curriculum, and students' access to information about course requirements for college. They analyzed the data, together with other information about the school's dismal graduation and college eligibility rates, and distributed their findings and recommendations to educational leaders and key community decision makers. They also incorporated what they had learned into popular education workshops for youth and family members in order to raise consciousness and build support. These activities created leverage for change by making school policies the subject of schoolwide discussion; they also enhanced the academic skills of the ICS participants.

ICS members are *learning to be powerful* in the sense that they are learning how to build and demonstrate the power of collective action. They inventory their current resources, do strategic planning to identify long- and short-term goals, establish timelines, and select the tactics that will communicate their power to those who can act on their demands. They ask, What would make it easy for decision makers to say "yes"? What would make it difficult for them to say "no"? They marshal large numbers of supporters in petition drives, phone or e-mail "jams," and marches; they get their story out via media or public testimony; they disrupt business as usual.

ICS members create strategic alliances with other groups that share their goals, thereby increasing their own influence. In the spring of 2005, ICS joined a coalition of about 20 Southern California groups to make California's college preparatory course requirements the standard curriculum for all high school students in Los Angeles. The coalition—Communities for Educational Equity (CEE)—included such disparate allies as the United Way of Los Angeles; Community Asset Development Re-defining Education (CADRE), a small multiracial group of activist parents in South Los Angeles; and Jose Huizar, the president of the Los Angeles Unified School District Board of Education. This broad-based alliance used grassroots organizing, community educational forums, media strategies, and marches and rallies. Hundreds of people showed up in front of the Board of Education offices in the summer of 2005 to cap a win for the right of all students to choose a college pathway.

ICS and the CEE have since partnered with the Los Angeles teachers union and district officials to make sure this victory is implemented well. New demands include the school conditions, resources, and support that students need to make effective use of a college preparatory curriculum.

ICS also allied with the speaker of the California Assembly, Fabian Núñez, and the Latino Legislative Caucus. Knowing that local victories are not enough to ensure college opportunities, ICS wants a say in state policies on admissions and financial aid. At a recent public event, Núñez acknowledged the vital role of ICS in school reform: "Your commitment to empowering students and parents has served as a catalyst for social change and educational equity."[3] He pledged to continue working with ICS to achieve educational justice in California.

The young people in ICS, along with adult activists, are developing the skills of civic participation—inquiry, organizing, and action. These skills will meet their personal needs for negotiating productive careers and lives, and will

California Assembly Speaker Fabian Núñez commending InnerCity Struggle's work as Maria Brenes and ICS Executive Director Luis Sanchez look on.

serve them well as they act as agents for creating quality schools and a robust democratic public.

The theory and evidence we offer in this book emerged from the work of young people, teachers, parents, and activists who, like ICS, use inquiry and organizing in their quest for educational justice. However, we did not come to our understanding of *learning power* by merely observing groups like ICS.

Over the last several years, the center we created—UCLA's Institute for Democracy, Education, and Access (IDEA)—has partnered with students, parents, teachers, and grassroots groups to learn about and promote a different approach to educational change. We have sought to carve out a unique researcher role for ourselves in these partnerships, providing data and analyses in response to specific questions posed by the groups; offering insights from previous research; sharing our knowledge of research methods; and forging connections among members of grassroots groups, reporters, researchers, and policy makers.

Engaging with young people and parents who experience educational inequality on a daily basis has made us less tolerant of reform methods that promise little difference and of research strategies that distance scholars from those who live the problems they study. Our partners impress upon us, with great moral and intellectual clarity, the dramatic inequality in our public schools. This inequality calls for radical change through radical means. With this in mind, we offer *Learning Power* as a new and compelling framework for urban school reform.

1

Unjust Schools

THE HISTORY of United States education is a remarkable tale of expanding schooling opportunities. It is also a story of clear and consistent advantages for White and wealthier Americans and disadvantages for low-income students of color. In the 19th century, Horace Mann believed that once common public schools were established, no evil could resist their salutary influence.[1] For Mann, universal schooling was to be the "great equalizer" of human conditions, the "balance wheel of the social machinery," and the "creator of wealth undreamed of." Poverty was certain to disappear, and with it the age-old discord between the "haves" and the "have-nots."[2] Horace Mann envisioned public schools as places where students of all backgrounds come together to share fair and equal opportunities for success in the educational system and, as a consequence, fair and equal life chances. The benefits would extend far beyond individuals and would advance democratic citizenship.

That, of course, was also the goal of the NAACP's legal strategy that led to *Brown v. Board of Education*, 50 years ago. The *Brown* case made clear that, despite Mann's compelling and extraordinarily popular rhetoric, America provided separate and very unequal educational opportunities to children who differed along lines of race. Contrary to Mann's vision, schools had not become "great equalizers." But the ruling in *Brown* was meant to change all that.

> In these days, it is doubtful that any child may reasonably be expected to succeed in life if he is denied the opportunity of an education. Such an opportunity, where the state has undertaken to provide it, is a right which must be made available to all on equal terms.[3]

The ruling that *de jure* segregation was unconstitutional was an accomplishment of great importance. Yet, only a few days after the *Brown* decision, W. E. B. Du Bois made a sobering and accurate observation about the decision and the future, "Great as is this victory, many and long steps on Freedom Road lie ahead."[4]

7

STILL SEPARATE AND STILL UNEQUAL

As we know too well, education "on equal terms" has not been achieved. In the decade following *Brown*, desegregation was met with foot-dragging at best and, at worst, with outright hostility and violence. Some progress was made by the early 1970s in eliminating dual school systems, particularly in the South. But even as some districts developed desegregation plans, school administrators and White parents often were quick to create separate course tracks that ensured that diverse groups of students attending the same campus were not enrolled in the same classes. Further, much of the progress that was made toward desegregation in the 1970s and early 1980s has since been reversed by the courts, federal and state policy, and education leadership—all of which have moved away from addressing segregation in its many forms. Today, the retreat of the courts, together with highly segregated residential patterns, means that African American and Latino students in most parts of the country attend public schools that are as racially segregated as they were before *Brown*.[5]

Efforts to equalize racially segregated schools through fiscal equity lawsuits have not fared much better. Politically powerful communities in many states, dubbing rulings that states must develop more equitable school funding systems as "Robin Hood" tactics, have made the development or successful implementation of such plans practically impossible. Multicultural and bilingual education reforms have often been implemented in flawed or superficial ways or, as in the case of California's 1999 "English for the Children" ballot measure outlawing bilingual education, have been halted altogether. As a result, racial inequalities persist in funding and in access to decent school facilities, qualified teachers, culturally and linguistically responsive curricula, and college preparatory programs. Gaps in schooling outcomes remain, not only in test scores but also in attainments that affect life chances, such as high school and college graduation.

California provides a powerfully discouraging example. In the mid-20th century, California's schools were the envy of the nation. The state boasted one of the nation's highest per-pupil spending rates, a surplus of qualified teachers, modern and well-kept facilities in most communities, and rising rates of high school graduation and college-going. Today, 30 years after a "successful" fiscal equity suit in the 1970s, *Serrano v. Priest*, the quality of California's schools has declined precipitously and inequities remain. California has fallen to 49th among all of the states in the number of students for every teacher and counselor, and it is last in the number of students for every librarian.[6] African American and Latino students are far more likely to attend schools with fewer opportunities to learn—schools with shortages of qualified teachers, fewer classes that count for college preparation, and overcrowded facilities. Put bluntly, California is unable to educate fully and fairly all its school children, and the growing population of African American and Latino children bear the brunt of the state's terrible schooling inadequacies.

Schools That Shock the Conscience

Washington Middle School, located in the center of one of California's large cities, provides a clear portrait of this inequality. In 2002, Washington enrolled 2,025 11- to 14-year-olds. Forty-two percent of the students were African American, 57% were Latino; 32% were still learning English; and 77% were from low-income families. These young adolescents faced extraordinary learning barriers at Washington, including a dire shortage of qualified teachers, abysmal teaching and learning conditions, a lack of the most basic instructional materials, and an appalling disregard of basic safeguards for the students' health and safety.[7]

Only 43% of Washington's teachers were fully certified by the state, and many of those were teaching outside the subjects for which they were certified. Some were woefully underprepared. One teacher, assigned to a "sheltered" class, had thought initially that the class "was for foster care students from homeless shelters"; she had no idea that "sheltered" instruction is a specialized teaching strategy used with English learners. In many classrooms, long-term substitutes filled empty teaching positions, and a succession of day-to-day substitutes filled others. The substitutes, in particular, often simply let the students play or watch movies.

There were not enough books at Washington for students to take home to do homework. English learners had nothing at school to read in their home languages. Science classrooms had no running water, lab tables, or supplies. Math classes provided no calculators (even though the state's math standards require them). In at least one math class, students spent time making their own graph paper. Some English classes had no dictionaries, thesauruses, or reference materials. Many social studies classes had no globes, and the atlases were falling apart. In one class, students had a map only because their uncertified teacher's supervisor "felt sorry" for them.

Teachers, who had too few and out-of-date textbooks for their average student load of 175, were limited to 150 photocopies a day and 500 sheets of copy paper a month. One of the school's two photocopying machines had been broken for nearly a year.

The school, designed for 20% fewer students and lacking adequate janitorial and maintenance services, was overcrowded, trash littered, dilapidated, and unappealing. Teachers "roved" between classrooms, carrying their supplies in all manner of conveyances, and some taught in spaces never intended to be classrooms. One science class was far too cramped for hands-on experiments, even if the supplies were available. The heaters in some rooms got so hot that they burned students who touched them, and the overcrowding meant that some desks had to be placed within arm's reach.

All 2,025 students ate lunch at the same time in an outside space with seats for about 500. Students said they often felt unsafe during the lunchtime chaos, and frequently there was not enough time to get through the food line. The water fountains were filthy, and many did not work at all. The playground equipment consisted of a few basketball hoops without nets.

Schools like Washington are found in poor, urban communities across California and the United States. Students at schools in mostly White, middle-class suburbs experience few, if any, of these problems.

We see the stark inequalities in the map shown in Figure 1.1. Each of the dots on the map marks the location of a Los Angeles area high school. The background shading of the map shows the racial composition of the neighborhoods in which the schools are located—the lighter the background, the greater the percentage of African American and Latino residents. The color and size of the dots indicate whether or not the school has serious limitations on the resources and opportunities it can provide to students—that is, whether more than 20% of its teachers lack full certification, if fewer than two thirds of its classes "count" toward students' preparation for college,[8] or if its facilities are so overcrowded that it cannot provide the standard number of school days for its students. On the map, schools with none of these problems are marked with a white dot. Schools with serious problems are marked with a black dot. The size of the black dot indicates whether the school has one, two, or all three of the problems. The map shows clearly that Los Angeles area schools serving large numbers of students of color tend to be the most in need of qualified teachers, the most deficient in college access courses, and the most crowded. The sobering reality is that 50 years after *Brown* and after decades of school reform, schools remain both separate *and* unequal.

Williams v. State of California

In 2000, some angry Californians joined together to ask the courts to remedy the inequities that many years of school "reforms" had left untouched and arguably had made worse. A group of young people and their parents filed suit in the California Superior Court in San Francisco on May 17, 2000, the 46th anniversary of the *Brown v. Board of Education* Supreme Court decision. Their case carried the name of Eliezer Williams, a student at a San Francisco middle school with many of the same problems as Washington. Nearly all of the 48 student plaintiffs named in the case were African American, Latino, or Asian Pacific Islander, and they all attended predominantly non-White schools. Most of their classmates qualified for free or reduced-price meals, and many were still learning English. The named plaintiffs represented a class of more than a million California students who experienced similar school conditions. On their behalf, Williams and the other plaintiffs sued California's Governor, the State Board of Education, and the State Superintendent of Public Instruction.

The *Williams* plaintiffs claimed that they, and many other California students like them, attend "schools that shock the conscience." These were schools

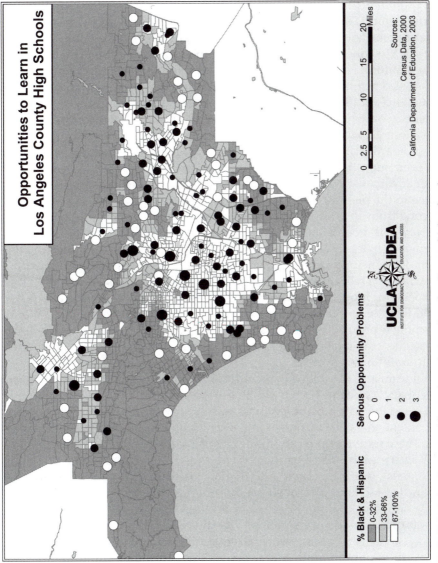

FIGURE 1.1. Opportunities to learn in Los Angeles County high schools.

with conditions so poor that no academic, or lawyer, or politician would want his or her own child to step foot inside them. In the words of the complaint, these schools lacked "trained teachers, necessary educational supplies, classrooms, even seats in classrooms, and facilities that meet basic health and safety standards."[9]

The plaintiffs argued that, by permitting such schools, California's educational system failed to meet its constitutional obligation to educate all students and to educate them equally. It is important to note here that according to the California state constitution, education is a fundamental right. California law also requires basic educational equality—that is, the state must provide all students with the essential elements of schooling that it provides to most students. Consequently, the *Williams* plaintiffs claimed that there is a constitutional floor below which no child's education should fall. They also argued that "substandard" schools are disproportionately attended by low-income African American and Latino students.

For a year and a half, we were part of a research team that examined evidence related to the plaintiffs' claims.[10] We studied the state's education policies and the conditions in California schools. We found ample evidence that not only were teachers, books, and facilities in short supply in California, but they were systematically less available to low-income students of color. Further, the different deficiencies (teachers or materials or facilities) were clustered in particular schools; a school experiencing one of the problems was much more likely to experience more or all of them, compounding their deleterious effects. We found that the problems were so widespread that they could not be seen only as "school problems" or even "district problems". Instead, the evidence pointed to systemic, state-level problems that schools and districts could not be expected to surmount on their own.

Our team also concluded that California state policy could and should guarantee that all students have basic educational resources and conditions. Only then could the state provide all students with a reasonable opportunity to learn the content and skills identified in the state's standards and to pass the state's tests. These resources and conditions include, at the very least, those named by the *Williams* plaintiffs—qualified teachers (as defined by the state's teaching credentials), sufficient standards-aligned instructional materials, and safe, uncrowded facilities. Although we did not argue that the mere presence of teachers, books, and decent school buildings would *guarantee* high-quality schools or high student achievement, we did contend that, without these conditions, students faced unreasonable educational barriers.

The group of experts hired by the state did not dispute the plaintiffs' charge that California schools lacked basic resources or that the system failed to provide those resources equally. They did not dispute that few California children in privileged neighborhoods suffered the conditions in the plaintiffs' schools. Instead, they argued, using econometric analysis, that providing more teachers, materials, and adequate facilities would be unlikely to increase the plaintiff students' test scores, and that this is what matters most. In other words, because test scores are the only readily measurable output of the education system, additional expenditures on educational inputs like teachers, textbooks, and facilities can only be justified if they are statistically correlated to increases in test scores.

The state's experts also argued that California's test-based accountability system—which they judged to be first-rate—provides incentives that motivate individuals to improve. This system, they reasoned, promised to create far more school improvement than providing all children with qualified teachers, appropriate materials, and adequate facilities. In essence, they answered the plaintiffs' broad plea for education on "equal terms" with a narrow technical argument about increasing test scores and with disparaging judgments about the needs and motivations of the plaintiffs, their families, and their communities.

The *Williams* case is important to the story we tell in this book. The findings of the plaintiffs' experts reveal that inequity pervades the most basic elements of the educational system. The arguments of the state show that merely documenting inequality will not, in and of itself, lead to more adequate and equitable schooling. Straightforward and obvious claims of injustice can be transformed, in the hands of lawyers, researchers, and policymakers, into highly technical disputes about statistical methods or esoteric debates about motivational theories. Scientific and technical arguments have a limited capacity to resolve matters that reach so deeply into cultural values and political contention. Indeed, as we explain in Chapter 8, the state's ultimate willingness to acknowledge the injustice of its educational system and settle *Williams* turned more on the political power of grassroots advocacy groups than on any findings of fact.

Inequality—Cultural and Political, as Well as Technical

In 1954, as the Warren Court ruled against the constitutionality of laws segregating schoolchildren by race, it declared that education must be made available to all "on equal terms." In addition to overturning the 1896 *Plessy* decision allowing separate-but-equal facilities, *Brown*'s unambiguous assertion of human rights, carrying with it the full authority and power of a unanimous Supreme Court, spoke symbolically to cultural and political equality as well as to the promise of education on "equal terms." Most significantly, it challenged an earlier court's view of who merits full consideration before the law. W. E. B. Du Bois observed, "100 years before [*Brown*] another chief justice declared [in *Dred Scott*] that Negroes had no rights which a white man must respect."[11] *Brown* rejected that judgment, and it revived the promise laid out in the Constitution's 14th and 15th Amendments of full citizenship for all.

Despite the broad cultural and political sweep of the *Brown* decision, three fundamental assumptions have dominated efforts over the past decades to realize its promise. The first is that equality can be achieved by working exclusively within the educational system. The second is that inequalities within the educational system are sustained by ignorance (or inadequate technologies) rather than by deep cultural beliefs and assumptions about race. The third, following from the first two, is that once educators are provided with knowledge and techniques for disrupting schooling inequality, salutary change will occur. These assumptions are grounded on the premise that, rather than reflecting the core of American society, racist practices are at odds with basic American values, and therefore Americans will, if given the opportunity, naturally move away from such practices.

Research over the past two decades on efforts to desegregate schools and to equalize funding among them illuminates the inadequacy of these assumptions and the corresponding reform approaches that have dominated the nation's equity efforts. That work reveals that when experts are asked to design and implement desegregation remedies, fiscal equity legislation, and compensatory education programs, they respond as if these are primarily technical challenges. Most education professionals, for example, have been trained in a professional milieu in which changes in schools take their guidance from traditional research, development, and diffusion approaches to innovation in business and industry. That is, professional reformers have focused their attention on the technical dimensions of the challenge and have responded by creating rules, structures, practices, and programs. Thus, they have developed student assignment plans (and transportation services) that achieve racial balance among schools and classes within schools, allocation formulas that reduce between-district funding disparities, training protocols in "human relations," supplemental academic programs, and so forth.

Similar insights emerge from research into efforts to eliminate racial disparities within schools, including "detracking" initiatives seeking to increase the access of students of color to high-quality and equitable teaching and learning. Here, too, we find that reformers have focused their efforts on developing structures and pedagogies that "work" in heterogeneous classes. Yet, the most formidable barriers reside less in the technical challenges of designing equitable schools, and more in the cultural norms about race, merit, and schooling that underlie the status quo and, for so many people, make specific equity reforms so difficult to accept. Equity reforms are often cut short by political struggles for comparative advantage, as middle- and upper-class parents seek to ensure that their children have the same absolute and relative social and economic privileges that they enjoy. The intractability of these norms and politics cannot be understood, let alone altered, absent consideration of the larger social, economic, and political milieu in which current inequalities between and within schools seem so sensible to so many of those who are privileged currently.

A technical approach to equity reform falls short of achieving education "on equal terms" because privilege and exclusion are not discrete problems that result from ignorance, but rather ideologies that are endemic to the logic of much of the educational system. Efforts to redress policies and strategies that sustain privilege and exclusion often encounter powerful interest groups. That is, it is not a matter of the better argument prevailing when the better (more egalitarian) argument runs headfirst into political force to sustain the status quo. Further, so-called egalitarian strategies are implemented unevenly. Because efforts to improve less privileged schools are often half-hearted and underfunded, and reform in privileged schools is typically sustained and more generous, technical "school improvement" often means more inequality. Hence, strategies designed to address gaps in opportunities and attainment often allow more privileged schools to increase their advantages. We have concluded, therefore, that the disparities we find among schools and within schools are at least as much a cultural and political problem as a technical one. And remedying these disparities is a far more complex cultural and political undertaking than researchers, educators, and policymakers assume or have the tools to accomplish.

We are not saying that professional reformers are unaware that eliminating gaps in opportunities and achievement among diverse groups of students is extraordinarily difficult. Neither are we saying that the central problem has been a lack of effort on the part of these reformers. Rather, no matter how hard people work at them, the usual approaches to school reform—technical reforms that change rules, structures, and practices—are simply not efficacious enough to counter the multiple forces that maintain the unequal status quo among and within schools.

Making schools more equitable—or, in Du Bois's words after the *Brown* decision, taking those "long and many steps on Freedom Road"—requires strategies that address the norms and politics of education and, inevitably, of the larger society from which they emanate.[12] That means that, in addition to the technical work of devising more equitable formulas for distributing resources and developing and implementing practices that "work" better for diverse groups of children, equity reformers must also deconstruct the prevailing beliefs and politics that sustain racial and class privilege. They must participate in changing the cultural belief that low-income communities of color want and need less from schools—as exemplified by the "experts" defending California in the *Williams* case who argued that providing more teachers, materials, and adequate facilities would be unlikely to improve the education of plaintiff students. Put bluntly, equity reformers must help alter the politics of educational policymaking that preserve advantages for wealthier and more powerful communities.

The prevailing assumption that racial inequality can be overcome through enlightened educational policy diverts attention from the inextricable connections between separate-and-unequal schooling and the larger separate-and-unequal social, political, and economic conditions that schooling mirrors. Moreover, this analysis is rarely part of the repertoire of the professionals who engage in educational reform. Thus, it is not surprising that education reforms have largely ignored the norms and distribution of power necessary to address inequality. Unfortunately, the neglect of the normative and political has guaranteed failure of the often creative and likely effective technical approaches that well-intentioned, equity-minded professionals have developed and sought to implement.

"STEPS ON FREEDOM ROAD": AN ACTIVIST PUBLIC

For guidance on this problem, we have turned to what may seem an unlikely source—American philosopher John Dewey. John Dewey's later work, in particular his political and educational writings from the 1920s and 1930s, suggests to us that the failure to realize *Brown*'s promise of education "on equal terms" can be attributed, at least in part, to an absence of a robust public sphere. That is, we have lacked what Dewey called the "public intelligence" to confront the dominant cultural norms and politics of privilege that sustain structures of inequality both in and out of school.

John Dewey's analyses of the public's role in establishing progressive social policy argue that realizing *Brown*'s promise demands an informed and energized public. Achieving education on "equal terms" requires all groups to speak on "equal terms" in ways that compel the powerful to account for what they hear.

> There is . . . nothing more radical than insistence upon democratic methods as the means by which radical social changes be effected. . . . Democratic means and the attainment of democratic ends are one and inseparable. . . . The crusade can win at the best but partial victory unless it springs from a living faith in our common human nature and in the power of voluntary action based upon public collective intelligence.[13]

Throughout his career, Dewey believed in the possibilities of a public intelligence advancing progressive social change. Early on, he looked to professional educators to gradually infuse intelligence into the broader political culture. He viewed this strategy as an end run around more confrontational political change. But, during the 1920s, Dewey became disillusioned with this approach as he saw how powerful interests could use mass communication to distort and subvert public understanding. His 1930s writing speaks to how participatory publics must engage public life more directly.

Dewey called for a public sphere in which experts and citizens[14] engage together in participatory social inquiry—in information gathering, exchange, interpretation, and debate. Structures and processes of social inquiry could cultivate a public intelligence about social problems affecting the daily lives of common people in a way that could reveal their causes and point toward viable solutions. Further, participation in inquiry could promote the organization and commitment necessary for those citizens most impacted by social inequality to push forward egalitarian reforms.

Dewey's hope for equality, then, turned on the intellectual capacity and political participation of common citizens. He argued that citizens engaged in public, social inquiry will better connect forms of educational inequality to their social, cultural, and political contexts and account for the ideologies of privilege that sustain those inequalities. More progressive policies can result, in Dewey's view, only from the full "flowering of human capacities" and the power of participatory politics.[15] Dewey did not dismiss expert knowledge entirely. Rather, he sought to forge close relationships between experts and common citizens so that each could inform the other in the process of inquiry. Such inquiry, he argued, creates new and useful systems of knowledge accessible to all. And that is where the promise to complete the project of American democracy rests.

Dewey's work provides considerable hope and guidance as we continue to pursue education "on equal terms" in the years ahead. Social understanding created in the public sphere (Dewey's "public intelligence") would be far more effective than conventional school reform in bringing more equitable policy. Reform strategies emanating from such public engagement could generate both the knowledge and the power needed to confront the dominant cultural norms and the politics of privilege that sustain structures of inequality both in and out of school.

However, Dewey provides little help with the circumstances under which such inquiry might occur, particularly in contemporary society. His 1930s writing offers few insights on how citizens might come together to examine particular instances of inequality or how that inquiry might lead to action and real change.

The kind of citizen engagement Dewey proposed, while antithetical to the technical approach of contemporary reformers, has been advanced in recent years by grassroots and advocacy groups using social movement and organizing strategies to achieve more equitable schooling. Strategies that challenge cultural norms and seek to alter power relationships are the stock and trade of social movements and grassroots organizations. Grassroots and activist organizations, seeking to build the power of low-income communities, engage students, parents, and community members in powerful actions aimed at exposing and disrupting schooling inequalities. These groups routinely target the prejudices and politics that sustain unequal schooling. Because grassroots "reformers" are also those who experience the broad range of social, economic, and political inequality, their centrality in reform forces the connections between education and broader social issues and struggles.

Although professionals must necessarily play a key role in the development and implementation of the technical elements of reform, social activists—students, parents, community members, organizers, and advocates—are far more likely to blaze a timely, effective, and sustainable route to ending educational disparities. Consequently, we propose that contemporary social-movement organizing is both a relevant model for pursuing equitable education and a realistic site for enacting Dewey's theory of a deep and effective public intelligence as the foundation of democracy.

Working as allies, researchers and educators can help such activists to understand the educational landscape, including the social and schooling barriers to equality; marshal evidence that allows grassroots groups to communicate these inequalities; and construct knowledge of what could be done to make schooling more equitable. Organized activists, however, must play a central role in this knowledge construction. And, they are best positioned to take action on this knowledge. Their demands on policymakers and other opinion leaders, and their appeals to the court, build the power to carry the struggle forward.

We have concluded, then, that Dewey's conceptions of social inquiry and social understanding employed in the context of contemporary social-movement and community-organizing strategies provide today's best hope for achieving the promise of *Brown*. Dewey's ideas point toward a model of inquiry-based organizing. They suggest how education researchers, educators, activists, and policymakers can join together in engagement, inquiry, participation, and empowerment. Dewey's emphasis on knowledge and the knowledge construction dimensions of civic participation and empowerment is particularly useful, suggesting that social movement and organizing strategies are most likely to result in equitable, higher quality schooling for all students if democratic learning processes accompany activities focused on building power and taking action.

Dewey's work suggests, for example, that social inquiry, conducted in the context of contemporary social-movement and organizing strategies, has the potential for creating new knowledge that defines high-quality education, merit, and achievement in racially inclusive ways. That knowledge gains power as low-income parents and parents of color participate in social inquiry and become actors in a movement for more equitable schools. Their engagement also helps frame a powerful "story" of parents and communities who want and deserve high-quality education and who know what education can and should be. As such stories take hold in the public consciousness, cultural and political obstacles to equity can be challenged more successfully.

In sum, participatory social inquiry is a process of knowledge construction that aligns research-based knowledge, newly acquired knowledge, and lived experiences. When applied to education equity, such inquiry forges new meanings and understandings about core educational ideas. Social movements rely on these same processes of knowledge construction as they build political power within previously marginalized groups. Realizing the promise of *Brown* undoubtedly requires both new knowledge and new power. As promising as these directions may be, they too face enormous cultural and political barriers. As we elaborate later, the scholarship on social-movement organizing around racial issues and the development of cross-racial movements raises cautions that education equity researchers and advocates should heed.

ELABORATING THE ARGUMENT: SOCIAL INQUIRY AND GRASSROOTS ORGANIZING

We arrived at this argument after years of research on inequitable schooling in the United States. The remainder of this book elaborates and provides concrete examples of the ideas we have introduced in this first chapter:

• The shortcomings of conventional reform strategies to realize *Brown*'s promise;
• Dewey's potential contribution to a new generation of equity strategies;
• Social movement organizing as a means of extending Dewey's ideas in the contemporary context.

In Chapter 2, we demonstrate through the example of a highly regarded high school how conventional approaches to reform offer a severely limited model on which to base efforts to equalize education across or within schools. We describe how this school has maintained its advantages over schools in less affluent communities, despite technical changes aimed at equalizing resources across schools. And we use the considerable research on tracking and detracking to make clear the woeful inadequacy of "technical" changes and change strategies in the face of the powerful norms and politics that sustain inequality within schools.

In Chapter 3, we explain how John Dewey's later work provides a more robust view of equity reform by highlighting the role of knowledge construction and application in the context of public engagement, social inquiry, civic participation, and empowerment. We also introduce our experience in using Dewey's ideas about social inquiry and action as useful and practical guides for respectful, productive, equity-based contemporary efforts with students, teachers, parents, and grassroots organizations. Our research group at UCLA's Institute for Democracy, Education, and Access (IDEA) has come to call these activities "social design experiments."

Chapters 4 and 5 offer two examples of IDEA's social design experiments. One is Futures, an intervention in which we used participatory social inquiry to realize more equitable schooling outcomes for low-income high school students of color. The second is Teaching to Change LA, which illustrates how participatory social inquiry can support teachers' development of more equitable curriculum and pedagogy for low-income students of color.

In Chapter 6, we confront the limitations of the two examples we have described and show how these limitations led us to explore democratic social movements and community organizing for ways that researchers, educators, activists, and policymakers can use social inquiry for policy change. We describe two of these policy-related experiences in Chapters 7 and 8. One is Parent-U-Turn, our collaboration with a group of low-income parents of color who have combined social inquiry with grassroots organizing to become a powerful force in local policy debates. Our other experience is with the Educational Justice Collaborative, a statewide coalition of advocacy and community-based organizations whose inquiry and activism have helped to shape California's equity policy agenda. These social design experiments are simultaneously research and interventions; they construct knowledge for the purpose of acting on it, and their actions become fodder for new inquiry. Of particular significance, however, is that none of these activities are owned exclusively by IDEA. To suggest otherwise violates the principles both of Dewey and of movement organizing and undermines the power of these ultimately democratic approaches to equity education reform.

We conclude with a final chapter that argues that Americans are most likely to realize equitable schooling by engaging in grassroots organizing informed by public inquiry. We maintain that the experiments we have described in this book provide promising and concrete examples of how that might occur, and that the time is ripe for such inquiry and organizing. We also predict some of the salutary changes we can expect if education professionals join together with activists in a new, inquiry-based social movement for educational justice.

2

The Limits of
School Reform

WOODROW WILSON HIGH SCHOOL is a large, diverse urban high school in a politically liberal university town.[1] A quick glance might indicate that the Wilson community would be a promising place to realize democratic and equitable education in a multiracial, multiclass state like California. Yet, it did not turn out that way.

Wilson benefits from being located in a diverse community with a large number of White and wealthy residents. These powerful residents, over the years, have used their considerable political influence and negotiating skills to keep their diverse schools among the most advantaged in the state—an accomplishment of which the community is very proud. At the same time, however, Wilson's schools have not escaped the insidious effects of pervasive cultural beliefs about low-income communities of color—that they value education less, that they are less "involved" with education, that their children are less able or less willing to achieve, and that their children's needs and futures are so different from those of the community's White and wealthy children that they require different educational programs. These prevailing norms, together with the political savvy of the community's most advantaged families, have created and maintained pernicious inequalities inside Wilson High.

This chapter uses the example of Wilson High School to illuminate how the norms and politics of White and middle-class privilege undermine the efficacy of reforms intended to provide high-quality schooling equally to all students. The persistence of racial inequality in the face of equity reforms is consistent with the contradictory role of schools in our capitalist democracy. Despite our prized cultural legacy of the common public school as a "great equalizer," American schools also serve the mission of preparing students for their "rightful" places in an unequal labor market and society. Because social hierarchies in this country are also racial hierarchies, stratified schooling opportunities and outcomes favor those from higher status racial groups.[2] Our experiences at Wilson help demonstrate the limits of technical approaches to equity school reform. Technical changes by themselves, even in the hands of committed and

21

skillful professional "change agents" or backed by court orders, are too weak to interrupt the intergenerational transmission of racial inequality. At root, the cultural norms of meritocracy and the politics of privilege are impervious to so puny an attack.[3]

Despite California's historic efforts to equalize education in the state and Wilson educators' impressive work toward equalizing opportunities within their high school, Wilson High embodies inequalities that pervade American schools. As we describe below, on the one hand, the norms and politics of American schooling protected Wilson's advantages during decades of statewide resource shortages and widening gaps among California schools and, on the other hand, created and perpetuated inequalities inside Wilson High. The outcomes both statewide and within Wilson have disadvantaged low-income students of color.

PRESERVING ADVANTAGE/ PRESERVING INEQUALITY

The students who attend Wilson are among the most fortunate high school students in California. Unlike thousands of their peers at the high schools whose resource shortages and dilapidated conditions were highlighted by the *Williams* case, Wilson's students benefit from above-average educational spending in the state, highly qualified teachers, ample instructional materials, a well-stocked library, plentiful college preparatory courses, and more.

In large part, Wilson High's advantages attest to the success of the Wilson community in staving off efforts to bring equity to California schools. As the state's schools reeled from the combined effects of its 1970s fiscal equalization court case and the "taxpayer" revolt that followed closely on the heels of the case, Wilson maintained its status as one of the state's best funded and most highly regarded school systems.

A Historical Glimpse at California School Finance Reform

The historical context of California school finance litigation and legislation provides the background for the modern inequities at Wilson. As we mentioned briefly in Chapter 1, California's high average levels of post–World War II educational spending masked stark disparities in the resources, conditions, opportunities, and outcomes between schools in Whiter and wealthier communities and those in communities of color and of poverty. The heightened attention to these issues in the 1960s triggered *Serrano v. Priest,* one of the earliest cases in a wave of lawsuits challenging different states to provide equitable school funding.

In 1971, the *Serrano* plaintiffs charged that California's educational finance system violated the Constitutional guarantee of equal protection because of the large variations in revenue that high- and low-wealth communities could generate through local property taxes when they taxed themselves at a given rate. In 1968–1969, students in high-wealth Beverly Hills attended schools spending $1,232 on each child while their peers across the Los Angeles basin in low-wealth Baldwin Park went to schools with only $577 to spend on each student.

Ruling in favor of the plaintiffs, the court directed the state legislature to equalize funding among districts. The legislature developed a complex formula that, over time, would diminish spending differentials among school districts so that the variation among them would not be more than $100 per student. However, before the impact of equalization could be felt, the state's 1978 Proposition 13 "taxpayer revolt" limited the property tax rate and decreased local tax revenues overall by 60%. It also required any new tax increase to be approved by a two-thirds majority of voters—a margin extraordinarily difficult to reach. The combined effect was that *Serrano* brought greater fiscal equity to California's educational system, but the schools got an equitable share of a dramatically smaller pool of funds.

Making matters worse, the funding mechanisms the state used to compensate for the loss of local tax revenue worked against the equalizing effect of the *Serrano* decision. Most new state funds came in the form of grants that were distributed to districts through a competitive proposal process. Districts with strong grant writers—most often districts with above-average funding—have been able to secure a disproportionate share of the new state funds. Thus, despite the requirements of *Serrano*, the state's responses to the constraints imposed by Proposition 13 undermined both equity and the overall quality of public education.

Wilson High's Funding

The Wilson community, in part because of its considerable wealth and political power, has protected itself from the worst effects of *Serrano* and Proposition 13. In 2004, for example, Wilson's district spent about $900 more per student than the state average and nearly $2,000 more per student than nearby districts serving predominantly low-income communities of color. Local fundraising efforts have produced grants from the city and private donations that add $1,600 extra per Wilson student, compared to as little as $68 in such local funds in nearby low-income schools. Wilson has also done quite well in capturing additional dollars made available by the state through the special categorical funding programs that are exempt from the *Serrano* limits. That Wilson captures another $1,200 per student from these funds (slightly below the state average) is surprising, given that nearly a third of these state funds are designated for programs serving students with special needs (for example, students with disabilities, those who need meal subsidies, and English-language learners). Wilson has only about half the percentage of English-language learners and low-income students as does the state as a whole.

Wilson also far exceeds state averages in its academic performance. Students' average test scores place Wilson High in the top tier of the state's high schools. Each year, about two thirds of Wilson's graduates qualify for 4-year colleges and universities—about twice the state average. Wilson sends many of its graduates to the nation's most prestigious universities. These graduates carry with them impressive academic records, high SAT scores, and promising futures.

Finally, Wilson High has been at the forefront of education reform. In the early 1990s, Wilson educators responded to widespread reports that escalating requirements for jobs in the new economy meant that schools had to prepare more students for college. A key step was to eliminate many of the low-level courses in which low-income students and students of color were overrepresented. Similarly, they converted the noncollege "general" track into a "regular" college preparatory pathway, making it more likely that all students could satisfy requirements to attend a 4-year college. Some of Wilson's reforms have been quite generously supported by grants from philanthropic foundations.

EQUITY REFORM AT WILSON HIGH

For years, troubling patterns of inequality lay just below the surface of Wilson's impressive statistics and reforms. As part of its reforms in the 1990s, the school's progressive principal, Rudy Stanton, called the public's attention to the "two schools" problem. By this, Stanton meant that most of the school's low-income African American and Latino students had very different learning opportunities and achievements than their White and Asian peers. Despite reforms that ostensibly created more opportunities for African American and Latino students, Wilson maintained a tracked curriculum with the same sorting effects as traditionally tracked schools.[4] The school maintained a two-tiered structure that channeled students toward very different futures. The school experiences, achievements, and college opportunities of students in the "honors" track (predominantly White and Asian students from the affluent north side of town) diverged dramatically from those in the "regular" track (mostly low-income Latino and African American youth living in the southern part of the community).

The school's segregated and differentiated opportunity structure was matched by racial disparities in outcomes. Almost half of the African American students and about 40% of the Latinos carried grade point averages of less than "C." Although the school routinely reported that about 85% of its graduates went on to college, significant race and social class disparities lay beneath this number. The large majority of Wilson graduates attending 4-year universities were affluent White, Asian, and Middle Eastern students. Most of the school's low-income African American and Latino students who went to college attended local 2-year schools, and these students were vastly overrepresented in the group that did not attend college at all.

These outcomes for Wilson's African American and Latino students are particularly sobering when compared with those for African American and Latino students in nearby districts with less qualified faculties and fewer educational resources. African Americans and Latinos at Wilson were no more likely to be eligible to attend a 4-year college than their peers in less advantaged schools. Further, because Wilson's students of color entered high school with far better scores on state achievement tests, they might have been expected to have much higher rates of 4-year college attendance than their peers in neighboring districts.

Moving Toward "One School" for All

Principal Rudy Stanton made the "two schools" problem *the* central object of reform. The superintendent, Sandra Nesbitt, also thought it was the right thing to do, and she was well positioned to undertake such a reform. The district was connected with national reform networks, highly regarded throughout the region, and supported by foundation grants. We served as the university partner to the district's reform.

Through a process of Wilson High faculty inquiry and experimentation with more inclusive practices, the school became somewhat more responsive to students of color. By 2000, a significant number of Latinos and African Americans began to participate in student government, and a few more enrolled in honors track and advanced placement (AP) classes. Some faculty-led interventions helped students of color navigate an unfamiliar and demanding college-preparatory curriculum. The Futures project we describe in Chapter 4 was one such effort. Compared to 5 years earlier, Wilson's African American and Latino students were more likely to receive college-eligible grades, participate in rigorous curricula (honors and AP classes as well as higher level math and science classes), and apply to and enroll in 4-year universities.

But the progress was modest. Although half of the school's population was African American and Latino, no AP or honors class in 2000–2001 contained more than 14% students of color. The "two schools" remained, even if the boundary between them was slightly more permeable than before.

Then Wilson's reform hit a wall. As some students and parents of color, along with supportive faculty, pressed against the "two schools" boundary, others shoved back. Claiming damage to the schools' traditionally high-achieving students from "watered-down" honors and AP classes, a substantial group of parents—nearly all White, several wealthy, and many with considerable power in the community—proposed adding another track called "mid-honors." This new track, they argued, would provide for the particular educational needs of students in the middle of the achievement range—those who want more academic challenge than the regular track provides, but who did not want a course as rigorous as honors or AP and were willing to forgo the extra grade points that AP provides. This proposed track would replicate a traditional school tracking system; only the names would change.

The Wilson story does not end here, and we return to it in Chapter 4. However, by this point it had become clear that the school's well-crafted reform process would not solve its "two schools" problem.

WHAT WENT WRONG?

At Wilson, as in California as a whole and across the nation, the struggle to achieve equality stumbled over a bumpy political landscape. As pointed out in Chapter 1, most reforms have proceeded from the assumptions that equality can be achieved by focusing exclusively on the educational system, and that a lack of knowledge is at the root of inequality. Throughout this period, court-ordered remedies and other equity reforms have drawn on traditional school improvement strategies to "treat" the prevailing inequality. Yet, they have done little to confront the broad social norms or the political arrangements that supported the inequality.[5]

Research That Lifted the Veil of Ignorance

By the mid-1980s, sociological research had made clear that some common school structures—tracking and ability grouping, for example—perpetuate unequal opportunities in racially mixed schools. The findings against tracking and all but the most temporary ability grouping are strong and unequivocal.[6] Schools' constructions of students' intellectual abilities, often based on race and socioeconomic status, have been found to play a major role in allocating learning resources and conditions. Elementary and middle school students whom educators judge to be less able or to have less "potential" are placed in low-level groups, classes, or remedial programs; those considered to be "bright" go to high-ability classes. Senior high school students are sorted into college preparatory courses or more general and vocational classes, based partly on their academic abilities and partly on how their abilities compare with those of other students. These decisions and placements determine the quality of the curriculum, instructional practices, and social relations that students experience. Students in lower classes, or tracks, typically get fewer of the resources and conditions that promote achievement and advancement than students in higher classes or tracks. They have fewer well-qualified teachers, less exposure to intellectually engaging curricula, and less access to technology and laboratories for investigation and problem solving.

Clear race and class patterns prevail, both between schools and within them. African American, Latino, and low-income students are consistently overrepresented in low-ability settings and less likely to participate in programs for "gifted" or college-bound students. These differential placements within schools cannot be explained by test scores; African American and Latino students are more likely to be placed in lower track classes than White students with comparable scores.[7] Unequal access to advanced classes occurs both between schools and within them. Most segregated schools serving low-income and minority students have proportionately fewer advanced classes than do schools serving predominantly White, more affluent students. Most desegregated schools disproportionately assign African American and Latino students to low-track classes.

As the evidence of the educational inequalities and racial stratification associated with tracking became known, many policymakers, educators, and advocacy groups advised that schools dismantle their tracked structures. During the 1990s, many educators took this advice and attempted to "detrack" their schools. Although some schools showed early success, detracking rarely got beyond small initial steps; at the same time, it brought great acrimony to the school's community.

The Failure of Knowledge and Technical Strategies to Disrupt Inequality

The research on detracking efforts is sobering. For example, Jeannie Oakes and Amy Stuart Wells conducted a study in the early 1990s that followed educators in 10 racially mixed schools over 3 years as they developed innovative course-taking structures and classroom practices for accommodating diverse groups of students.[8] They documented how reformers at each of these schools had come to see the pattern of putting students of different racial and ethnic groups into largely separate and quite unequal classes as deeply problematic—both pedagogically and morally. Made uncomfortable by their experiences, these educators were prompted to action by the research and by the judgment of professional and policy organizations that tracking works against expectations for all students to meet high academic standards.

These educators shared the research with their colleagues, and they used the lessons of the school change literature to support reform. They found new resources (often grants for "restructuring" schools), technical assistance, and professional development. They took their time, creating strategic plans for gradual implementation. Most believed that those who opposed the reforms would eventually see that tracking is at odds with core American values and quality education. They thought that their schools and communities, if given a well-crafted and successful alternative, would be eager to abandon discriminatory practices.

They were wrong. Their efforts to make their schools more equitable were fought bitterly and often crushed. Some colleagues in their schools and districts remained highly skeptical; a few were outright hostile. Even some who valued racially mixed schools worried that detracking undermined the educational chances of high-achieving (usually White) students. Wealthier White parents applied enormous pressure to keep the status quo; they worried that democratizing the high-status curriculum would jeopardize their children's chances for admission to prestigious universities. Many middle-class White parents associated their daughters' and sons' increasingly scarce opportunities with the "problems" caused by minority students in their schools, most of whom were poor.

Detracking collided with (mostly) taken-for-granted conceptions of racial differences in intelligence and ability and deeply entrenched traditions that define a valuable curriculum and appropriate practice at the schools. Moreover, the proposed changes were redistributive—that is, they fundamentally altered how the schools allocated their most precious resources, including teachers, materials, and high-achieving students. They challenged traditional ways of thinking about merit and which students "deserve" the best that schools have to offer.[9] As these schools struggled to break free of tracking, the pull of social stratification proved too strong.

Increasingly, researchers have documented how these norms and politics (beliefs and power) mobilize privileged parents to maintain the status quo ability grouping and tracking practice and ensure their children's position in advantaged classes.[10] While the process of resistance to equity is well documented, there is little in the research on tracking or in the educational change literature that helps reformers counteract powerful parents and school officials who simply do not like the changes and know that they have the power to thwart them.

This is what happened at Wilson High. The school's reform strategies were strongly supported by the evidence, but when reason met power, power won. Like so many other schools, Wilson's reform had been successful enough to become a threat, and therefore it had to be stopped. Very quickly, the reformers' attention shifted from their proactive equity initiatives to reactive scurrying to hold on to gains. To buy some time, the faculty urged the parents to postpone their demands until they could see the results of the teachers' intensive professional development on accommodating all students' learning in more heterogeneous classrooms. However, "improvements" from professional development would not be persuasive because there were few complaints about specific curricular or instructional disadvantages that students experienced from diverse classrooms. Some parents inferred that the high-achieving students learned less, thought less rigorously, and were less well prepared for college. They were not persuaded by the school's data showing no declines in academic achievement, college entrance exam performance, and acceptance to elite colleges. More to the point, parents most frequently complained about classroom distractions, lack of attention, or a less comfortable classroom or school environment. These less tangible but deeply felt concerns were not supported by the school's data on discipline and safety.

THE LIMITS OF ENLIGHTENMENT AS A CHANGE STRATEGY

Schooling's continued role in the reproduction of race and social class inequality is mediated by cultural norms and political processes that are complex, mutually constituted, and, on their face, racially neutral. Measures of academic abilities, definitions of high-status academic language and knowledge, norms governing appropriate school behavior, and relations between schools and families are all expressed as race-neutral, meritocratic means for allocating opportunities and identifying achievement. Children who match these norms are presumed to deserve schooling advantages by dint of their individual merit, even though this assessment conflates intelligence with the skills and knowledge that educationally and economically privileged parents pass on to their children.[11]

Rather than blaming racially skewed schooling outcomes on norms and politics that lead to disparate resources and opportunities, our society often blames those who do not fit the prevailing ideologies of intelligence and merit. Social science itself has played an unsavory role in reifying concepts that soon serve as conceptual and linguistic proxies for race, such as "culture of poverty," "at risk," "nonverbal learning style," and "oppositional behavior," to justify the persistence of inequality. All contribute to the fear and loathing of the racialized other, and allow subtler but powerful forms of inequality to fill the gap left by the end of *de jure* segregation and "in-your-face" racism. For example, it has become taboo to assert that Whites are intellectually superior or to exclude students from educational programs solely because of their race and social class. Yet, unequal and stratified schooling continues to make deep, unquestioned sense. Scratch the surface of many common critiques of schools serving poor students of color—that they practice "social promotion" at the expense of academic standards, for example—and one finds assumptions resting on class and race rather than on the more obvious inferior learning opportunities provided by the school.[12]

The educators at Wilson High School, like many highly professional faculties, sought guidance for their work from the educational change literature, which includes several decades of research on the sorry and familiar story of school reform gone awry. Much of this literature purports to offer understandings and strategies that aid in the successful adoption, implementation, and institutionalization of new structures and practices. For example, chapters in the 1998 *International Handbook of Educational Change* document this empirical work.[13]

In fact, any student of the school change literature would likely applaud Wilson's careful attention to the lessons learned from the past decades of research. They adopted an inquiry approach to professional development. The principal and a fairly large group of teachers sustained often difficult conversations about achievement, race, and learning, hoping that faculty could develop equitable structures and practices that would bring Wilson's "two schools" together. A significant number of faculty participated. Wilson educators worked to secure other teachers' "buy-in" to the reform. They updated the school board and parent groups regularly. They sought allies in teacher union leaders, and they made slow, incremental changes to ensure that their reform enthusiasm did not outstrip the school's technical capacity. Wilson High's reform was not halted because the reformers neglected the lessons from this literature.

It turned out, however, that the educational change literature had little to say about the particular types of changes Wilson's reformers sought—reforms that challenged social norms and redistributed resources and opportunities on behalf of the least advantaged students and communities. Although some scholars do venture beyond the strictly technical aspects of the change process, this normative and political analysis focuses largely on the microcultural and micropolitical obstacles to change *within* the community of professional educators.[14]

The vast change literature says little about strategies for disrupting social inequality through school reform. Theorists and change agents have not treated equity reforms as distinctly different from other school improvement initiatives. Efforts to create cross-disciplinary curriculum teams also may entail controversy, but they elicit far less political or self-interest backlash. To the extent that the change literature addresses reforms meant to benefit less wealthy Latino and African American students, it assumes that schools are filled with well-meaning educators who need some assistance or prompting to achieve greater equity and more efficacious structures and pedagogies.

Consequently, reformers have proceeded with planned educational change strategies to increase educators' technical capacity and make schools' structures and organizational cultures more hospitable to effective practices.[15] This approach is consistent with the prevailing industrial/technical model of schooling that focuses almost exclusively on schooling's instrumental role in producing academic achievement or workforce preparation. In this view, educational structures and practices must be engineered, adopted, and implemented to accomplish those ends. And, in fact, most change studies focus on educational reform as the process of improving the means in order to improve the outcome. Although many change scholars and change agents also consider the quality of life in schools or individuals' satisfactions and frustrations, these dimensions of schooling are usually treated as part of the instrumental mix for improving outcomes.

We conjecture that this "practical" bent to school reform contributes to researchers' and reformers' focus on change *within* schools instead of looking to the community or the larger political economy as a field for analysis and action. Thus, even work such as Hargreaves's recent exploration of the anxieties teachers experience when parents challenge their competence stops short of addressing race- and class-linked parental objections like those raised at Wilson High.[16]

The net effect of this apolitical approach to educational change is to overemphasize the importance of enlightening or persuading educators (often referred to as "buy-in" or "taking ownership") and to provide the rosy view that technical changes will result in necessary and profound benefits to all students without disruptions or redistribution. As in the business world, these change strategies make sense as long as all parties to the reform share a common goal. But efforts to address race and class inequality uncover conflicting interests. Wilson High thus made some equity progress as long as the principal could keep equity firmly attached to the school's bottom line. Progress halted when equity lost this privileged position and simply became a negotiable instrument— desirable, but not essential—to benefit the school's sense of itself as an elite institution.

Our research has taught us that technical knowledge is insufficient to bring about equitable education, even when attention is paid to changing the school's professional culture. Quite simply, educational equity is entangled with cultural and political dynamics that extend beyond the school; therefore, equity reforms must engage issues of power by extending beyond the school. Treating such reform as a strictly professional matter belonging exclusively to educators is the key error of school reform.

Not accustomed to seeing their work in terms of cultural and political struggle, educators are caught off guard by the quickness and virulence of the resistance of those who see reforms as a threat to their status, cultural norms, and political and economic positions.[17] Our research further suggests that educators cannot do this work alone even when they understand how their own school is embedded in this wider web of culture and politics. In many school systems, we have watched low-income African American and Latino communities remain silent or be silenced while powerful White and wealthier parents and policymakers dominate the reform debate. If equity-focused educators step in and advocate for less powerful and silenced communities, they are easily brushed aside. Without political pressure for equity brought to bear by the public, educators cannot serve an appropriate professional role of balancing multiple legitimate, if conflicting, public demands. Further, when educators step in and speak and act *for* less powerful communities, they do nothing to build the local community power necessary to change the cultural and political asymmetries that sustain the very schooling inequalities they seek to disrupt. Finally, teachers and principals make themselves vulnerable when they become closely identified with the less favored student groups. Thus, their status, influence, and job security can be jeopardized—putting them at risk for transfer to less favored schools, teaching difficult or ill-equipped classes, or getting fired. Without a constituency comparable to the opponents of reform, most just do not last long in the battle.

Because of a political dynamic in which the existence, let alone the distribution, of power is never explicitly addressed, technical change strategies tend toward consensus rather than conflict. They aim at engendering a sense of ownership among all members, rather than a fundamental realignment of advantage. As a result, much reform energy typically dissipates in attempts to bypass or finesse explicit cultural struggle. A consensus-based, politically neutral approach to educational change served Wilson High School well until the reforms began to disrupt the distribution of resources and opportunity that favored White, middle-class students. At that point, the reforms challenged deep-seated norms about what White and wealthy students "deserve"—classes where they are sheltered from less "meritorious" peers. The standard reform literature offered no insight on how to counter these undemocratic, yet highly political, claims.

Put bluntly, although equity reforms required technical knowledge, Wilson educators' primary challenge was political—elites needed to relinquish features of schooling that they perceived to be to their advantage. The reformers had to persuade this powerful constituency that extending opportunities to low-income students of color would not undermine the status and educational preparation the school provides White and wealthier students.

The consensus-based school change literature provided little guidance for winning conflict-based struggles for equity reform. Only a few studies—such as Datnow's work on the gender politics of school reform, Wells and Serna's research on the cultural politics of detracking, and Welner's study of community battles over court-ordered detracking—have illuminated the murkier waters of educational change when reform evokes larger social tensions around race, social class, and gender.[18]

The reform-minded educators at Woodrow Wilson High School, their supporters at the district office, and their university partners were savvy about these issues. Their inquiry about the "two schools" problem enabled them to move beyond a neutral perspective regarding the reform. Yet, they had few actual tools to convince middle-class parents that high-quality educational opportunities for their own children did not have to come at the expense of other children. Consequently, Wilson educators found themselves attempting to counter middle-class White parents' fears about enrolling their students in classes with lower income students of color by explaining that new curricula and teaching techniques promised a high-quality education that could continue to meet the needs of middle-class children.[19] But for these middle-class parents, "quality education" (like "merit") had meaning only as a *relative* concept. An education could be good only if it were better than what disadvantaged students were getting. They could not distinguish loss of advantage from loss of quality. And because low-income African American and Latino parents did not have a powerful public voice in Wilson's reform, the White and middle-class parents never were forced to confront the contradictions between their effort to maintain advantage and their espoused belief in equal opportunity.[20]

REFORM THAT CHANGES LITTLE

As the story of Wilson High School illuminates, knowledge advances, technical innovations, and organizational change strategies have brought only limited progress toward education "on equal terms" for all American children, either among schools in different communities or within schools for different groups of students. Efforts to end even the most egregious *de jure* segregation have been met with delays, hostility, and reversals. Since the 1980s, the courts, federal and state policy, and education leadership have all moved away from addressing segregation in its many forms. Other structural remedies (e.g., fiscal equalization, affirmative action, detracking) to inequalities in resources, conditions, and opportunities—however well researched and designed—have been resisted and rejected almost as virulently. Research-based classroom technologies aimed at bringing culturally and linguistically inclusive curriculum and instruction to American children (e.g., multicultural curriculum, culturally responsive pedagogy, bilingual education) have, for the most part, been gutted in favor of "standards-based" reform with high-stakes tests to "motivate" students and teachers to do better.

Fifty years after *Brown*, segregated schools and racial inequalities in educational opportunities remain. Despite the considerable research and development of technical advances designed to bring more equitable schooling, the struggle to realize that goal has brought retrogressive action and inertia by elites, anger among nonelite Whites who see themselves as the losers in such reform, and the growing disillusionment among excluded groups themselves about the possibility of racial equality and the desirability of racial integration.[21] Rather than abating over time, resistance to reforms aimed at realizing the promise of *Brown* has persisted, and perhaps has grown stronger. Playing out as privatization and threats of withdrawal from the public system, the resistance has further undermined America's commitment to the common public school.

Clearly, new conceptions and methods of equity-focused education reform are badly needed. We offer some of our thinking, research, and experience toward such ends in the remaining chapters.

3

Participatory Social Inquiry
What John Dewey Offers
Equity Reformers

Show me a democracy that devalues the public, devalues the non-market realities that transcend the privatistic, hedonistic, materialistic proclivities that the
market often, though not always, but often reinforces, show me a democracy
that downplays the public, thereby downplays public education, public conversation, public health, public transportation and I'll show you a democracy in
deep decay and decline, beneath the meretricious glitter and superficial surfaces
of its grand economic performance.

Cornel West paraphrasing John Dewey's argument in
The Public and Its Problems[1]

IT IS FITTING to look to John Dewey for insight on equity reform, given that
the struggle for an egalitarian democracy lies at the heart of his life work. John
Dewey believed that inequality could only be overcome by confronting deep-
seated values; he understood that ideology underpins unequal resources and
social arrangements. According to Dewey, philosophy's long-standing tendency
was to "become unconsciously an apologetic for the established order, because
it . . . tried to show the rationality of this or that existent hierarchical grading
of values and schemes of life."[2] Dewey reasoned that such rationalizations are
inevitable where unequal social arrangements exist:

> Special privilege always induces a standpat and reactionary attitude on the part
> of those who have it; in the end it usually provokes a blind rage of destruction
> on the part of those who suffer from it. The intellectual blindness caused by priv-
> ileged and monopolistic possession is made evident in "rationalization" of the
> misery and cultural degradation of others which attend its existence. These are
> asserted to be the fault of those who suffer; to be the consequence of their own
> improvidence, lack of industry, willful ignorance, etc.[3]

Dewey recognized similar patterns in efforts of scholars to defend stratification through the emerging science of intelligence testing:

> Just as Aristotle rationalized slavery by showing how natural it was for those superior by nature to constitute the ends for others who were only tools, so we, while marvelling perhaps at the callousness of the Greek philosopher, rationalize the inequities of our social order by appealing to innate and unalterable psychological strata in the population.[4]

If Dewey was correct that deep-seated values undergird inequitable structures, then equity-minded school reform must work on a normative and political as well as a technical level. Successful equity reform must attend to changes in power and relationships that both derive from and shape social arrangements. Here, we look to Dewey's later work to find further insights into

- The relationship between educational and political equality;
- The processes for educational and political change aimed at realizing equality;
- The relationship between developing knowledge and building power for progressive social change.

DEWEY ON EQUALITY

From his early forays into social theory in the late 1880s to his robust engagement with social democracy in the 1930s, Dewey offered a vision of equality that, like *Brown*, asserted the importance of both educational opportunity and full civil rights.[5] "Each individual" requires a social environment that provides him with the "opportunity for release, expression, fulfillment, of his distinctive capacity."[6] Decent housing, public health, and tools for learning are all critical to such an environment.[7] The creation of citizens "in the fulness [sic] of their capacities" in turn demands that "free human beings [associate] with one another on terms of equality."[8] Relating to fellow citizens on the basis of equality does not imply a "mathematical equivalence" in which all must participate in the same way. Rather, it means that hierarchical understandings of individuals as "greater and less, superior and inferior," must give way to a "metaphysical mathematics of the incommensurable in which each speaks for itself and demands consideration on its own behalf."[9]

Dewey, of course, recognized that American society is far from this vision of equality, and he placed the battle against inequality at the core of his philosophic and political project. He imagined participatory social inquiry—what Hilary Putnam referred to as the "full application of intelligence to the solution of social problems"—as the most powerful tool for progressive change.[10]

Such inquiry demands that all citizens be "equipped with knowledge and competent method."[11] It also demands that "every human being must count" and be "taken into account" to realize the cognitive advantages of diverse experiences and distinct voices.[12]

Dewey's Early Efforts to Grapple with Social Change

But how is it possible to work against inequality when the primary engine for progressive social change—a "kind of knowledge and insight which does not exist"—requires a high degree of social equality?[13] Early in his career, Dewey responded to this problem by adopting a progressive historical narrative that imagined the next generation developing new forms of intelligence through democratic schooling. By constructing environments for young people to apply the tools of intelligence in everyday experience, educators could provide students with practice in egalitarian social relationships and "command of the fundamental methods of inquiry and the fundamental tools of intercourse and communication."[14] Dewey envisioned this educational project promoting equality in two ways. First, it promised equal access to knowledge, thereby "restoring to the common man that which . . . has been embezzled from the common store and appropriated to sectarian and class use."[15] Second, the citizens who "la[y] hold of" this new knowledge and intelligence in their "childhood and youth" would be prepared to "locate the source of our economic evils" as adults.[16] Dewey was careful to note that such understanding may not immediately translate into radically new industrial or political conditions. "But," he reasoned, "it does mean that we may produce in schools a projection in type of the society we should like to realize, and by forming minds in accord with it gradually modify the larger and more recalcitrant features of adult society."[17]

Dissatisfaction With Evolutionary Social Change

In the 1920s, Dewey began to question the strategy of evolutionary social change through education as he saw new forms of mass communication undermine public intelligence. The new science of public relations, which emerged after World War I, left the public unable and often uninterested in discriminating between "sound and sense" or "lay[ing] hold of the realities beneath the froth and foam."[18] Further, Dewey recognized that powerful interests often view the expansion of educational opportunity as a political threat that must be challenged. For example, in the late 1920s, Dewey explained the persistence of African American illiteracy as the product of a system that sought to sustain White supremacy:

> Unless there was a general Negro question, social, economic, and political, there would be no such excess of Negro illiterates as now exists. Racial prejudice, fear

of racial equality, dread lest education would render the black population "upstarts" who would clamor for the use of the vote, and make them less tractable as cheap labor, are definite factors in maintaining a large illiteracy in our black population.[19]

A REVITALIZED PUBLIC

Dewey responded to the failures of public intelligence by calling for more intelligence and a revitalized public. He pointed to the values inherent in the scientific process—willingness to constantly test beliefs, openness to alternative ~science~ ideas, and systematic analysis—as general principles for guiding the work of publics. These values, he hoped, would encourage skepticism about the source and distribution of knowledge and power in society. Dewey also encouraged publics to adopt the "method" of science in assessing social policies. He called for groups of citizens to treat "policies and proposals . . . as working hypotheses . . . subject to constant and well-equipped observation . . . and ready and flexible revision."[20] This experimental approach—and more important, an experimental attitude—would educate the public, providing them with the "tools . . . of observing, reporting, and organizing" which "can be evolved and perfected only in operation."[21] Similarly, Dewey attributed an educative role to the direct "consultation and discussion" that occur within participatory social inquiry.[22] Following Alexis de Tocqueville, he pointed out that public dialogue "forces a recognition that there are common interests, . . . [and it] brings about some clarification of what they are."[23]

Dewey believed that these common interests would reflect the authentic needs and concerns of working people when participatory inquiry was freed from "vested bias and prejudice."[24] As Deborah Morris argued, this belief was in part connected to Dewey's faith in "science's immense social and political utility . . . to undermine dogma and entrenched privilege."[25] Moreover, Dewey's publics were inherently populist in their composition.[26] He placed common people in the foreground of public inquiry and marked out a limited role for experts. Experts could support lay publics by "discovering and making known facts."[27]

Dewey warned that when a "class of experts" is "removed from common interests" it "become[s] a class with private interests and private knowledge, which in social matters is not knowledge at all."[28] In addition to creating a new "intellectual aristocracy," this elevation of experts "shut[s] off" the social intercourse so crucial to the problem-solving process.[29] Experts thus should imagine themselves like the skilled shoemaker who realizes that it is "the man who wears the shoe [that] knows best . . . where it pinches."[30] They must join lay publics in dialogue about both problem and method and treat these sessions as serious consultations from which they might learn.

TOWARD AN EDUCATIVE POLITICS

In his theoretical writing, Dewey offered little advice about what set of actions—political, educational, or intellectual—would lead to the development of revitalized publics.[31] But, during the Depression, Dewey articulated a model of activist, educative politics for building a new and egalitarian social order. In the words of the *New York World Telegram*, Dewey moved "out of the classroom" and into the "hurly-burly" of politics, playing a leadership role in the movement to create a third political party and participating in vibrant public dialogues with progressive educators and labor leaders.[32] In each of these sites of activism, Dewey encouraged mass education and organization of powerful publics that would restore "hope for politics" and provide "equality among human beings irrespective of race, color and creed."[33]

Throughout the Depression, Dewey called for "educational tactics" to provide "spiritually and mentally starved American workers" with sustenance that was as necessary as "food for the physically starved."[34] "We submit," he wrote in a funding appeal for Brookwood Labor College, "that no activity can be more important than . . . giving workers themselves the vision of a new world and some comprehension of the means by which it may be achieved."[35] In advocating "educational tactics," Dewey did not mean "a cloistered withdrawal from the scene of action." Rather, he called for political education that "translate[s] . . . ideas and knowledge . . . into emotion, interest, and volition."[36] For this to occur, ideas "must be linked to the practical situation"—the everyday "troubles and aspirations of the mass of the population."[37]

> Teachers can learn something about the defects and requirements of existing types of organization by the study of economic and sociological literature and by reading such newspapers and periodicals as state the facts honestly. But the understanding thus gained is cold and at arms' length compared with the understanding and sympathy that would spring from direct and vital contact with . . . productive workers.[38]

Dewey's appeal for greater contact between teachers and workers resonates with his persistent call for greater "organization" among allies in the struggle for equality. He proposed that organizing liberals was harder than organizing conservatives. Whereas conservatives "hold together not so much by ideas as by habit, tradition, fear of the unknown," liberals "depend upon ideas . . . and when persons begin to think upon social matters they begin to vary."[39] To build common cause, Dewey argued that liberals must do more than agree in principle; they must act together. "Organization of standpoint and belief among liberals can be achieved only in and by unity of endeavor."[40]

Dewey described the benefits that accrue to citizens who forge alliances and take joint action in ways that sound like contemporary theorists of social capital: "Working shoulder to shoulder in a unified common movement" energizes participants and builds their commitment to one another as well as their shared cause.[41] These commitments provide participants with "backbone" and protect them from the conservative backlash that inevitably comes to struggles for equity.[42] Here Dewey invoked the familiar slogan: "Divided, we may fall. United, we shall stand."[43] Further, he argued that, "combin[ing]" with allies, participants gain a stronger voice "to impress [their ideas] upon public opinion."[44] Finally, Dewey recognized that participation in joint activity is educative. Through alliance, individuals "develop the character, skill and intelligence that are necessary to make a democratic social order a fact."[45]

THE LEGACY OF DEWEY'S EDUCATIVE POLITICS FOR CONTEMPORARY SCHOOL REFORM

Dewey pushed beyond traditional understandings of knowledge and knowledge diffusion. Knowledge that provides insights on inequality—what Dewey at times referred to as "economic literacy"—is necessarily practical knowledge, bound up with problems of everyday experience.[46] Acquiring this literacy requires engagement with academic texts *and* "vital contact" with workers who bring special insight about their own troubles and aspirations.[47] Consistent with his overlapping views of learning and democratic politics, this literacy must be honed in joint action.

In sum, Dewey asked researchers and reformers to create a space for joint public work—a space that is both for the work and defined by it. This "public sphere" has membership, but no ownership. Participation is the price of admission. American freedoms, ephemeral at best outside the sphere, are rediscovered and regenerated, and become concrete within it. Here is where the civic participation of experts and citizens can shape policy through information gathering, exchange, interpretation, and debate—the hallmarks of Dewey's vision of participatory social inquiry. Further, the problems created by inequitable social policy are the correct content of this inquiry.

To this end we offer the following four principles, built on Dewey's legacy, about how, in today's context, participatory social inquiry might guide reforms seeking more equitable schools.

- *Engage Those Most Affected by Inequality.* Participatory social inquiry focused on making schools more equitable must foreground the engagement of those people most affected by unequal schools and social policy. The engagement must include meaningful and sustained relationships with experts. The foregrounding of the role of common people, however, requires that experts play a limited role. Experts can support lay publics by "discovering and making known facts."[48] In Dewey's framing, experts thus should imagine themselves like the skilled shoemaker who realizes that it is "the man who wears the shoe [that] knows best . . . where it pinches."[49] They must join lay publics in dialogue about both problem and method and treat these sessions as serious consultations from which they, as experts, might also learn.

- *Ensure Access to Knowledge and Its Construction.* First, and foremost, expert knowledge must be made accessible so that common people can recognize within their own experiences that which experts have appropriated with their elite and often incomprehensible framing. Or, in Dewey's words, the process should restore "to the common man that [knowledge] which . . . has been embezzled from the common store and appropriated to sectarian and class use."[50] Second, an "experimental" method and attitude must drive social inquiry. Participants reveal their experiences and perspectives, gather new information, and generate and test hypotheses, adopting the "method" of science in assessing social policies. They treat "policies and proposals . . . as working hypotheses . . . subject to constant and well-equipped observation . . . and ready and flexible revision."[51] They constantly test beliefs, remaining open to alternative ideas and encouraging a proclivity toward systematic analysis. This experimental approach and attitude educates the public, providing them with the fundamental methods of inquiry. Dewey believed that this approach and attitude give the public "tools . . . of observing, reporting, and organizing" which "can be evolved and perfected only in operation."[52] Finally, the knowledge construction process must both draw from everyday experience and, in turn, test newly constructed knowledge in that context. This demands that knowledge of all types be legitimate—from traditional research to participants' own multiple experiences and perspectives. Inquiry into social problems should draw upon book learning, authentic dialogue, and the "troubles and aspirations" of lived experience. It must include opportunities for knowledgeable and engaged citizens to demonstrate their "watchfulness, concern, and activity in the points and places where government . . . touches the life of the people."[53]
- *Adopt a Critical Stance.* Those who participate in democracy must examine the politics of knowledge construction. Because economic elites largely control public relations, they can place before the public "facts" and ideas that "rationaliz[e] . . . the misery and cultural degradation of others. . . . These are asserted to be the fault of those who suffer; to be the consequence of their own improvidence, lack of industry, wilful [sic] ignorance, etc."[54] The hegemonic reach of prevailing ideologies extends in unpredictable and idiosyncratic ways to include even those who are clearly disadvantaged by current practices. Therefore, all participants need the opportunity to learn that the schooling problems they hope to change have a current and historical context. "How did things come to be this way?" "Whose interests are (and are

not) being served by the way things are?" are questions that help frame this critical inquiry. In Dewey's words, participants must "locate the source of our economic evils."[55]

⟡ ***Develop a Transformative Goal.*** Participation fosters a sense of collective identity as people discover shared interests around which they might act jointly. Inquiry and dialogue allow groups to construct a story of who they are, what they do, and why they do it. That "story" motivates the group to strategize about ways to realize the more hopeful possibilities they have framed. Such stories can be considered "disruptive knowledge" because, upon hearing them, the listener can no longer hold on to prior conceptions that depend on uncritically accepted beliefs. Disruptive knowledge challenges the facts that people hold. But perhaps as important, disruptive knowledge overturns complacency and makes it more likely that the listener will be moved to moral action. Participants also forge a shared theory of change and a common "end in view." Through inquiry, they can create a "vision of a new world and some comprehension of the means by which it may be achieved."[56]

SOCIAL DESIGN EXPERIMENTS

At UCLA's Institute for Democracy, Education, and Access (IDEA), we have applied and tested similar principles of participatory social inquiry to bring about more equitable schooling. We have created and studied settings where researchers, educators, citizens, and students together employ a critical stance to construct, report, and use knowledge to transform unequal schooling policies, practices, and outcomes. Our goal has been to understand whether such approaches to research and reform can redistribute power on behalf of those usually marginalized and silenced. We have come to call these activities "social design experiments."

We take the concept of a "design experiment" from the work of psychologists Ann Brown and Alan Collins, who moved their studies of learning out of the laboratory and into the classroom.[57] Their goal was to exercise systematic observations of phenomena that could occur in relatively conventional settings and to test hypotheses of what might happen when the "experimenters" altered the conditions in selected ways. In this way education researchers could both create educational innovations and test them in classroom reality. So, instead of testing their ideas about learning in the pristine setting of the laboratory, the researchers, in collaboration with teachers, created an environment in which the research questions could be asked in the messy context of real classrooms. Additionally, as they learned from their experiments, they could change the setting to allow them to ask and answer new questions. It occurred to us that the design experiment collapsed multiple research-to-practice steps (hypotheses, experimental design, theory building, practical applications, etc.) into a process that produced scientifically valid results at the same time it contributed to practice. Notably, in these design experiments, the relationship between researchers, practitioners, and students was unconventional. Rather than considering teachers and students only as the subjects of their research, practitioners were participant informants and, in some cases, co-designers.

Design experiments by Brown, Collins, and other psychologists have examined students' cognition and learning. Our appropriation of this idea adds the word "social," recognizing our interest in using the method for examining how constructing settings for participatory social inquiry might help us understand the intersection of the larger political and social context of schooling and specific efforts to make schools more educative and equitable for low-income students of color. In addition, we use "social" to emphasize the vital role of participants in shaping the purpose and character of our shared work.

In the chapters that follow, we share more concretely how we developed this line of work in two different "cases" of social design experiments. Our Futures experiment at Wilson High School, described in Chapter 4, focused on increasing the access of low-income students of color to 4-year colleges and universities. Our Teaching to Change LA experiment, described in Chapter 5, sought to explore with teachers how curriculum for urban students might engage young people constructively in understanding and struggling against the unequal schooling in their communities.

In different ways, these two cases positioned UCLA's IDEA researchers both as a source of research-based knowledge and as participants attempting to blend the existing knowledge base, new investigations, and the knowledge from students' and teachers' first-hand experiences into actions that could build power and prompt changes that could make schools more equitable.

We do not offer our examples as exemplary (or even replicable) cases of equity reform success. Rather, these are carefully grounded narratives that convey the personal experiences of the participants—the identities, histories, and ongoing works of students and teachers—as they seek to disrupt inequitable social environments. The narratives also document empirical findings about the barriers and facilitators of educational change. Futures and Teaching to Change LA illustrate how education research and theory, along with many other forms of knowledge, become part of a struggle toward education "on equal terms."

4

Futures

Students Disrupting
High School Inequality

Turning the tables on reporters at the Democratic National Convention in 2000.

Nina Melendez entered the United States as a 12-year-old with only a few words of English. Her parents, wanting more for Nina than they could provide in Mexico, brought her to California without legal documentation and left her in the care of her 21- and 19-year-old sisters and her 15-year-old brother, who had crossed the border earlier. The four siblings lived in a tiny apartment near a beachfront hotel where Nina's oldest sister worked as a maid. They lied about their address to enroll Nina in a highly rated middle school, even though it meant that she would need to ride multiple buses to school each day. She enrolled in classes for English language learners, and would stay in these special classes through her ninth-grade year. Nina's family expected her to be their first college graduate; never mind that none of them knew how higher education worked in the United States or how to prepare for it. Not long after we met her as a Wilson High School ninth grader, Nina asked us for advice: "My sister tells me that college is like repeating high school, so I better pay attention in high school so I won't have to go to college . . . is that right? . . . So college gets you prepared to go to a university?"

African American Tasha Thompson came to Wilson High School as a 14-year-old struggling with family troubles. Tasha, her mom, her five siblings, and a nephew lived in a neighborhood south of Wilson known for drug activity and gang-related violence. They were just glad to be together. Tasha's mom's earlier bouts with drug and alcohol abuse led her to relinquish custody of her children to an aunt. Now sober and having regained custody of her children, Tasha's mom both worked and went to school. Fiercely proud of her mother's recovery, Tasha cared for the other children, helping them with their homework, meals, and baths, and getting them to bed each night. Her mom emphasized that education was the key to "succeeding in this world" and that Tasha should be the first college graduate in their family. They used a false address to avoid the neighborhood school and enroll Tasha at Wilson High. They had no idea that the courses Tasha was taking would not prepare her for college.

Arturo Alvarez, like Nina, was undocumented. Arturo's dad found work as an upholsterer, and the family struggled to pay rent in the Wilson neighborhood, where the children could attend good schools. As a fifth grader without English, Arturo struggled alongside his White and affluent classmates. Feeling rejected because he was "not from here," Arturo believed that his lack of English was seen as a lack of intelligence. As a ninth grader entering Wilson High, however, the lanky teenager was proud of both his Zacatecan roots and his school achievements. Nicknamed "Flaco" (skinny), he sported a thin dark mustache, dressed in long sleeve shirts buttoned to the top, and wore a large cross hanging from a chain around his neck. By then, he had learned English, gotten very good grades, and was a model of good behavior. It was not uncommon to hear Wilson administrators and teachers question, "Why aren't more of them like Arturo?" Nobody, however, had suggested that Arturo take honors classes or plan a path to college.

Olivia Velasquez, a California-born Latina, was the oldest of her immigrant parents' four daughters. Her dad, a Wilson High alumnus, earned enough as a bus driver to pay for a small three-bedroom, second-floor apartment overlooking a gas station near the school. As a ninth grader, Olivia worked hard to balance her schoolwork with her responsibilities as the oldest child. Her parents wanted her to prepare for college, and they pressed her to study hard, but they also needed her to miss school from time to time to help out at home or to translate for her mother at doctor's office visits. Olivia often stayed up late, finishing her homework after her parents and siblings had gone to bed.

African American Imani Edwards grew up hearing a lot about Wilson High School, even though she lived nowhere near the school. Both her single mother and her older brother had gone to Wilson, and both had been expelled. Despite this unhappy history, Imani and her mom were convinced that Wilson was the best place for Imani to get the good education they both wanted so badly for her. They used Imani's grandmother's address to prove local residency, and the two of them got up at 5:30 each morning to avoid rush hour traffic on the long drive to school. Imani knew that she was college bound. Strikingly articulate and assertive, she made her plans clear to everyone, and she won a coveted spot in a ninth grade honors English class. Once admitted, however, this self-identified "excuse expert" repeatedly missed school on test days and turned in assignments late. Sadly, her astonishing verbal fluency and sophistication had never produced for her the learning opportunities or confidence she needed to succeed with academic writing. Imani hid her struggles and poor grades with characteristic bravado, fooling her classmates into thinking her path to college was smooth.

IN CHAPTER 2, we described Wilson High, the school these five students attended. In many ways, they were very lucky to be at Wilson, with its ample resources, college-prep course offerings, well-qualified teachers, and commitment to education equity. So few teenagers like them attend such schools. Yet, despite all these advantages, Nina, Tasha, Arturo, Olivia, and Imani were caught in the second of Wilson's "two schools." This was the school characterized by low expectations and enrollment in courses that would not qualify them for 4-year college attendance. They entered Wilson as "typical" and "average" students and, except for Imani's spot in honors English, they were placed in regular-track classes.

As pointed out in Chapter 2, although nominally approved as college preparatory, Wilson's regular-track classes were designed for students with poor prospects for higher education other than the local community college. The extensive honors and Advanced Placement (AP) course offerings made up the track where students were groomed for elite 4-year colleges and universities. The school climate had few expectations that students, once placed in the lower track, would move to the higher track. There was no policy—written or in practice—that asked school personnel to initiate, persuade, cajole, argue, or in any other way motivate students to reach beyond the school's original diagnosis of their low potential. So, although half of the ninth-grade class was students of color, only 5% of those enrolled in ninth-grade honors English were African American or Latino.

THE FUTURES PROJECT

In the spring before Nina, Olivia, Arturo, and Imani enrolled in Wilson as ninth graders, Wilson's principal Rudy Stanton and district superintendent Sandra Nesbitt participated in inquiry groups exploring how to solve the "two schools" problem. As research partners in the school's reform efforts, we facilitated the inquiry discussions and encouraged the educators to examine the different trajectories that regular and honors-track students travel through Wilson. We asked:

- How do students get sorted into these different tracks?
- Do students in the regular track—particularly students of color—conceive of and pursue their pathways through high school and beyond differently from students in the honors track?
- What will students in the regular and honors track be doing years after graduation?
- What knowledge and skills will they be using?
- How, if at all, will their different Wilson experiences connect to their futures as citizens, community members, and workers?

We raised these questions as rhetorical prompts to encourage a broad reexamination of Wilson's tracking patterns. The Wilson educators took the questions seriously. They expressed interest both in learning more about the trajectories and in the possibilities of transforming them. We suggested a strategy for pursuing both of these goals—engage a group of students from the regular track in studying the trajectories of Wilson students. Our thinking was that if regular-track students themselves investigated these questions, they could generate new, and much-needed, insights. We also thought that engaging regular-track ninth graders in studying these questions might be a good way to smooth their own transition to high school and support their preparation for college—if, of course, that was what they wanted. Principal Stanton lent support to these ideas and suggested that we work with a new ninth-grade humanities class targeting students of color who needed extra support and encouragement. We agreed to collaborate with teacher Christopher Antonopoulos in designing the class and the students' study.

That next fall, Antonopoulos's ninth graders began studying a diverse group of Wilson seniors who came from both the regular and honors tracks. They also studied some students who had gone to the district's continuation school

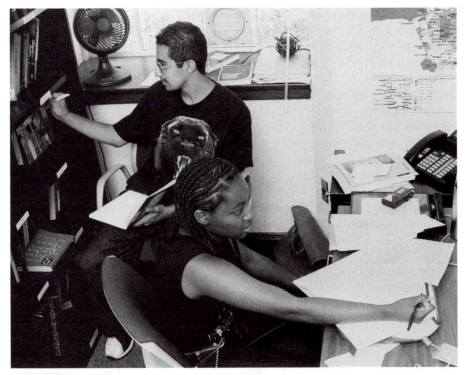

Collecting data in telephone interviews with older students and educational researchers.

(a small program for students who, for behavioral or other problems, had difficulty succeeding in the large high school) or who had dropped out altogether. The ninth graders interviewed their "subjects" about their post–high school plans and how their experiences as Wilson students had helped shape them. They evaluated the 12th graders' academic transcripts and shadowed them throughout the school day. The ninth graders analyzed their data in class together, looking at the relationships among student background, school experiences, and long-term goals. In the process, the Futures students learned how to create data collection protocols, to conduct interviews, to do observations, and to code data. They also sought to make sense of the powerful stories that emerged about students' lives. Most of the Futures students saw for the first time the vastly different paths that students take through high school and what those paths mean for life's chances.

By the end of the year, we realized that there was a great deal more to be learned about this "experiment" we had created. Further, we noticed changes in the Futures students' knowledge and views of their school that few of their peers experienced. For some, we had helped awaken interests and spark knowledge that would be a shame to abandon. We began to speculate that the students' experience as researchers of the high school dynamics that they were also living might foster academic skills, educational insights, and greater commitment to school success. If that were accurate, the project could be a site for Wilson educators to develop new structures and pedagogic practices that could address the "two schools" problem.

Antonopoulos agreed to collaborate with our UCLA research team and to stay with the students, if they wanted, for another 3 years. He asked Nina, Olivia, Arturo, and Imani, along with the others in his humanities class, if they would like to continue their work together over the next 3 years as the "Futures Project." As Futures students, they would have Antonopoulos as their social studies teacher every year, and together they would continue their study of students' pathways through high school and would support one another as they followed those pathways themselves. The 19 girls and 11 boys who agreed to participate (including Tasha, who, although not in Antonopoulos's class, begged to join the group) were students of color—20 Latino, 9 African American, and 1 South East Asian. All were from working-class families; two thirds had qualified for free or reduced lunch in middle school. Their middle school grades were mediocre (averaging a grade point average of 2.66, or roughly C+) and, if they went to college, all but two would be first-generation college-goers. Half resided inside the high school district, and half attended with or without "out of district" permits.

Over the next 3 years, the 30 Futures students became members of a new sort of research community. Together, in their social studies classes and in summer research seminars at UCLA, the students, Wilson teachers, and our UCLA research team studied high school students' aspirations, course taking, and achievement; social stratification; the distribution of educational opportunity; and policies aimed at achieving educational equity. We considered concrete phenomena at Wilson High School; national schooling patterns; and theoretical constructs related to such topics as differential access to resources, tracking, schools' relationships with families, and student resistance.

We also posed questions about the Futures students themselves:

- Would learning the "secrets" of college preparation help the Futures students translate their aspirations into action?
- Would the students recognize the power of intellectual work by studying their peers' (and their own) pathways through high school?
- Would they become more engaged in school?
- If so, how would this engagement affect Wilson's structures and opportunities?

We observed the students and Antonopoulos in classrooms, and we interviewed them, their parents, their teachers, and even ourselves. We collected and analyzed school documents, and we sat in on teacher gatherings, in reform meetings, and in many informal sites for students and parents. These more conventional data-gathering activities produced volumes, shelves, and garages full of data, but much of our understanding came from working directly with the students and with Antonopoulos, regularly attending Antonopoulos's classes—participating, coaching, and counseling. As indicated in Chapter 3, we called the Futures project a "social design experiment," and, throughout we moved dialectically between designing strategies, collecting data, building theory, and participating.

Futures participants systematically documented the students' day-to-day project experiences in the attempt to capture the factors that influenced their education and learning. Teacher Antonopoulos's field notes and memos often recorded factors influencing students' academic achievement (family, personal, and social issues) and the critical moments when they identified themselves as a college-going (or non-college-going) student. Through data collection and analysis, the project itself was continuously reexamined as a site of learning and teaching.

PARTICIPATORY SOCIAL INQUIRY

At the end of Chapter 3, we outlined the principles of participatory social inquiry we draw from Dewey's scholarship. Although we certainly will not claim that we designed the Futures project to align neatly with these principles, they were in our minds. Throughout, Dewey's thinking informed the Futures work.

Engaging Those Most Impacted

Dewey stressed that social inquiry must engage those who are most affected by inegalitarian social policy. The 30 student researchers, diverse as they certainly were, all faced dim prospects for navigating the school's curriculum toward eligibility and admission to 4-year colleges. They entered Wilson High School with weak academic preparation and limited access to social networks with college knowledge. And they experienced all the barriers and risks that American high schools present for students of color, students with low income, students with limited English, and undocumented students.

In a loose and undeveloped way, the students, many teachers, and the researchers shared a goal of altering the students' trajectories through high school from one that led simply to graduation, if that, to one that led to admission to and success in a 4-year college. Could these students make that switch? How? Were there lessons for schooling generally? Was Dewey correct in believing that sharing and distributing inquiry among those who had a stake in the knowledge derived would produce more useful knowledge than inquiry that treated students as traditional research subjects?

We were not so naive, however, to expect these students, on their own, to provide an understanding of their stratified American high school. We knew that only with the support of highly skilled teachers and experts familiar with research and theory could (or would) the students construct knowledge that would be useful either to their school or to themselves. Like Dewey, we sought a defined (though not necessarily limited) role as and for experts. We began working with the students when they were 14 years old. Regardless of how we might have presented ourselves initially, we gradually became teachers and allies, as well as researchers.

We thought that Wilson teachers and our university research team could contribute best as partners with the students in a new kind of research community that worked side-by-side over time, asking questions, exploring hunches, scrutinizing existing knowledge, and using the tools of research to generate new knowledge. The teachers and researchers could use their expertise by "discovering and making known facts," but we would not claim exclusive authority for asserting the meaning of those facts. The students would employ their own expertise to make sense of what we learned in light of their own school and life experiences, and would test out those ideas in dialogue with one another and with the adults who, admittedly, had very different experiences. The bottom line was that the students, like Dewey's man trying out the shoemaker's newly constructed shoe, would know "best . . . where it pinches."

The students participated as research apprentices working alongside university researchers who were investigating the sociology of urban education. This student–researcher relationship was pivotal to much of the Futures project. The apprenticeship model enabled researchers to position their "self-interest" with accuracy and dignity. The project was never about "helping" needy students. The passion and curiosity the researchers had for their work provided a credible model for the students' participation. A project such as this could easily devolve into separate, self-focused missions. Instead, the academic core of the researchers' life work (not at all unrelated to the students' interests) provided a space for mutual engagement. This work was seen by all as a social good that belonged neither to the students (as recipients of a service) nor to the researchers (as consumers of information about students) alone.

As students assumed the identity and the tools of educational researchers, and as they developed their intellectual prowess, they became core participants in a research-oriented community of practice.[1] The students participated in serious consultations in which experts as well as students learned. In Dewey's words, instead of gaining an understanding that is "cold and at arms' length," we wanted the "understanding and sympathy that would spring from direct and vital contact."[2] The collaboration was incredibly fruitful for the adults as well as the students.

Reviewing data analysis with IDEA researcher.

To speak of communities of practice and apprenticeships does not capture the "direct and vital contact" that takes place in an authentic community of caring adults and young people who are eager for learning, schooling, and emotional support. As the students studied their regular schoolwork together, as they worked together on the Futures research, and as they hung out together, they developed strong relationships. These bonds buffered the conflicts that arose when they tried to act like college-bound high school students and simply did not know how, or felt it was impossible. When a student seemed to be drifting away—perhaps out of the Futures project altogether—the others could regroup and draw that individual back in. The students' development was not uniform, and there were always some students who were doing brilliantly well and some who were hanging on the precipice. Much insight was gained in figuring out another's success or troubles. And, of course, there were always adults nearby to scaffold the academic and social learning.

In her sophomore year Tasha began to characterize Futures as a "family" and as a "home" where, although "everyone isn't always happy with each other," people were free to express themselves. She credited these trusting relationships with keeping her from quitting school in the 10th grade:

> I was going to drop out and no one really knew but Mr. Antonopoulos. I would get up in the morning, get dressed, get all the kids dressed, walk out of the house with them like I was going to school, wait maybe 30, 45 minutes and come right back home. I wasn't motivated. School wasn't a place I wanted to be. I was like an outsider in a weird way. I knew everybody, but I didn't want to hang with those people. . . . I came to school one day, and Mr. Antonopoulos just talked to me; he just sat down, and he had a real conversation with me, and told me that I needed to be there. I think a couple of days later we were in class and one of the girls in Futures said something and we had this really deep conversation and she started to cry. From that day everybody started opening up. I don't know exactly what I shared, but [I stayed in class] from everybody reaching out to me and from Mr. Antonopoulos being there at the right time when I needed someone to tell me "you need to go to school and do this."

By her junior year, even Imani, who had earlier proclaimed that "no one" at Wilson could offer her academic or personal support, came to depend on the community:

> Futures is a great network of people who we've grown to trust. And it's their supporting us . . . [that] makes going through a system that we're learning is unjust and against us . . . a little bit easier.

Olivia articulated how their common understandings led the Futures students to be able to help one another negotiate their taxing senior year:

> Futures was also a place where we vented a lot, especially during our senior year. We were doing all this research and learning all this different stuff. We also had school going on and everything else that comes along with being 17. When we got together we kind of let all our emotions out. We learned how to support one another. We learned that we were all going through the same things—financial problems, family problems, school problems. I mean, those are heavy burdens, especially. One of the things that helped a lot of us get through difficult times during our senior year was that we had to help one another. I think it had to do with the topics we were studying, but I do think that it was because we spent so much time together.

The relationships that were created and fostered were not confined to the classroom setting. As juniors and seniors, Futures students made overnight trips to visit colleges and to do research presentations. The travel time provided opportunities for wide-ranging discussion on topics that often led to heated disagreements—topics that, in Tasha's words, "hit home with everybody." These intense discussions fused the intellectual and the personal, deepening students' connections with one another.

Project-provided computers and Internet access allowed students to engage in a lively electronic network with each other and with the Futures adults. Their cyberspace community and support network took their joint academic work and personal relationships beyond the traditional school day. This increased the students' opportunities for supporting one another, opened new channels for mentoring, and gave teachers new insight into students' lives outside of school. Students confided problems, doubts, and insights, and teachers offered encouragement, assistance, and advice in ways that went beyond the norm of face-to-face classroom interactions. Even as late as finals week of the students' senior year, Chris Antonopoulos used instant messaging at 12:30 a.m. to persuade one Futures student to stay up that night to write a final paper and become the first in his family to graduate from high school. He did.

Ensuring Access to Knowledge and Its Construction

At Wilson High School, knowledge about navigating a college-bound pathway was the near-exclusive property of the privileged. White and wealthy families not only had more familiarity with the content of the curriculum, they had considerably more information about college preparation and access. Moreover, they routinely used their knowledge to secure advantages for their own children—negotiating regularly for the "best" teachers, for honors class placements for children who had not met the stated criteria, and for more.[3] Accordingly, Futures sought to equalize access to knowledge by providing the students and their families with support in learning the content of their courses, with access to the "secrets" of navigating high school, and with a chance to engage sociological scholarship that could help them better understand their current place within the unequal patterns of high school success and college participation.

The specific content of the students' social studies classes with Chris Antonopoulos changed from year to year to meet the college-preparatory curriculum requirements. The curriculum engaged the students in rigorous intellectual work characteristic of honors classes. As 10th graders, for example, they explored world history by studying the biographies of leaders and everyday people across the world and in several historical periods. These biographies laid the groundwork for the students to write biographical sketches of their own family histories—sketches that frequently followed family members across national boundaries. Next, the students wrote educational autobiographies and drew on social theory to make sense of critical moments in their own development.

Each year, the students delved into the type of "college knowledge" that their more advantaged peers accessed around the family dinner table. We created "Futures and Families," a monthly seminar where students, alongside their parents, learned about multiple types of colleges and universities (i.e., technical colleges, community colleges, first- and second-tier state universities, and independents), as well as what courses, grade point averages, and tests various schools require for admission. Students developed 4-year academic plans and identified potential barriers and solutions to their own college eligibility. They helped one another apply for admission to honors courses, studied for SAT and ACT college admissions tests together, and went on college trips. As seniors, the group took on learning about financial aid applications.

Beyond the nuts and bolts of college preparation, the students investigated research and theory about the systemic barriers facing low-income students of color and strategies for grappling with them. This crucial work gave the students a nuanced understanding of why their struggle was something more complex and daunting than simply learning the steps or following the protocols one might find in a self-help pamphlet. On one occasion, UCLA sociologist Daniel Solórzano introduced the students to his research on the "academic pipeline," documenting the high rates of attrition among Chicano secondary students and their low enrollment and matriculation rates within higher education. In another instance, Wilson's African American principal, Rudy Stanton, discussed academic theories of negotiating between home and school cultures, includ-

Discussing social reproduction and critical race theories with UCLA professor Daniel Solórzano.

ing "code-switching" between standard and nonstandard English. He shared stories about how he applied these theories in his own life.

Complementing their Wilson schoolwork, the Futures summer seminars at UCLA plunged the students more deeply into the sociology of education. Each summer, they read excerpts from seminal books and articles from research journals. They found sociology—particularly work on social stratification and inequality—quite astonishing. Although most students recognized inequalities in their lives and schools, they had no broad understanding of the historical or structural bases for inequality. Students often blamed themselves for the inequality, and most students lacked the language to describe their experiences. Not surprisingly, they were taken aback by empirical studies showing systemic patterns of inequality, and they were intrigued by sociological explanations. One of their first and most moving encounters was with Jay MacLeod's study of low-income teenagers of color in *Ain't No Makin' It*, particularly with his use of Pierre Bourdieu's capital theory.[4]

The students received college credit for their participation in the UCLA summer seminars—credit that bolstered their high school academic transcripts and academic standing as entering college freshman. Observers commented that the seminars resembled graduate school courses more than undergraduate work, and that the seminars were nothing at all like what students experience in high school.

An Experimental Approach. An experimental approach, and more important, an experimental attitude, Dewey believed, would provide the public with the fundamental methods of inquiry—"tools . . . of observing, reporting, and organizing."[5] Participants must reveal their experiences and perspectives, gather new information, generate and test hypotheses, and adopt the "method" of science in assessing social policies.

The Futures summer seminars relied on tools of systematic inquiry and helped young people use those tools to subject their ideas "to constant and well-equipped observation . . . and ready and flexible revision."[6] That's a tall order for teenagers whose classmates were at the beach. But these students' friends were with them on the UCLA campus, and their work seemed to them not quite as formidable as John Dewey might have described it.

In the summer of 1999, the students formed four research groups—each examining a sociological topic related to their own schooling experiences: the influence of family on education, the importance of language in schools, the links between popular culture and school curriculum, and student resistance. Each group formulated a research question, created a research design, collected and analyzed data, generated findings and implications, wrote up their results, and presented them using PowerPoint slides.

In the summer of 2000, the students used the Democratic National Convention in downtown Los Angeles as a site to study public policy issues affecting

Conducting a content analysis of contrasting news stories about the 2000 Democratic National Convention.

them: youth access to education and to the media, the living wage movement, and civic engagement in urban centers. Tasha and her research group investigated youth access to the media. Equipped with data collection protocols, tape recorders, and video cameras, the students interviewed members of the press in the streets of downtown Los Angeles, inside the Convention Center, and in the main offices of the *Los Angeles Times* and the Spanish language newspaper *La Opinión*. Their data collection focused on how reporters decide which stories are "news" and how they portray youth.

Legitimizing Multiple Sources of Knowledge. Futures brought multiple experiences and perspectives to all matters under discussion—from traditional research findings to participants' own experiences and insights. Including the students' experiences was not at all like the intellectually dismissive attitude assumed by some teachers when working with teenagers—making the work "relevant" by getting the students to think about themselves rather than the larger or more general problem. Rather, the students' experiences could inform their inquiry into social problems, because by this time they could embed those experiences in theory and a scholarly perspective, and vice versa. This work combined, in Dewey's words, book learning and the "troubles and aspirations" of those experiencing the problems,[7] and the result was construction of new and useful knowledge.

For the Futures students, these multiple sources of knowledge gradually became iterative, not simply additive. That is, theory, dialogue, empirical grounding, research, experience, ideology, and more can be learned and "collected," but without a critique that exposes, tests, and makes flexible and conditional— without an "experimental attitude"—it is impossible to construct something useful out of the knowledge that has been experienced or received.

Increasingly, students drew meaningful and generative connections between personal stories and larger patterns and structures of inequality. Tasha, for example, came to understand her own experience in the light of sociological knowledge: "Before I became a member of the Futures Project I had no idea that I was being tracked; I did not even know what tracking was or that tracking existed." She came to appreciate the value of drawing on both personal experiences and knowledge generated through systematic inquiry:

> It is important that we share stories so that we can work together to solve all the problems that are going on. But we also need more people to go out there and research why minorities are in low positions in our society. If no one goes out and finds this data, then how are we going to try and change things? We will not have any proof that anything is wrong.

In some very concrete ways, Futures recalls Dewey's early work directing his laboratory school at the University of Chicago. The Dewey school encouraged young people to apply the tools of intelligence to everyday experience while practicing egalitarian social relationships.

The Futures students' research culminated in their senior-year government class, where they undertook a class research project entitled, "Futures versus the State of California." The project combined the students' prior research on the inequitable distribution of AP classes with new information about student rights and state educational law. It also followed on the heels of our recent work as experts in a civil rights lawsuit (*Daniel v. California*) challenging these inequities.[8] The students' research assessed their own schooling circumstances in light of legal and theoretical foundations, and, in Dewey's terms, they applied their intellectual tools to the real problems of their lives.

Futures students investigated students' access to AP courses at Wilson by bringing to bear their own multiple sources of knowledge. They considered personal experience, study of a contemporary lawsuit on course availability, publicly available data, interviews, and, of course, by then, their own development as "experts" in the broad arena of socially just schooling. For example, Arturo was a highly qualified student who initially was not encouraged to take the advanced courses that neither he nor his immigrant family had knowledge of.

After interviewing Wilson students taking AP psychology courses, Arturo and Tasha learned that the White students had far more knowledge than the students of color about gaining access to AP classes, the benefits of those courses such as weighted grades and increased college access, and the potential to skip introductory courses in college.

Adopting a Critical Stance

Dewey believed that knowledge construction was not simply technical and neutral, but influenced by powerful interests. Elites controlled what knowledge was considered sensible and whether this knowledge would become widely socially embraced as "facts." To no one's surprise, the facts that prevailed in this construction enterprise were those that gained or preserved the elites' advantages. Dewey noted with some concern the increasing power of public relations professionals to shape and put into circulation knowledge that favors elites. As pointed out in Chapter 3, he argued that the public must look critically at social facts and explanations that "rationaliz[e] . . . the misery and cultural degradation of others."[9]

By the time they were seniors, the Futures students had developed a strong critique of the "facts" about school achievement, college preparation, and college admissions. Alongside their inescapable induction into mainstream social, political, and economic thinking in which competition, merit, strong individualism, and so on, constituted the "even playing field" of American democracy, the project introduced the Futures students to critical social theory that would, at least, allow them to consider alternative explanations of disparities among groups of students. We wanted the students to be able to use social theories to recognize the structural and historical contexts underlying their educational experiences, or, in Dewey's framing, to "locate the source" of everyday problems.

Social reproduction theory, for example, gave the students a theoretical tool to consider the pathway from college readiness to college enrollment as something other than a matter of individual volition (and all that this might imply for assigning individual blame). Instead of viewing the path to college as transparent, objective, and inclusive, the students could, first, identify advantages conferred by access to private information, exclusive networks, and money; next, they could imagine counterstrategies that would add some counterweight to their own less-favored status. The students discussed whether, as Bourdieu's theories would suggest, advantaged Wilson High students and their families can use their wealth and social connections to gain critical college-access information. Advantaged students, they concluded, may either acquire this information directly from their families (cultural capital), access the information from networks of friends (social capital), or pay someone who has the information they need (economic capital).

Like most of the Futures students, Tasha came to see the value of a critical lens in understanding her own experience:

> I draw upon my personal experience and on critical social theory. . . . I use social reproduction theory to make sense of my position as a working-class African American female who struggled to gain college access. The critical research influenced me by giving a name to my experiences and helping me to understand that these oppressive cycles can be broken.

The students were also profoundly affected by recent resistance theory and critical race theory (CRT), and they used these theories to investigate how students' negative attitudes and behavior at school might reflect and embody larger economic, religious, gendered, racialized, and political structures and cultural norms.[10] They were particularly impressed with studies of how students' resistance need not be self-destructive but could actually propel them toward positive ends. The following hopeful passage from Solórzano and Villalpando really struck home:

> Students of Color can redefine their marginal location as a place where they can draw strength. They are then able to identify strategies to succeed in a place they perceive to be oppressive. Moreover, in order for Students of Color to complete a degree and accrue other experiential benefits from college, they engage in oppositional behavior by learning and using critical skills to navigate through the system.[11]

The Futures students used Solórzano and Delgado Bernal's resistance model to identify four different forms of resistance and, more important, to understand what transformational resistance looks like within a contemporary high school context. They concluded that students who engage in transformative resistance need to have a high critique of social oppression and take positive action to promote social justice. This frame enabled the students to add a positive attribute to their emerging identities as persons with a public purpose.

Nina shared her prior belief that low academic performance resulted from a lack of effort, a form of students' self-defeating behavior:

> As I conducted research, I was both academically challenged and personally enriched. I learned to critically analyze my experience as a student of color in an "integrated" high school, like Wilson High.
>
> It really opened my eyes. . . . Because I was a recent immigrant . . . I wasn't aware of how the school system works. . . . From the theories we studied, I was more understanding of other students' experiences, I looked at it differently. . . . Before, I would have first blamed the students. Second, I'd blame the school system. Now, not just the school system, but the whole society.

The students began to see their efforts to gain information and help with their own college access as a means of deliberately appropriating the strategies used by more advantaged students whose capital made such strategies seem natural.

Constructing a Transformative Goal

The ultimate goal of Futures was to test whether or not engaging regular-track students as a community of researchers seeking to understand and disrupt race and social class patterns of inequality in school success and access to college would be transformative. First, would participation in that engagement alter students' paths through high school and beyond; would the paths be different from those predicted for them as ninth graders? Second, would the project influence the school to instantiate new structures and practices that would disrupt common patterns of inequality?

Drawing again from Dewey, we had imagined that the Futures team would develop a collective identity as they acted jointly on their shared knowledge and aspirations, that they would construct a story of who they are, what they do, and why they do it. We thought that their collective identity and "story" would allow them to envision and realize more hopeful futures for themselves. By uncovering common structural elements of their isolated or incoherent grievances, we thought they might transform their knowledge, experience, commitments, and relationships into useful "capital" for achieving their goals. We also thought that by sharing what they had learned and become, the Futures students could press the Wilson community to reconsider policies and practices that limited the academic progress of low-income students of color.

Constructing New Identities. Futures created a space that gave the students an opportunity to shape, construct, and negotiate identities different from the ones that their placement in Wilson's "second school" gave them. And, in fact, they took on identities that were bound up with knowledge and skills related to college-going and to the research process through which they had developed their knowledge and skills. As their academic skills improved, their interest in higher-level courses increased and their understanding of the system deepened; the students began to see themselves as college-going individuals. This shift was quite different from "increased confidence" to take demanding courses. The new identity countered, but did not eliminate, a powerful and enduring *lack* of confidence. Frequently, the students struggled to keep up; daily, they shared classes with students who were better prepared for the norms and challenges of those classes. Indeed, theirs was the identity of persons who belonged in challenging classes, were realistically less confident, but would persevere both on their own behalf and for others like them.

They also came to see and talk about themselves as "critical researchers." Notably, their years of participation in critical social science research provided the Futures students with a broader sense of what college access and degree attainment might mean. They came to see the university as more than an extended social opportunity or another set of hurdles to jump on the way to a profession. Several of them came to see themselves as critical college-going students seeking to prepare themselves to give back to their communities and help recreate schools as democratic institutions.

Nina's critical stance and her goal to achieve academically and attend college became entwined. She began to see her academic achievements as a means to work for change within the educational system and community. Despite how flawed she found the system, she desperately wanted to achieve and meet success within it, and she believed that Futures could help her do just that:

> [Futures] is really preparing me to survive in this world especially in a country like this one because there's a lot of injustice. There's really nothing that has been done to repair all the damage. Being aware and knowing what your rights are [is preparation].

Capitalizing Their Knowledge, Experience, and Commitments. In the most immediate sense, the Futures community became a source of capital for the students; that is, it generated resources they could exchange for valued outcomes. One of the most striking examples was the community of support they developed around taking Wilson's most advanced classes. Partly because the Futures students knew that they could count on one another and the Futures adults for support, the students enrolled in more and more honors and AP classes. Their collective enrollment went from 7 classes in 10th grade, to 22 classes in 11th grade, to 41 classes in their senior year. Most significantly, the connections between the Futures adults and the rest of the faculty enabled seven of the Futures students to negotiate placement in the same AP English class. Because they were clustered together, the students were more confident about participating in challenging classes where students of color were rarely enrolled.

The students found ways to turn their transformative resistance into capital that had exchange value in the college-going process. This confirmed that they did not have to give up entirely their "neighborhood" identity or become indistinguishable from middle-class students and their values and identities. As a junior, Nina joined the staff of the school newspaper, where, despite some opposition from the student editors, she created the first Spanish language news column in the 105-year-old newspaper. "My articles are mainly based on issues affecting students of color, including ESL [English as a second language] students whose issues are not taken into consideration and who often times are marginalized." Although Nina saw this column as a way to express herself and give back to her community, her column was also useful "capital" that would enhance her college applications.

Several Futures students developed their leadership capabilities as they created safe and transformative spaces for younger students of color within the school and the community. They were elected to student government, facilitated sessions at a retreat on race relations, and founded a new organization for indigenous students. Tasha joined the activist group "Teens Against Violence and Abuse" and a young women's discussion group. Olivia created "Club Unidos" with another Futures student. The club began a tutoring program at an inner-city middle school. This transformative work helped bring the knowledge and experiences of high school students of color into Wilson High School's mainstream.

The students had the worth and status of their knowledge confirmed when they presented their research findings to various audiences both in and outside Wilson High. Without this evidence that their knowledge was broadly useful, they might have been more inclined to see themselves as anomalies among students of color—special students with arcane knowledge. Instead, they shared their insights with Wilson student, teacher, and parent groups, as well as with graduate education classes and at education conferences. They also thought that their actions could lead to change. They believed, for example, that their enrollment in AP courses would blaze a trail for other low-income, minority youth in the school setting.

Sharing Disruptive Knowledge. The seminars of 1999 and 2000 culminated in comprehensive oral presentations by the student-researchers. These presentations were delivered to an audience of UCLA faculty and graduate students, school administrators, school board members, state officials, community organizers, and parents. "I had never heard my child talk like that before," marveled one mother. A number of professors agreed that the student presentations represented college-level work. Professor Daniel Solórzano, whose work the students had studied, was particularly impressed, "I think they were able to grasp this field called the Sociology of Education generally. . . [I]t's not like we have a group of our graduate students, and we're talking about them. We're talking about 10th graders."[12]

With the presentation of the results of their inquiry, the Futures students became agents with voices. They still encountered efforts to marginalize them, but they found small cracks in the barriers of injustice through which their command of the tools and methods of inquiry gave them legitimacy. Increasingly, they elbowed for themselves narrow spots at the tables of power from which they would not budge; often enough, they were welcomed.

Shortly after the shootings at Columbine High School, Vice-President Gore held a press conference on the Wilson campus. Imani, along with four other Futures students, was invited to be part of the audience of about 100 students in the school library. Imani recalled the event:

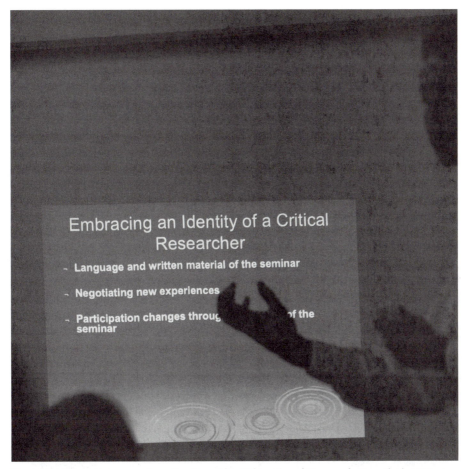

Presenting Futures research at the American Educational Research Association Meeting in 2003.

Vice-President Gore visited my high school following the Columbine incident. The meeting was described as a dialogue between students and politicians to combat teen violence within schools, but Gore conveniently announced his run for the presidency at a press conference in the front of the school. During the dialogue, the Vice-President asked what we as a society could do to make students feel more at ease in school. I raised my hand and responded that there are students who are not represented in the curriculum and asked what steps we could take [on] a state and federal level to make all students feel represented. Gore proceeded to ignore both my questions and the round of applause I received from my peers.

To be sure, most of the Futures students had public moments where they could be proud of their knowledge, their articulateness, and their power to disrupt commonplace thinking. More poignant, however, was their rising to the daily challenges that generate little applause and may go no further than their family and friends. Tasha told us:

> The hard thing is trying to make my family aware of what is happening to them. Yes, I understand what social reproduction is because I had the Futures class that taught me what I needed to know. It also influenced me to learn many other things on my own. However, my siblings are still going to schools that Oakes talked about, where they are tracked. So how do you tell someone that the classes that they are in are not classes that will help them? How do you explain to your family what tracking is? Most parents don't have the time to do the research that I did. They are too busy trying to provide for their families, so they don't have time to learn information like this. How are you going to get them on the level that they are truly supposed to be on when they have been tracked for so long that they are far behind and think they are on the track they are supposed to be on?

Transforming Wilson High. The Futures students could not help but see themselves as both affected by and partly responsible for Wilson's English department's move to ease restrictions for 11th- and 12th-grade honors English classes. Therefore, their collective breath was taken away when, as seniors, the predominantly White and affluent Parent Teacher Student Association challenged the English department to create more tracking and therefore more isolation of students of color. As we described in Chapter 2, these parents believed a new honors track of English courses between AP and the regular college-prep English courses would provide their students with an appropriate curriculum. At the same time, these same parents pressed the social studies department to create a 10th-grade AP world history class. The social studies department, proud of its economically and racially diverse sections of world history, knew that an AP course would likely increase segregation.

The tracking debates that ensued were conducted on high-volume Web sites and e-mail list serves, as well as in presentations at school meetings. Futures students were well aware that these discussions implicated their activism and push for college access. At one point, Imani and one of her fellow Futures students were challenged to a debate on tracking in their AP English class by a Harvard-bound classmate. They cited evidence from empirical research and challenged their counterparts to provide data to back up their arguments. They tried to advance theories about why advantaged students might hold tightly to the myth of meritocracy. They were ignored.

Later, in the Futures class, they recounted the passionate argument while the rest of the group listened attentively and provided critical feedback. Angry, the

Futures students decided to take the issue to the student government. They rehearsed their arguments and prepared their case to the student body officers with several research articles about tracking. Once again, they were dismissed:

> Every time we schedule a time to discuss the articles, the Associated Student Body president and the student school board representative always say we have something else to do today and "we can discuss it later." They also keep asking for some articles in favor of tracking, before they have even read [the original tracking article they provided].

The student government never engaged in an open and sustained dialogue. The advantaged students who thought they had much to lose by de-tracking classes had successfully filibustered the dialogue with plans for the prom, Krispy Kreme Day, and the fashion show. Transforming Wilson High turned out to be far more difficult than even we had anticipated.

WHAT HAPPENED TO FUTURES?

As ninth graders, most of the Futures students viewed their regular-track courses, their relatively low status at school, and their teachers' perceptions of them (as not college bound) as a natural and inevitable outcome of their social and personal worth. This changed as they studied the trajectories of their older peers, read in the sociology of education, and drew connections between their own experiences and the structures, practices, beliefs, and politics that sustain or disrupt patterns of inequality in the schools. Increasingly, they risked signing up for honors and AP classes, sought leadership positions at the school, and developed ways to share their knowledge with other students—what they called "giving back."

In the spring of 2000, all but one of the Futures students graduated from Wilson—a pretty remarkable feat. The Futures students far outpaced the high school graduation and 4-year college-going rates of a matched comparison group of African American and Latino students who began ninth grade with the Futures students but who did not participate in Futures.[13] The high school graduation rate of the Futures students was 97% compared with 75% for the comparison group of students. The Futures' average cumulative grade point average at the end of 12th grade was 2.52 compared with 2.37 for the matched group. The small difference in grades becomes significant when we consider that the Futures students took far more challenging courses than their peers. Further, in all likelihood, the additional 15% of students in the matched group who dropped out were those with the lowest grades. Had they stayed in school at the rates of the Futures students, the difference between the two groups' grades would have been much larger.

The Futures students' grades were not uniformly stellar, in part because they had taken very challenging courses, but 25 of the original 30 had 4-year college acceptances in hand. In fall 2001, 16 enrolled in 4-year schools, 9 others went to 2-year colleges, and 2 enrolled at a technical or vocational school. Consequently, in the fall following high school graduation, 90% of the Futures students were enrolled in some form of higher education: 4-year university, 2-year college, or a vocational program. In these outcomes, too, the Futures students did far better than their comparable Wilson peers.[14]

Notably, of those students attending 2- or 4-year colleges or universities, all but three attended with another member of the Futures cohort—a decision most students made intentionally as a way to stay connected.

GAINS THROUGH STRUGGLE

The success of the Futures students did not come easily. Throughout high school they struggled in school and out. By their own accounts, however, being a part of Futures helped them both to navigate high school and to understand the barriers they faced in the process. All the students left Wilson with a strong sense of themselves as young intellectuals who belonged in college and who hoped to return ready to contribute to their home communities.

Hurdles at Wilson

Olivia's good grades were the product of enormous effort. She stayed up to finish her homework after the rest of her family was in bed. She took extra summer school classes to jump from her basic math track into college-preparatory classes. She challenged herself in honors and AP classes even though she felt extraordinarily uncomfortable in them. But, in at least one case, the pressure of being in a "White" class was too much:

> I was hesitant to ask questions because I did not want to wrongly represent my race or ability. I did not want students to believe I was slow or "stupid," causing them to believe that all Latinos were incapable of this work. I was in the class for a couple of weeks, during that time I wrote an essay, which earned a "B." I was discouraged when my class began to read *The Odyssey*. The book was difficult, and I felt I was the only student who did not understand. It was for this reason that I soon left. Soon after, the other Latina in the class left. She described to me that the class was intimidating and she was the only "dumb" one there. Later, I learned I was not the only student who did not understand the book, but in actuality many students were having a rough time.

Despite the students' developing college readiness skills and advanced-level competencies, however, they continued to face academic and behavioral challenges in their regular Wilson High classes. Some of these challenges speak to the conservative logic and pedagogy of the school's conception of academic preparation. Their challenges also reveal the comprehensive high school's resistance to marginalized students of color who engage as college-goers. As Olivia told us:

> It was hard sometimes to make transitions between our other classes and this class because I think our other classes were much more structured in the sense that we had to think a certain way. In Futures we had freedom to [go] beyond what was in the textbook. You know, we did research, and we had the opportunity to think beyond certain limits. In other classes, you can't really do that. You can't really question certain things. You just had to go with whatever the textbooks say to get a good grade in the class. I think that was one of the hardest things about Futures during high school.

With the support of Futures, Olivia navigated the challenges successfully. She graduated from Wilson and was accepted to several 4-year universities.

Imani, despite intellectual interests and considerable skills that were obvious to everyone (and irritating to some), had an enormously difficult time conforming to the academic and behavioral expectations of her teachers. She often let her anger overwhelm her commitment to become eligible for college, and she graduated from Wilson with an erratic mix of remarkable successes and equally remarkable failures. For one semester, in fact, her grades slipped below a C average. She also incurred the wrath of several Wilson teachers who, absent the intervention of Antonopoulos and Futures researchers, would have barred her from classes she needed. The Futures adults, acting much like upper-middle-class parents, also went outside the normal admissions channels to get Imani an admissions interview at a private liberal arts college. After talking with her for nearly an hour, the college admissions officer was sufficiently impressed to give her a conditional college acceptance despite her high school record.

Hurdles Outside School

Futures could do little to relieve the enormous burdens most students bore outside of school. Futures students had family responsibilities that increased even as the demands of college preparation intensified. For example, when Tasha turned 16, she began working at McDonald's after school before going home to her nightly family responsibilities. Only after others were asleep could she study. Nevertheless, she kept a B average, partly out of her commitment to be a model for her siblings to follow. "If I don't go [to a university]," she told us, "how will they know it is possible?"

Nina learned in a very hard way that outside of high school, all that seemed to matter was that she was "illegal," and nothing she learned in Futures could change that. Nina's undocumented status was not known to the Futures team until her junior year, when she asked Chris Antonopoulos for advice. Not knowing how much of a problem this might be, the team sought out an immigration attorney, who encouraged Nina to file for legal status. Acquiring legal status would require her parents' filing as well, which was an impossibility. So, she did not address her status, studied even harder, finished her coursework, got outstanding grades, stayed involved in school and community activities, filled out applications, took college trips, and hoped for a scholarship. In fact, her strong record of scholarship and her respected newspaper column had earned her several Latino scholarships and a Centennial Award for influential campus leaders. It was not enough.

If she enrolled in the elite public universities she qualified for, she would have to pay the hefty $30,000 out-of-state tuition because her status made her ineligible for public financial aid. One of the Futures adults wangled an extremely late April admissions interview for Nina at a private liberal arts college in northern California. They were delighted to accept her, but there too she would have to pay the international tuition rate of $35,000 each year. Efforts to persuade a wealthy public figure to establish a private scholarship failed, and Nina's hope faded. This outstanding student barely passed her classes, and she decided not to participate in graduation—not even the private ceremony planned by Futures.

At the last minute she changed her mind and attended graduation, where she received accolades for her academic success. Then she went to work, using a false social security number to get a job selling shoes at the local shopping mall. But she did not give up her dream of college. Three years after leaving Wilson, Nina received an associate's degree from a local community college and enrolled as a junior at an elite public university. Changes in California law have allowed her to pay much lower in-state fees, but she remains ineligible for financial aid or any of the student jobs she needs so desperately.

Arturo faced the same challenge, although he was luckier than Nina. His high grades and thoughtful application essay won him an acceptance at a private Jesuit university, whose own commitment to social justice led them to provide him a full scholarship. The only provision the school made was that he obtain status as a legal resident during his first semester. Arturo's family—who, unlike Nina's, lived in the United States—was eager to help. Nevertheless, the slow and difficult process forced Arturo to leave the university for a full semester.

As of this writing, the Futures students are 4 years beyond high school graduation, and most of those who started college are still in school. Arturo, Tasha, Olivia, and Imani all earned bachelor's degrees in spring 2005. Ten other students were enrolled at 4-year colleges or universities, including Nina, who was finishing her junior year at the elite public university she transferred to after earning her associate's degree at the community college. Five others were enrolled at community colleges. These numbers reflect a persistence rate of 78% in higher education overall, and a rate of 88% at 4-year institutions. These figures compare favorably with national averages.[15] They are particularly laudable given that nearly all of the students have struggled to balance their academic pursuits with financial and familial responsibilities; 53% of the Futures students attending college work either full- or part-time. Surely, they have defied those who judged them as ninth graders to be unsuited for 4-year college preparation. Ten of the original 30 students are not enrolled in school and are working full- or part-time. We have lost contact with only one.

Notably, the link between education and social responsibility remains strong. Most of the Futures students have been involved in campus or community organizations that promote political identity, understanding, and action, or provide services to youth or the community. Many have built networks in their colleges similar in some respects to Futures. They keep in touch with their fellow Futures students and draw on them for academic, political, and spiritual support. Social justice, concern for others, and the confidence to act upon their best knowledge are commitments that still characterize their lives. Tasha, for example, shared a story of how a conversation with an employee at her local grocery store late one night turned to the topic of college:

> I was in Food for Less and he was working there. He was a Latino gentleman and . . . he was talking about school and I was like, "Oh, yeah, I'm in college." And he was like, "I'm really trying to find out." So, I went to my campus and I got an application. I got an EOP [Educational Opportunity Program] application and everything, and I gave it to him, and I showed him how to fill out the FAFSA [Free Application for Federal Student Aid] form and everything, and he's waiting right now to find out if he got in.

TRANSFORMING STUDENTS BUT NOT SCHOOLS

At every turn, we see barriers that schools and society raise to block the pathways to college and to hopeful futures for poor students and students of color. Our social design experiment demonstrates that, in the short term, students can adopt college-going identities that enable them to navigate, avoid, or jump over those obstacles and, when they stumble, get up and carry on. We have also seen that when students combine with "professionals" (in this case, some researchers and educators), they can accomplish quite a lot, but they are not likely to sweep clean the obstacle-filled terrain of schooling and leave it a much more equitable and hopeful place. The Futures story gives a glimpse of the enormous intellectual power and hope for a good society that lies within a sector of our population whose contributions are now cut short. The achievements of the Futures students call attention to that potential, and they shine a harsh light on what is missing.

It is probably still too early to assess the long-term academic outcomes of the Futures students and the role that their Futures experience has played in those outcomes and in the social contributions they will make. It is clear, however, that participatory social research

- Supported the students as they contended with challenges and obstacles;
- Provided them essential networks of social support and information;
- Yielded critical understandings of educational inequality that helped them navigate their paths through high school;
- Shaped their knowledge, skills, career aspirations, and social commitments.

It is not too early to assess the outcomes of the Futures experience on Wilson. Although it was not transformative, Futures did have a significant effect on Wilson. Partly as a result of watching and learning from the students, the school administration committed to a default college-preparatory curriculum for all students. They restructured the counseling department to provide new training for counselors, better access to all students, and a shift in counseling practices. The school implemented a summer bridge program for underrepresented students challenging themselves with AP classes for the first time. It committed to doubling the size of the AVID program, a support class for "average" students seeking to become prepared for college. However, as we noted in Chapter 2, the school's equity reforms were under constant scrutiny and faced open resistance from powerful community members who saw the reforms as a threat to the high-quality, if exclusive, opportunities their own students in Wilson's "first school" enjoyed. Today, Wilson still struggles to be both equitable and responsive to the interests of the school's most advantaged students and families.

Teaching to Change Los Angeles

Teachers Bringing Social Justice to Urban Classrooms

Studying the "Freedom Train" in Cicely Bingener's kindergarten class.

SHORTLY AFTER school began in September 1999, 12 teachers from across Los Angeles drove to UCLA to talk about their work in urban schools. These graduates of UCLA's Teacher Education Program had agreed to join us for dialogue and pizza. They came after long hours in the classroom, where they had grappled with the challenges and responsibilities of professional work that were still new to them. But these teachers carried a mission to promote social justice in urban schools. And they recognized that this goal required new knowledge and commitments that could only be forged in shared inquiry.[1]

Most of the 12 taught in schools with conditions like those in Washington Middle School that we described in Chapter 1. "You walk around campus," explained Romeo Bueno, "and there's trash everywhere." In his classroom, the blinds were falling apart, and the textbooks were trashed and unavailable for the students to take home. Other teachers did not expect their textbooks for several weeks. Although these teachers had taught for only 3 or 4 years, they were among the most senior teachers at their schools, so high were the rates of teacher turnover and uncredentialed teachers.

Conditions like these and worse made the teachers worry that their energy for social justice would fade as the year and their careers went forward. They felt isolated within faculties that blamed students and parents for the school's poor conditions and outcomes. Recognizing the force of this logic on her own beliefs and practices, Wendy Rios said, "I thought I'd be a certain kind of teacher. . . . I'm not sure I like the educator that I am right now; it's not where I want to go."

Rios and her colleagues welcomed the chance to refuel their commitments to social justice by participating in and leading inquiry groups with other teachers. "Just talking to other people," noted Rios, "helps me see where it is that I'm changing." In addition to the value of frank group discussions for renewing energy, letting off steam, and gaining greater self-awareness, inquiry provided Rios and other teachers with insight about the sociopolitical dimensions of their daily work.

Cicely Bingener taught kindergarten in Inglewood, a community of mostly low-income African Americans and Latinos just outside the Los Angeles city limits. She recognized immediately that the prevailing logic within her district was "antithetical to what UCLA is trying to teach." She believed that inquiry could lead teachers to become "a force" that could counter the district's logic. Like Bingener, social studies teacher Elizabeth Minster believed that teachers needed to think and act more politically. She singled out the antibilingual and scripted curriculum policies "passed down to us from the district and even the state" and noted that teachers feel "like we're not able to teach in the manner that we'd like." Although teachers did not like the policies, Minster had not yet "seen any cohesive force uniting to voice discontent." She wondered if teacher inquiry groups might move in that direction.

This chapter explores the efforts of Rios, Bingener, Minster, and other teachers to use participatory social inquiry as a strategy for realizing more equitable schooling. We facilitated their work through two related social design experiments. First, "teacher inquiry" brought together this group of teachers to reflect critically on their practice and serve as leaders to other groups of teachers with similar intentions. It built on Dewey's insight that the essential step in reclaiming public life is to improve the "conditions of debate, discussion, persuasion."[2] Second, *Teaching to Change LA* (*TCLA*), an online journal that grew out of the teacher inquiry, provided a public site for the research of urban teachers and their students. *TCLA* differed from the more introspective and professional "teacher inquiry" in that it made public students' and teachers' inquiry and added parents' voices as well. It reflected Dewey's belief that public life requires continual inquiry *and* full and free reporting of the results of this inquiry.

We designed these experiments to correct what Dewey termed "the eclipse of the public," or stated more modestly, to create a fertile environment through which we could study purposeful efforts to bring Dewey's public into well-lighted view. Dewey was looking for average citizens who could recognize their common interests and organize themselves into publics capable of "forming and directing" public policies.[3]

The problem of the public for Dewey, and us, is both cognitive and political. The would-be public is "bewildered" by forces that seem far removed from their immediate experience and far too powerful to challenge. It does not recognize that the public has a role to play in shaping these forces. The cognitive problem calls for "a kind of knowledge and insight which does not yet exist . . . an obvious requirement is freedom of social inquiry and of distribution of its conclusions." The political problem requires moving beyond understanding toward collective action. It demands strategies for bringing together a "scattered, mobile and manifold public [so that it] may recognize itself as to define and express its interests."[4]

Both "teacher inquiry" and *Teaching to Change LA* focused the energies of teachers (and through them their students) on the cognitive challenge. Along with our teacher collaborators, we envisioned the social design experiments as processes for forging new personal and public insight. We also hoped that by working on the cognitive side, we would create not just an informed body of youth and teachers committed to social inquiry but also the "cohesive force" that Elizabeth Minster imagined.

TEACHER INQUIRY

Teacher inquiry first took shape in our partnership with Wilson High School. We began meeting with Wilson educators in inquiry groups in 1995, exploring why the "two schools" problem existed and how it could be overcome. These groups generally met every other week for 2 hours during the school day, with John Rogers facilitating. The sessions were loosely structured, beginning with participant reports about emerging insights and issues, moving on to discussions prompted by an organizing question, and closing with some agreement for what the participants would seek to discover or test out over the next couple of weeks. For example, we talked about, and experimented with, connecting the formal curriculum to youth popular culture, and then analyzed how the resulting student work demonstrated (or did not demonstrate) the academic growth of previously silenced students. With John's support and navigation, the groups' dialogue explored difficult, but critical, questions about the relationship among beliefs about learning and race and patterns of inequality at Wilson.

The Wilson inquiry groups were a robust site of learning that led us to incorporate many of these same processes within our teacher education work. In 1997, we began monthly meetings with a group of first-year teachers from our Teacher Education Program. Here, new teachers could grapple with the meaning of social justice education in schools plagued by material deprivation, institutional structures aimed at sorting and controlling, and constraints on teaching and learning in the midst of current and historical racism and economic inequality. The teachers welcomed the chance to ask far-reaching, if sometimes naive, questions without fear of being exposed as ignorant or being punished for voicing taboos associated with race and culture. The understanding in each group was that members be of good will, not that they be sophisticated and conversant with progressive norms.

The participants imagined inquiry as a space for making sense of the broader enterprise of urban schooling as well as their own roles as equity-minded teachers—an identity they recognized did not fit well with the general school environment. Inquiry was a space, in the words of one, "to realize why I'm there." Many participants in these early sessions noted the striking difference between this space for "inquiry" and the official and unofficial sites for dialogue and meaning-making at their schools. Administrators (and other colleagues) frequently discouraged self-reflection in all the ways of the "social pathology" that Dewey described:

> There is a social pathology which works powerfully against effective inquiry into social institutions and conditions. It manifests itself in a thousand ways; in querulousness, in impotent drifting, in uneasy snatching at distractions, in idealization of the long established, in a facile optimism assumed as a cloak, in riotous glorification of things "as they are," in intimidation of all dissenters—ways which depress and dissipate thought all the more effectively because they operate with subtle and unconscious pervasiveness.[5]

Inquiry brought the teachers a new recognition of how administrators and other teachers squelched the free exchange of experience and data needed to address their schools' many equity issues. These new insights prompted discussions of how to take their marginalized values and knowledge into the broader school culture, and they realized that they could accomplish this by extending their culture of inquiry. Together with the teachers, we constructed a social design experiment around teacher inquiry. We would hold monthly seminars for teachers—essentially, inquiry groups for facilitators who then would conduct inquiry with other new teachers. We invited a broad range of teachers to join new inquiry groups led by these facilitators. We predicted that this "home-grown" scaling-up of inquiry would be received differently than the typical professional development activities conducted by outside experts who were selected by and beholden to school administrators.

Practicing Egalitarian Social Relationships

Five inquiry groups of 8 to 12 teachers began meeting in 1999. Two or three members from each of these groups served as facilitators and met monthly at UCLA in a "facilitators group." This group, which John facilitated, developed a loose curriculum and shared practices for their own inquiry groups. That curriculum was anchored by a book or reading on the theme of social justice chosen by the facilitators. The practice of inquiry began with dilemmas posed by these books or by the stories that teachers shared about their daily lives in schools. Facilitators tried to pick up on themes that, in the words of Romeo Bueno, "had the most meat." Deborah Meier's book *Will Standards Save Public Education?* spawned conversations on the narrowing effects of testing on the curriculum; Freire's *Teachers as Cultural Workers: Letters to Those Who Dare Teach* opened up conversations about how to reach out to students who seemed alienated by the school culture. Participants often found that the "questions came up naturally" as the problem facing one participant connected with those of another. "Before I knew it," remembers Kristin Lyons, "someone had said something that had tapped into the core of an issue I had been considering too."

Telling and hearing similar stories in inquiry groups enabled teachers to move beyond the sense of isolation that Dewey associated with the eclipse of the public. Lily Kim said that inquiry helped "me recognize I am not alone." Kim came to see herself as part of a community in struggle that other participants described as "safe and supportive" and "critical and challenging." For Romeo Bueno, these qualities came in the form of "shared convictions for social justice education in urban schools. Our discussions had grit because we brought the same concerns about our schools and students to our discussions even though we didn't always agree with one another's opinions."

Constructing Knowledge

Sharing stories, reading articles, and raising questions, the inquiry participants clarified and tested out new understandings about the meaning of social justice teaching in schools heavily burdened by inequality. The teachers recognized, for example, that reading about sociocultural theory or critical pedagogy did not offer self-evident guides to practice. They responded by looking at each aspect of their work and asking, "What am I doing? Why am I doing it?" These were not rhetorical questions simply to express frustration, but the beginnings of a nuanced understanding of how to disrupt inequitable education patterns. Their constant questioning and comparing helped teachers develop conscious and reasoned pathways to "come to where I believe I should be."

Inquiry enabled the teachers to recognize patterns of inequality or inadequacy across schools and the larger policies and structures that gave rise to these patterns. Sharing stories often brought to light the widespread nature of substandard conditions (such as the lack of available textbooks) that had seemed idiosyncratic to one's school. Articles on educational policy (such as Linda Darling-Hammond's "The Right to Learn and the Advancement of Teaching") provided the inquiry groups with a way to locate the origins of these problems in the failures of district or state authorities, rather than in the children and their families.[6] This understanding contrasts with the experience of many teachers who, like Dewey's "bewildered" citizens, "are caught up in the sweep of forces too vast to understand or master."[7]

Adopting a Critical Stance

Sometimes we spoke of our inquiry process as "critical inquiry" to underscore the centrality of equity and justice to our dialogues.[8] Readings exposed teachers to Freire and other critical pedagogues, to policy analyses highlighting the inequitable distribution of educational resources, and to critical studies of urban schooling's history and political economy. Elizabeth Minster recognized the power in grounding current conditions in politics and history: "You have to understand the origins of unequal schooling in order to change it." Inquiry participants began to understand their own complicity in educational inequality, and to use that knowledge productively.

Cicely Bingener said that inquiry could "push us to look at what it is in ourselves that allows us to accept . . . [and] participate in" the troubling practices of urban schools. Bingener pointed out that because teachers "are products of that same [troubled] school system," it is not surprising that teachers embrace a number of unconscious racist and classist beliefs. Inquiry helped teachers expose and challenge these biases. Being part of a group of teachers willing to challenge one another on tough issues transformed this introspection from personal accusation to shared struggle for justice. Bingener noted that members of her inquiry group were willing to "bounce off . . . perceptions of [biases] . . . because we are searching for a common thing—social justice and equity." Through such reflection, inquiry participants like third-grade teacher Charalene Asis shaped their teacher identities to be consistent with effective participation in environments in many ways hostile to educational or social change. Asis described herself as "*still* thinking, *still* being critical, and *still* asking questions."

Exploring Los Angeles schooling inequality and its impact on teaching during an inquiry session at UCLA.

Developing a Transformative Goal

The teachers who created and led the inquiry groups saw inquiry as a strategy for revitalizing public life as well as for renewing individual teachers. They hoped teacher inquiry would spread disruptive knowledge and help teachers become a force for equity in Los Angeles schools. But how could a small number of teacher groups foster change beyond the members of those groups? Cicely Bingener argued that the combination of knowledge and anger created through inquiry could serve as a "spark" for broader political action. Complacency, she reasoned, was only an option for teachers who did not reflect critically on the school system. "It's like [if] none of us knew that there was something called social reproduction . . . we'd be oblivious to it and might be actually happy and not frustrated like we are. But we do know what it is. And now we're forced to deal with it. . . . Once you become aware . . . there's this whole new level of accountability."

Many of the inquiry group participants responded to their heightened consciousness of inequality by focusing on making a difference where they felt most efficacious—their own classrooms. "I think the one thing we have control over is what we do in our classroom," remarked first-grade teacher Ramón Martínez. "That's sort of the beauty of teaching." Teachers across grade levels shared critical information with their students about how inequality plays out in schools. Martínez talked with his students about how new state legislation violated their rights by limiting their access to Spanish-language materials; social studies teacher Elizabeth Minster informed her students that new accountability measures were narrowing the curriculum at their school in ways that did not happen in more affluent communities. Teachers also engaged students in discussions about school practices and structures. Kate Thompson encouraged her Wilson High School students to talk about why the regular- and honors-track classes looked so different from one another. As Thompson noted, "inquiry carried over [into the classroom] all the time."

As teachers got a firmer sense of how classroom and school inequalities were integral to structures at work in the community, it made sense to them that they take their critique into the community. "I don't think I'm a born leader or a born activist," acknowledged English teacher Kristin Lyons. "But I feel like I need to learn how to do that. I can make changes in my classroom in those four walls that I have, but I want to do more." Yet, like so many of her colleagues, Lyons was unsure about how to move forward. "Inquiry helps and it raises all these thoughts and ideas and thoughts of change and talk of change, but when do we do that change? When do we go out there?" Elizabeth Minster suggested that inquiry at least "empowered us individually" to go and talk with other teachers about "things within schools" that usually go "unquestioned." But even Minster did not view this approach as a systematic way to communicate to the broader body of "disempowered" teachers. They needed a vehicle to make public the results of inquiry.

TEACHING TO CHANGE LA

In March 2001, a local public broadcasting station in Los Angeles televised a half-hour segment featuring *Teaching to Change LA* (*TCLA*). Joanna Goode, a math and computer science teacher, explained that a group of teachers had created the online journal with UCLA's Institute for Democracy, Education, and Access (IDEA) to make public the ideas and insights that emerge from classroom inquiry. "Often the conversations we are having stay in our classrooms . . . so we wanted a place where we could share our work in a broader venue."[9]

Many of the 15 teachers who met with us in the summer of 2000 to create *TCLA* had been involved in teacher inquiry, and all wanted to publicize knowledge that previously had been, as Dewey expressed it, "cooped up" within teacher groups or classrooms.[10] The teachers imagined the online journal as a medium for making known their ideas and those of their students. We agreed to be the institutional home for the journal and to explore this novel way of extending inquiry about schooling into the public sphere.

Our first issue of *TCLA*, "Democracy 2000," came out in the wake of the presidential election. Teacher editors asked other teachers and students from across Los Angeles to share discussions and analyses about the election and the meaning of democracy. The second issue, published in June 2001, centered on the "Digital Divide"—a problem we encountered first-hand as we attempted to share our online journal with youth and adults who did not have adequate access to the Internet in their schools and community centers. As with our first issue, our teacher editors solicited teacher and student work about the digital divide from Los Angeles teachers and students as well as community members and researchers. These first two issues produced modest interest beyond the contributing classrooms, with roughly 2,000 visitors a month logging on to the journal.

Since 2002, *TCLA* has explored a different theme each year—a "Student's Bill of Rights," participatory school accountability, the historical struggle for educational opportunity in Los Angeles, and youth political participation. *TCLA* publishes several issues on the theme throughout the school year and, at the end of the year, convenes a city-wide youth summit to highlight the research students have done. IDEA scaffolds classroom and community inquiry by providing an array of online resources about the theme and by offering teachers a year-long teacher seminar on the topic. Student and teacher articles now reach readers across the Web, with almost 50,000 visitors coming to the site each month.

Engaging Those Most Affected

The inaugural issue of *TCLA* opened with an audio clip of high school senior Alejandro Nuño reading Walt Whitman's "Chants Democratic." Whitman envisioned a place where people of "common words and deeds . . . enter the public assembly."[11] Following Whitman, the first issue of the journal provided a virtual "assembly" for those often excluded from public life to share their ideas about democracy. Students submitted alternative speeches that politicians could make if they *really* cared about conditions in South Los Angeles, reflections on the significance of the presidential election for urban youth, and Whitmanesque poetry singing democracy's praises. Fourth-grader Rahel Abebe wrote: "Democracy / I like it / Ask me why / Because it gives everyone's voice a chance / Because it's part of my life and soul / Because I can be heard / Because / That's why / I like Democracy."[12]

Kristy Cooper, a fifth-grade teacher and *TCLA* editor, created a forum called "LA Voices" to share students' ideas. She sent questionnaires to schools across the region, asking students what they would like to change in their school. Students responded by articulating a broad agenda for educational change. Some questioned why their schools were installing security cameras; others raised concerns about the lack of upkeep of their school facility; still others lamented the lack of textbooks and other resources students need to learn. For the most part, students conceived of "voice" as separate from action. That is, they talked about what they would change *if* they had the power to effect change. Their inquiry did not explore how to communicate these concerns with decision makers, let alone how to exert pressure on these decision makers.

Teachers used *TCLA* to articulate the challenges facing youth in the communities they served. Ramón Martínez's commentary decried the effects of legislation outlawing bilingual education for his first-grade students who had limited English skills. "They are being instructed in a language they don't understand."[13] Martínez had often shared this critique within his inquiry group, but the journal gave him a vehicle to encourage others to "step up and take a stand" for educational justice.[14] *TCLA* also allowed him to engage in online debates with those who were critical of his article (see Figure 5.1).[15] In Dewey's terms, such dialogue allowed Martínez to test the knowledge he had forged in the course of inquiry.

The editors selected *TCLA*'s second theme after confronting the technological gap in Internet access among different groups. We invited students across the city to document the availability and use of computers in schools and the broader community. This prompt engaged youth in different ways than the "Democracy" issue had. Instead of only soliciting students' voices, the "Digital Divide" issue encouraged students and their teachers to gather and analyze data connected to their daily experiences.

Such inquiry clarified and gave a context to students' understanding of "where the shoe pinches." Armando Soriano, a high school student in Los Angeles's Eastside, came to the project on the "Digital Divide" with a sense that he and his friends did not have sufficient access to computers. But, mapping the available computers in his neighborhood confirmed and made concrete that "computer access in my community has been, and continues to be, a scramble."[16] Students at Lennox Middle School tried to make sense of this

:: [sent 3/2/01]

On March 19th, Wayne Bishop offered his comments after reading Ramón Martínez's article. Ramón replied to Wayne's comments, and both responses are listed below:

In spite of his inflamed, even outrageous rhetoric, "we must begin to challenge the educational policies that serve only to harm them," the harm would appear to have been being done but that progress might finally be getting underway. I believe in everyone's right to speak, including that of reactionary, head-in-the-sand teachers, but why does something that calls itself "UCLA's Institute for Democracy" give them a microphone? If anything, we need phonics police, English police, and math police to keep such teachers from impeding the progress already being recorded. Low-SES Hispanic kids should have a realistic opportunity to the American dream as well as the rest of us.

- Wayne Bishop, Cal State LA

>> [replied to 3/7/01]

Mr. Bishop,

Thanks so much for your response to my article. Although I definitely disagree with the way in which you've chosen to characterize me ("reactionary, head-in-the-sand teacher"), I welcome the chance to dialogue with you on the issues presented in my opinion piece.

Perhaps one of the reasons that UCLA's Institute for Democracy, Education and Access chose to publish my piece was because it runs counter to the hegemonic discourse (so prevalent and unquestioned at present) that equates school reform with more tests and increased punitive measures. While I certainly don't know enough about you to attempt to characterize you in any way, I assume that you have accepted such discourse as true and unproblematic. Your reference to improved SAT9 scores suggests that you operate on the assumption that the test is an objective and accurate measure of student learning. Unfortunately, while most politicians and educational policymakers share your views, there are many qualified and experienced teachers who do not.

Incidentally, before you accuse teachers of impeding the progress of "Low SES Hispanic kids," you would do well to visit those teachers' classrooms (so that you might have the opportunity to search for some substantial evidence on which to base your preposterous accusations). Were you to visit my classroom, for example, you would be surprised to find that my students are actually making substantial progress and that I am able to assess their progress (using multiple measures) without the help of norm-referenced standardized tests.

You should also know that my opinions do not represent an isolated voice, but rather a growing social movement to transform public education. The Coalition for Educational Justice is a citywide organization of parents, students and teachers who are organizing at the grassroots level to ensure an equitable education for all students. Although I am usually suspicious of people who preface their pronouncements with the phrase "I believe in everyone's right to speak," (I've found that people who make such statements often do so to conceal the fact that they believe the very opposite.), I invite you to respond to this email, so that we can engage in constructive dialogue. Finally, for the sake of clarification, you should know that "reactionary" is not defined as anyone who disagrees with your personal views and opinions.

Looking forward to your response,

Ramón Martínez

FIGURE 5.1. Teachers take on a public role through *TCLA*'s virtual forum.

"scramble" by interviewing community members and university "experts" about the costs of computers and their use in the workplace. Their inquiry led them to conclude: "There are not many opportunities for people to use computers [because] many people in Lennox do not have enough money to buy computers. There are not enough jobs that use technology in Lennox or jobs that offer competitive salaries which would make it more affordable for people to buy computers."[17]

Studying computer availability from the vantage point of their own communities led students to develop generative questions that they posed to experts and school district officials. The answers melded "divide" issues with "equity" issues. "Why do some schools have better technology than others?" "Why does the digital divide negatively affect poor people and people of color?" "Are poor Whites in the same condition as poor non-Whites? If so, is anything being done for them?" "Why is so much of the information on the Net mainly for men?"[18] These questions were more than academic for the students. Hence, students at Compton High School, who faced among the worst school conditions in the state asked: "How can you help public schools with no Internet access? How long will it take?" Because they came to this inquiry from communities with broad and complex interests, the students' questions were not confined narrowly to education. Lennox Middle School students asked: "How can we raise wages so computers can become affordable?" Similar questions prompted a robust public conversation about what Dewey termed "all the conditions" affecting the public.[19]

Accessing Knowledge and Its Construction

The 50th anniversary of *Brown v. Board of Education* offered a unique opportunity for teachers and students to examine the struggle for education on "equal terms" in Los Angeles. There is a long history of activists, academics, and journalists using the occasion of *Brown*'s anniversary as a springboard for public reexamination of the nation's commitment to racial equality and educational opportunity. Martin Luther King, Jr. was well aware of this symbolic capital of *Brown* when he traveled to the steps of the U.S. Supreme Court to deliver a major address on voting rights on *Brown*'s third anniversary.[20] Newspapers, popular magazines, and academic journals cover every major anniversary of *Brown* as both a moment for historical remembrance and a chance to assess contemporary conditions. Clearly, Los Angeles teachers could count on providing their students a number of public remembrances of *Brown* in spring of 2004.

Yet, many Los Angeles teachers wanted their students to be more than mere consumers of this inquiry. They joined us in a participatory public history—the "Equal Terms Project"—hosted and supported through *TCLA*. Together with the teachers, we reasoned that it was particularly appropriate for urban students to be at the center of a reexamination of *Brown* because, at its core, this decision addressed the rights of all youth to participate fully in public life. Classrooms from early elementary school through high school constructed knowledge about the historical and contemporary struggle for educational justice within their local communities. We disseminated this knowledge online and at community forums, creating a robust public dialogue on how to achieve *Brown*'s promise in the here and now.

Kindergarten teacher—and *TCLA* editor—Cicely Bingener took the lead with us to provide teachers with background information, primary sources, and strategies for participatory research through a monthly seminar. Our goal was to provide teachers and students access to knowledge about Los Angeles's distinctive racial justice history. Bingener's great-grandfather, a prominent African American minister, had played an important role in this history, responding in the early 1940s to a searing incident in which White students burned the effigies of the six African American students at Fremont High School.[21] Few historians (let alone teachers or students) were familiar with such incidents of racial violence in Los Angeles schools during the pre-*Brown* era. And many teachers and students did not realize how different Los Angeles's post-*Brown* history has been from the dominant national narrative. That is, during the same period that schools in the Jim Crow South gradually moved from racial segregation toward desegregation (or at least less segregation), Los Angeles schools became dramatically more racially segregated.

The broad outlines of this social history of Los Angeles were captured in a compilation of readings for teachers and their students that included academic articles on California school segregation, policy briefs on contemporary inequalities in California schools, texts of key legal cases, and an array of original articles from local newspapers. In addition to this reader, *TCLA* carried an online library of historical and contemporary information about Los Angeles schools and communities. These materials allowed teachers and students to track their schools' changing demographics since the middle 1960s and to see graphically the changing racial composition of their community through a series of Geographic Information System maps. *TCLA* pointed teachers and students to current data on how their own school measures up on particular educational opportunities such as access to qualified teachers, as well as how these opportunities vary in California depending on the composition of the student body.

Offering an Experimental Method of Inquiry

The materials on *TCLA* provoked, contextualized, and sustained broad inquiry. The demographic maps and school enrollment data from previous decades frequently surprised students who had come to view the racial composition of their neighborhood and school as "natural" and inevitable. Third-grade teacher Charalene Asis recalls that her South Los Angeles students suddenly began to wonder: "Why aren't there more Whites and Asians at our school?"[22] At Farmdale Elementary, where more than 9 of 10 students are Latino, third graders wondered what the school was like when its student body was more diverse. Students at other schools found themselves drawn to a particular moment in their school's history recorded in newspapers or other articles. Fremont High School students, now Latino and African American, were surprised to learn that mobs of White students had once used racial violence and intimidation to keep the school all White. They explored what lessons this incident held for the school's current racial tensions between African Americans and Latinos— because the school has not enrolled White students for several decades. Similarly, when Roosevelt High School students read about the historic student walkouts of 1968, they wondered whether the forces that led to mass student protest then might produce the same result today.

These compelling questions framed each classroom's data gathering. Many classrooms analyzed old yearbooks and school photos. They coded pictures and learned the difference between undisciplined observations and data on which they could base conclusions that others would pay attention to. The students debated the ethics and practicality of placing people into particular racial categories. Fifth graders at 99th Street Elementary in South Los Angeles "triangulated" their data— using their own tabulations of students' demographics from school photos alongside the school district's "official" racial and ethnic survey and data from the United States census. The yearbooks yielded other information of great interest to students. Students at Bethune Middle, a school currently undergoing transformation from a predominantly African American to a predominantly Latino student body, examined the yearbooks with an eye to how the school promoted cultural identification. They found clubs celebrating African American culture and pictures captioned, "Black Is Beautiful." At multiracial Wilson High School, the student researchers wanted to learn about how the school encouraged or discouraged interracial relationships outside the classroom. They closely analyzed pictures of clubs, athletic teams, and dances, noting the racial composition, where different students stood, and other forms of nonverbal communication.

The most powerful data came from oral history interviews students conducted with people who had attended their school in years past. Our teacher seminar offered teachers some guidance on oral history interviews that they then crafted into lessons for their students. These lessons ranged from practical advice (always try to find a quiet site for the interview to optimize sound quality of tape recordings) to broader discussions about how to strike a balance between letting the subject's voice be heard and directing them toward the research questions. Such discussions helped students become more conscious of what it means to take on an experimental method. In addition, the interviews themselves often provided students with the sense of confirmation and discovery that often accompanies this method. Both of these feelings were evident at Roosevelt High School, where Jorge Lopez's students listened to activists from 1968. These now middle-aged parents and grandparents talked about school problems that the students had anticipated (in part because they expe-

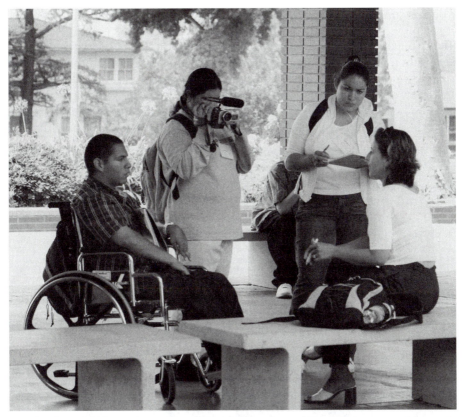

Conducting oral history interviews with a community resident about race and inequality at their school in earlier decades.

rienced the same problems today). But the students were surprised to learn that the protesters were badly beaten by police—as this story had not made its way into the newspaper reports the students had read.

Across all grade levels, the quality of the oral history interviews was quite striking. Students were especially adept at getting adults to share painful, hopeful, and deeply evocative stories about their schooling. This capacity to draw out submerged stories is likely tied to the students' roots in the same communities as their interview subjects. Perhaps these connections established lines of trust that are critical to oral history interviews. It is likely that Carlos Montes of the 1960s Chicano activist group Brown Berets saw himself in Jorge Lopez's students at Roosevelt High School. Or, perhaps the students' very presence prompted adults to call up forgotten memories of their own experiences at the same school. Certainly, the students and the adults noted the power of youth who bring an inquiring attitude and authentic questions.

Legitimizing All Forms of Knowledge

The public history project called on students to look to secondary literature on segregation, primary documents such as newspaper accounts, quantitative data such as census records, and the stories that the students gathered from their interview subjects. No one source of information was held up above the others, and no single source was deemed sufficient. Rather, students used the oral histories as a "check" on the limited reporting within the *Los Angeles Times*, and they continually assessed their own racial censuses (from yearbook counts)

Wearing an "Equal Terms" T-shirt at a student research summit.

against those created through official channels. This approach to the data encouraged students to reflect on the particular strengths of the data, the weight to be given to the data, and how they would allow the data to enter their analyses. And it often left them balancing the plausibility of one set of claims against another. Students at Bethune Middle School, for example, noted that teachers and site administrators held a more "positive outlook" on their school's condition than did parents. The students drew on other data (from reading and from data on *TCLA*) to conclude that indeed their school did lack a number of fundamental resources.

Taking a Critical Stance

The public history project encouraged students to challenge the practices and rationale that hold educational inequality in place. At Farmdale Elementary, teachers Marian Wong and Lydia Acosta related stories about the cultural insensitivity they experienced as students at the school in the 1960s.[23] Student researchers also heard a wide range of adults questioning the fairness of the educational system today. A teacher interviewed at 99th Street Elementary told the students: "Where you live determines how your school is. People don't have the same education and the same supplies."[24] This implicit standard—that everyone deserves education on "equal terms"—provided students with a marker for judging their own schooling. It enabled Kim Min's third-grade students to "recognize and express their discontent" with the inadequate instructional materials at their school.[25]

In addition to knowing that conditions were substandard, student researchers forged new, more structural explanations for their schools' problems. At Bethune Middle School, African American and Latino students who previously blamed one another for the school's poor conditions now saw that their communities shared a common experience of discrimination. Their public history project wove together stories of school officials excluding African Americans and Mexican Americans from local schools and quoted civil rights activists from both communities. In the words of their teacher, Cynthia Gonzalez, "they were able to see the inequalities that surround them now in a more critical way." Similarly, at Roosevelt High School, students noted that their newly acquired critical history did not appear in the textbooks: "the books just teach you what they want you to know."

Constructing a Transformative Goal and Transformative Identity

TCLA's public history project aimed to both inform and transform the public. We believed that by participating in the inquiry, students and their teachers would develop a deeper understanding of why educational inequality exists and how communities have struggled to overcome it. We also imagined that students and teachers would develop the skills and sense of entitlement to communicate their new knowledge with the broader public. Our hope was that as young people shared this knowledge, they would spawn broader community dialogue about Los Angeles's failure to realize *Brown*'s promise and what would be required to create education on "equal terms" today. We hypothesized that if such dialogue were sufficiently robust, it could energize and organize a complacent and diffuse public toward action.

Perhaps our clearest finding is that the project was a site for learning and relationships in which many young people assumed powerful public identities. Their sense of their "proper" place—whatever that may have been—was replaced with the certainty that they had a right and the worth to be taken seriously in all matters that affected their communities and their education. Their research helped them recognize that they did not simply occupy a moment in time, but they were part of history. High school social studies teacher Tom Lascher noted that many of his students had never thought that their "community, family, and friends might be proper subjects for study." Similarly, middle school teacher Argentina Rodriguez reported that her "students learned that they live in an important historical location." These understandings opened up broader realizations that the everyday experiences of people in their communities have been profoundly shaped by legal cases, policy actions, and the struggles of young people like themselves.

Debbie Sonu saw her third-grade students "talk openly about social issues and express their thoughts in coherent ways." The students' public presence impacted the adults with whom they interacted. Eighth-grade teacher Cynthia Gonzalez reported that her administrators "took notice" of the students' sophisticated understanding and questions. Yet, the student researchers did not conform to middle-class models of polite public discourse. Sonu recalled that her students "spoke emotionally," and Roosevelt teacher Jorge Lopez remembered his students were "very passionate and angered" when presenting their work. Lopez noted this passion as an outgrowth of the students' very real sense that "they are being cheated out of a quality education" and a sign that they were participating authentically in a dialogue that "spoke to" their interests.

For many students, this anger at unequal conditions was paired with a commitment to take public action for change. Lopez's Roosevelt students were "inspired" by the student activists of 1968 and by Mexican Americans who filed legal challenges in the 1930s and 1940s to state-sanctioned segregation in many California districts. "I want to do something like that and help my community," noted one of Lopez's students. "They did that to give us a better place." Similarly, Charalene Asis believed her third-grade students had internalized "for the rest of their lives" *Brown*'s lessons about the need to struggle and demand equal treatment. Finally, transformation is a human phenomenon that happens in

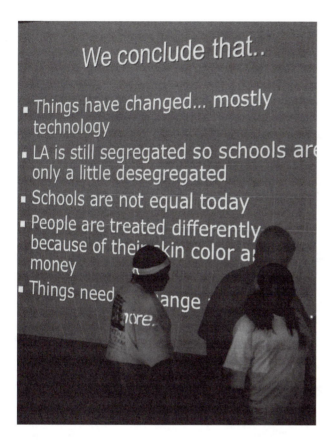

Fifth-graders using PowerPoint to present public history project findings at UCLA and community centers.

communities. The teachers and IDEA researchers worked together to create much more than a "site" or "context" in which this transformation and disruptive knowledge could take place. These were learning "communities" in the fullest sense—communities with a common sense of respect and purpose.

Spreading Disruptive Knowledge

Participating in the public history project helped students develop a body of critical knowledge about their schools and social policy that they shared through *TCLA* and at public forums. Students—particularly those in South and East Los Angeles—came to a deeper awareness of certain "social truths" that rarely received public attention. They acknowledged that their schools were in fact segregated by race and class. And they recognized that their schools received fewer resources and offered fewer opportunities than schools with majority White populations. Perhaps most fundamentally, students learned that the conditions in their schools and communities are not inevitable, but rather the product of a broad set of policy choices that are open to change. In part, this lesson was carried through demographic maps and yearbook pictures showing that "this community" or "this school" did not always look the way it does today. It was made more evident through the study of policies and their impacts—such as the effect of the 1978 Proposition 13, which greatly reduced property taxes and funding for public schooling. Students at Bethune Middle School were thus able to conclude that "achieving the legacy of *Brown* [requires] changing the ways schools are funded."

In June 2004, 150 students came to UCLA to share the findings of their research about the historical struggle for educational justice in Los Angeles. The audience included parents, community members, civil rights advocates, educators, and archivists. The student presenters ranged from third graders to high school seniors. They gave minilectures, shared spoken word performances, presented plays, and read letters. The students also participated in a public dialogue with Sylvia Mendez, the plaintiff student in *Mendez v. Westminster*, the case that overturned school segregation in California in 1947. Throughout the day, the students' work highlighted the persistence of inequality and struggle. As students from Bethune Middle School summarized, "students still do not have access to similar resources."[26]

The students published their research in *TCLA*, where it received a large (and geographically broad) readership. Yet, sharing Dewey's belief that "vital and thorough attachments are bred only in the intimacy of an intercourse which is

Kim Min and her third-graders posing with Sylvia Mendez after presenting their research on the Mendez family's landmark California desegregation case.

of necessity restricted in range," we encouraged and helped create opportunities for the students to present their findings to public forums in their own communities.[27] Laurence Tan's fifth-grade class at 99th Street Elementary in South Los Angeles traveled to the local high school to participate in a district-sponsored spoken word festival. The students' performance of "Equal Education Now" combined poetry, hip hop, and dance. It communicated both a nuanced understanding of history and a powerful demand for change.

Schools back then were . . .
Not fair.
Segregated
RACIST

Schools today are . . .
So VIOLENT and not so peaceful.
They are UNFAIR because there are some teachers that don't care about
   our education.
Some schools are not equal to others and are better off.
They are SUPPOSED to be desegregated and equal but some are better
How can schools be desegregated when LA is STILL SEGREGATED?

Students deserve . . .
More opportunities
EQUAL RESOURCES of education
Equal RIGHTS
Fair treatment
Better EDUCATION
More challenging classes
Students deserve to be treated in the right way and not in the bad way
RESPECT from their teachers and school
STUDENTS DESERVE to be treated like PEOPLE.

We want . . .
We want resources and education to be equal
Our schools to be mixed and fair for all
To get treated like everyone else
Better food
We want teachers to start LISTENING to their students
We want RESPECT and ATTENTION
We want TO BE HEARD
PEACE in our COMMUNITIES
We want JUSTICE, EQUALITY, and a GREAT EDUCATION
Because . . . WE DESERVE IT!!![28]

Across town, a multiracial community gathered at a forum cosponsored by a youth center, the local branch of the National Association for the Advancement of Colored People (NAACP), and UCLA's IDEA. Several teachers, district officials, and school board members rounded out an audience of high school–aged youth and community members. Students from the youth center and LaSonja Roberts's African American literature class presented research on the history of race relations and current challenges to equal opportunity, including the low rates of African American and Latino participation in advanced placement and honors classes.

The most compelling findings came from a pair of student surveys. One highlighted the large number of students and, in particular, students of color, who do not believe the school promotes integration and multiracial understanding. In the other, a sizable percentage of students, again disproportionately students of color, reported that they lacked tutoring or resources like graphing calculators that are critical to college access. These findings prompted a vigorous dialogue among forum participants about the causes of continued inequalities and potential policy responses. Within a week of the forum, a member of the youth center summarized the policy recommendations from these discussions and passed them on to their school's Board of Education.

Yet, neither the School Board nor their administration ever took action on the recommendations from the forum. Neither did any policy changes emerge from the event in South Los Angeles or from the other public forums commemorating *Brown*'s legacy. The teachers and students certainly felt more knowledgeable and more empowered through their public participation. And many community members, including more than a few elected officials and educational leaders, heard and learned from these presentations. But there was no organized group positioned to push forward the initial findings. That is, there was no organized and activated public who could transform the disruptive knowledge into action. Public inquiry alone could not create this public. As Dewey noted:

> Systematic and continuous inquiry into all the conditions which affect association and their dissemination in print is a precondition of the creation of a true public. But it and its results are but tools after all. Their final actuality is accomplished in face-to-face relationships by means of direct give and take.[29]

Spreading disruptive knowledge is a necessary but not sufficient condition for the kind of social change needed to accomplish equitable schools.

6

Building Power
What Grassroots Organizing Offers Equity Reformers

Let me give you a word on the philosophy of reform. The whole history of the progress of human liberty shows that all concessions yet made to her august claims have been born of earnest struggle. The conflict has been exciting, agitating, all absorbing, and for the time being putting all other tumults to silence. It must do this or it does nothing. If there is no struggle, there is no progress. Those who profess to favor freedom, and yet deprecate agitation, are men who want crops without plowing up the ground. They want rain without thunder and lightening. They want the ocean without the awful roar of its many waters. This struggle may be a moral one; or it may be a physical one; or it may be both moral and physical; but it must be a struggle. Power concedes nothing without demand. It never did and it never will. Find out just what people will submit to, and you have found the exact amount of injustice and wrong which will be imposed on them; and these will continue until they are resisted with either words or blows, or with both. The limits of tyrants are prescribed by the endurance of those whom they oppress.

Frederick Douglass, letter to an abolitionist associate, 1849

If real democracy is to be achieved, it will start with grassroots action. As diverse people respond to local circumstances, they must build broader movements which confront and change the policies and structures which dominate our lives. The power of the Highlander experience is the strength that grows within the souls of people, working together, as they analyze and confirm their own experiences and draw upon their understanding to contribute to fundamental change.

Highlander Center, 2005

OUR WORK with the Futures students and with the teachers in inquiry groups and *Teaching to Change LA* (*TCLA*) affected all the participants—including us. The students learned about social theory and engaged in serious intellectual work. Most of them navigated their way into college, even though their high school did not think of them as "college material." The teachers participating in the inquiry seminars deepened their knowledge of urban schools, and they engaged their students in studies that illuminated their political and economic surroundings while building vital intellectual skills. In short, the participants across these projects built personal power as they learned about power.

We were proud of these accomplishments. But we also understood that this approach to social inquiry had little impact beyond the participants themselves and those closely connected with them. The students' and teachers' powerful personal transformations caused some ripples of influence among their immediate friends and colleagues but brought few structural or normative changes to their schools.

The work of individuals paled in comparison to other powerful forces pressing schools toward offering unequal opportunities and scripted curriculum and pedagogy aimed at increasing standardized test scores. In some cases, the teachers were viewed as "exceptional" (meaning that their accomplishments could not be expected from others); in other cases, the teachers were judged to be troublemakers. Similarly, the Futures students were both greatly admired and somewhat disparaged. Their successes were often explained away as anomalies or as the products of a resource-intensive intervention that could not go to scale in any practical way. It was suggested that the very highest performing Futures students simply had what it takes to excel in school and would have done just as well without the program.

In fact, on the few occasions when Futures or Teacher Inquiry work challenged prevailing structures, norms, or political arrangements, the proposed changes elicited renewed support for the status quo or outright backlash. Even when these teachers' and students' ideas garnered reform enthusiasm within their school, outside forces countered these initiatives, leaving them no better than the detracking reforms we described in Chapter 2. Put bluntly, exploring and understanding power were not the same as enacting power.

Our work, along with that of many others, has demonstrated the technical feasibility of enabling vastly more students to receive a high-quality education that sets them on a pathway to college and engaged citizenship. However, the social inquiry that had so compelling and powerful an effect on teachers and students was unlikely to challenge successfully the institutional structures, norms, and politics that hold social inequality in place.

Our social design experiments were limited by our traditional focus on transforming schools in and of themselves and relying on education insiders to accomplish that transformation. Though we and the teachers had engaged parents, and supportive school administrators sought to buffer outside opposition, our change strategy did not veer far from the schoolhouse. We had convened some public meetings to consider the work of students and teachers, and we distributed this work widely on our Web site, www.teachingtochangela.org. However, these public engagements were never fully exploited to develop the face-to-face relationships upon which meaningful social action rests. They did little to balance the social capital between those who have the schools they want and those who do not have the schools they need. Our work confirms several of John Dewey's propositions for effective, socially just, democratic reform. Principally, he insisted social betterment requires participatory social inquiry among those who bear the burden of inequality most. These participants would analyze their everyday problems with an understanding of the social, cultural, and political contexts that sustain inequality and support the ideologies of privilege. Such participation, Dewey argued, would create new and useful systems of knowledge. The learning associated with this participation would entail an iteration of expert knowledge becoming more everyday-like, and common knowledge becoming more expert-like. Likewise, the knowledge would become a basis for social action, and participation in social action would inform the knowledge base.

Yet, for all of its insights, Dewey's educative politics is limited by his own standpoint. In the words of Cornel West: "Dewey writes from the vantage point of and in leadership over that rising professional fraction of the working class *and* managerial class that is in sympathy with and has some influence among an exploited yet franchised industrial working class in the United States."[1] Hence, much of Dewey's activist writing was directed to teachers rather than those he referred to as "the masses." Concerned with the tendency of teachers to hold themselves above and apart from workers, Dewey aimed to replace their aloofness with connection. His worries about teachers enacting and imposing class privilege led Dewey to say little about the role of leadership or organizing within social movements. He called on citizens to "unite to inform themselves," but neglected to address the critical role of organizers in bringing people together for education and shared action.[2]

Dewey's "standpoint" also made him wary both of agitational methods that move beyond dialogue and of political engagement that transcends electoral politics.[3] He offered no strategies or tactics that would place an angry public face on the problems of inequality. These shortcomings did not allow Dewey to answer a number of essential questions suggested by his theory. For example, In what settings might public inquiry occur? What process might be transformative—that is, might enact knowledge through social action?

As we sought to answer these questions, we looked for empirical evidence, an ideology, or a tradition that bridged the inclusive knowledge-gathering and constructing processes that we had been exploring in our design experiments to an instantiation of democratically powered knowledge-in-action. Could there be an educative politics that was informed, on the one hand, by critical inquiry and conventional research, and, on the other hand, by the strategic actions associated with successful attempts to mobilize power in pursuit of social justice? The search for this combination led us to the arena of social movements and grassroots organizing.

After much study and our own inquiry into the theories and practices of social movements and grassroots groups, we began to experiment. Slowly, and with intention, we began to build alliances with organized groups that were engaged in activism around making state policies and local school practices equitable: advocates, community members, and parents and youth. With them, we have explored the proposition that social movement and grassroots organizing provide the most promising contemporary venues and practical strategies for placing in action the sort of social inquiry that Dewey imagined (and with which we already had some success). In the context of the groups' work, we investigated the hypothesis that broad-based and democratic public engagement benefits from inquiry and action as well as from participation among scholars, activists, and foundations that support equitable schooling.

In Chapters 7 and 8, we describe two projects of the Institute for Democracy, Education, and Access (IDEA) in which we examined the fusion of social inquiry and activism. In these projects, we have explored how advocacy and grassroots groups as education outsiders can variously encourage, pressure, and scaffold educational insiders' equity reforms. We have also investigated how and why the organized participation of parents, students, and community activists might be more efficacious in reform than action by elite policymakers, professional staff developers, or program designers. Our hunch, as we discussed in Chapter 1, was that grassroots and advocacy groups would create settings and employ strategies for understanding problems and posing solutions that challenge norms and build political power. That is, the external setting of community organizing, with its explicit focus on political and normative change, would transform policy and practice toward equitable ends better than insider-driven, technical change.

Further, mindful of the iterative nature of inquiry and action, we believed that as inquiry added a deeper knowledge of schooling, this knowledge would result in more powerful organizing. Stated simply, knowledge alone is not power, but it can contribute to the expression of power through informed and activated participants. We also anticipated that those engaged in grassroots social movement organizations would be reluctant to separate schooling from other social, political, and economic institutions and conditions that are profoundly entwined with schools. Because members of grassroots community groups experience multiple forms of inequality simultaneously, we thought they were less likely than education professionals to seek a "silver bullet" education reform that could dramatically improve students' learning and their life chances in the absence of attention to other social needs. Conversely, we imagined that community members would feel more urgency for immediate relief of the most egregious inequalities than would insiders whose inaction might be framed as progress over the long term.

In the rest of this chapter, we look at augmenting Dewey's ideas about engagement and learning with organized social action. We first review some basic elements of social movements and grassroots organizing. Then we explain how movement organizing maps well onto Dewey's ideas, and how movement organizing extends Dewey's ideas in useful ways.

SOCIAL MOVEMENTS

Over the past few decades, social scientists have helped us understand why movements arise, how they work, what impacts they have, and why. We believe that there are insights in this work that are far more useful for achieving equitable education than the ideas and practices that underlie most school reform.

Consider the following in light of what we have learned about the limits of the technical focus of conventional school reform: Social movements, born of conflict and discontent, are meaningful efforts to bring about progressive social change. Social movements gain force as informal networks of individuals and groups exchange information, resources, and expertise based on shared beliefs, a sense of solidarity, and collective identity. Social movement networks make demands on the established order through public protest and other collective actions that go beyond conventional politics. As they seek concrete changes in social policies and institutions, social movements also seek to construct new cultural norms and create new political arrangements that advantage nonelites.[4]

Social movements focused on expanding opportunities and public participation—such as the Civil Rights, feminist, and labor movements—can help us envision the possibility of an "education equity movement." Just as (potential) constituencies for the established movements existed prior to their coalescing into political forces capable of altering the political and social landscapes, there is a broad array of people and ideas awaiting a collective effort to become organized into a similar force for educational justice. Because social movements focus explicitly on normative and political goals and processes, their methods contrast dramatically with the largely technical approach of professional educators, who follow a far more linear and consensual research, development, dissemination, and adoption model of innovation. Strikingly, social movements zero in on the very dimensions of equity education reforms that make them so difficult to adopt, implement, and sustain as professional innovations—that is, their explicit challenge to prevailing cultural norms and the distribution of resources and opportunities that advantage elites.

GRASSROOTS ORGANIZING

Sociologists Susan Stall and Randy Stoecker conclude that "behind every successful social movement is a community, or network of communities."[5] Organized groups are the key building blocks of social movements. These groups are made up of people, intent on building power, who have come together in more or less formal ways to refine their understanding of specific problems, agree upon solutions, and devise strategies for realizing these changes. Knowing that neither a righteous cause nor a sound technical solution will in itself achieve their goals, these groups seek widespread support so they can confront, negotiate with, or persuade the people and institutions that stand in their way or can help.

Grassroots community organizing is a natural source of movement "building blocks." Rinku Sen asserts in *Stir It Up* that "long-lasting social change is made by large-scale movements . . . [and] movements emerge from organizations that . . . build and activate . . . constituenc[ies]."[6] Such organizing is a process whereby low-income community members, often with the support of professional organizers, build locally controlled and inclusive organizations that seek social change on behalf of members. A number of centers have emerged around the country that train individuals and groups with the accumulated knowledge and skills for successful organizing. One training manual boils organizing down to its very basics: "The process of finding out what people want as individuals and then helping them find collective ways of getting it."[7]

Stall and Stoecker define community organizing as "the work that occurs in local settings to empower individuals, build relationships, and create action for social change."[8] Similarly, Marshall Ganz, former civil rights and farm worker organizer and now lecturer at Harvard's Kennedy School of Government, argues that organizing activities seek to create networks that can sustain a new activist community, to frame a story about the network's identity and purpose, and to develop a program of action that mobilizes and expends resources to advance the community's interests. Ganz argues that these three domains of activity—building relationships, developing common understandings, and taking action—combined into campaigns, are what enable ordinary people to develop the knowledge, capacity, and power that social change requires. Ganz's conceptualization is particularly useful in that it helps us see how organizing picks up where Dewey left off.[9]

Relationships

"Organizing is overwhelmingly about personal relationships. It is about changing the world and changing how individuals act together," asserts the Midwest Academy's manual for activists.[10] Organizers develop relationships by linking community members to one another in local groups and networks of groups. Some small local groups, for example, develop relationships through "door knocking" campaigns, wherein group members canvass neighborhoods, talking one-on-one with residents about their concerns and aspirations. At the other end of the spectrum, national and global organizations engage in e-activism. Groups like Greenpeace and MoveOn.org use Web sites and listservs as mechanisms for connecting like-minded activists as members of virtual communities.

The largest national networks of local face-to-face grassroots groups working on behalf of low-income communities and communities of color are the Association of Community Organizations for Reform Now (ACORN), the Pacific Institute for Community Organization (PICO), and the Industrial Areas Foundation (IAF). ACORN is a national network of neighborhood-based citizens' groups that grew out of the 1970s War on Poverty programs and whose original focus was on ensuring the rights of welfare recipients.[11] Both the IAF and PICO are national, faith-based alliances of congregations, schools, and other community organizations.[12] In 2004, the IAF had 55 affiliates in 21 states, each made up of religious congregations, labor locals, parents' associations, schools, and other community groups. IAF has approximately 150 professional organizers. IAF's and PICO's institutional membership approach grows out of the theory that existing relationships among people in churches, schools, and other stable institutions provide the strongest base for building the power and problem-solving capacities of low-income communities.

Many community organizing groups also forge common cause with other groups around a particular goal or a broader agenda. Such supportive alliances enable small groups to marshal resources and achieve "wins" far beyond what their own size and strength would allow.

The relationships fostered in organizing groups extend beyond achieving short-term policy goals. Nearly all such groups have as a long-term goal the building of stable, efficacious organizations that use democratic processes to develop the problem-solving capacity and commitment of less powerful communities.[13] The Midwest Academy training center, for example, teaches power and confrontational tactics to organized groups so that they can "win tangible improvements in people's lives." Also central to the academy's mission is to "make people aware of their own power" and to "alter the relations of power between people, the government, and other institutions by building strong permanent local, state and national organizations."[14] They explain further,

> When we say that we want to "alter the relations of power", we mean building organizations that those in power, at all levels of government, will always have to worry about. Whenever they decide to do anything that has an impact on your group, they are going to have to say "wait a minute", how will that organization react to this? We also know from sad experience that what is won this year can be taken away next year if the organization that won it disappears or is weakened. In Direct Action Organizing, building an organization is always as important as winning a particular issue.[15]

In organizing, then, relationships become power—often described by sociologists as *social capital*—that can be used as a resource for social action. These social ties create norms of solidarity and reciprocity among community members. Members can count on one another to keep commitments and to work on one another's behalf.[16] In low-income urban communities, such networks of trusting relationships can be useful for solving a wide range of social problems, supporting political action, sustaining the group through difficult struggles, and disseminating information among members.

Unlike conventional advocacy strategies where professional advocates (lobbyists, for example) struggle on behalf of powerful groups, organizing seeks to build leadership among the people who actually experience the problem and engage them in direct action for social change.[17] Ideally, organizers let go of the leadership in order to locate responsibility and power in the group's membership.

Understanding

Organizing nearly always engages participants in inquiring into how their immediate problems fit into the larger social, economic, historical, and political context; identifying likely solutions to those problems; and constructing an agenda for change. According to Ganz, understanding comes from the fusion of local knowledge with facts and broader social theories that help communities see their own particular circumstances in a larger social and political context.[18] Connecting to broader social theories builds their understanding of problems and potential solutions. It also enables members of grassroots groups to generate wholly new ways of thinking and plans of action—what sociologist Francesca Polletta calls the "innovatory" and "developmental" elements of democratic participation.[19] Polletta argues that members of grassroots groups constantly develop new strategies and skills in the course of political action as they share leadership, exchange ideas, and negotiate consensus. This model of organizing is quite similar to the social inquiry Dewey argued for.

Also much like Dewey, Marshall Ganz claims that understanding comes as organizers and community members engage one another in dialogue about their own situations and as they generate more hopeful alternatives.[20] Dialogue not only reframes problems; it also fosters a sense of collective identity among the group as people discover shared interests around which they might act jointly. It allows participants to construct a story of who they are, what they do, and why they do it. That "story" often challenges prevailing narratives that may explain away unequal distribution of resources and power as natural and inevitable. The participants' counternarratives motivate the group to strategize about ways to realize the more hopeful possibilities they have framed.

Action

Political action often arises episodically as communities react to policies they do not like. Such action rarely reshapes the underlying conditions giving rise to the policies. Fundamental social change requires that organized groups of people mount proactive campaigns carried out with planned "tactical" actions that move their agenda forward. Such actions must be persuasive to authorities who have the power to enact change. They also must be seen as legitimate in order to garner the support of large numbers of people who need to rally behind the cause. Moreover, they must be satisfying to the activists themselves, so that the activists will continue to engage in collective action even when the outcomes are disappointing.

The creation of an activist community begins as organized groups target a particular objective—often a small one at first. They select the most promising strategies and tactics for mobilizing resources and acting collectively to achieve concrete "wins" that take them closer to achieving their goals. Collective actions include such disparate tactics as mass postcard mailings, boycotts, vigils, strikes, face-to-face confrontations, and intentional law-breaking. Some organizations focus on protest, whereas others seek to build strategic relationships that enable them to negotiate with people in power. Still others use sophisticated media strategies to garner widespread public knowledge and sympathy for problems. Nearly all rely on unconventional tactics as well as more conventional political actions.

Social movement researchers categorize various direct "actions" as reflecting three different theories of action: numbers, material damage, and bearing witness. Actions based on the power of numbers include marches, rallies, petitions, letter writing, and mobilizing voters. Like democratic political processes, such actions attempt to persuade elites that there is large public support for or against a particular policy. Actions reflecting a theory of "material damage" include, boycotts, strikes, blocking traffic, disrupting business, and, at the extreme end, damage to property. The theory here is that actions will be powerful and persuasive if they cause some noticeable impact on the economy or disrupt normal processes. Actions based on "bearing witness" include forms of civil disobedience such as hunger strikes, burning draft cards, refusal to pay taxes, and chaining oneself to a tree. These strategies seek "to demonstrate a strong commitment to an objective deemed vital for humanity's future" by engaging in behaviors that involve personal risk or cost.[21] The logic here is that such dramatic actions will generate support for social causes and persuade policy elites that change is warranted.[22]

All three of these theories of action also embody the belief that those directly affected by the problems can make the most compelling case for solving them. Activists put their bodies alongside their ideas to create persuasive force. Such activists present themselves as legitimate constituents rather than greedy professionals, meddling outsiders, or fuzzy-headed academics.

THE ROOTS OF CONTEMPORARY ORGANIZING

Multiple traditions have shaped contemporary community organizing in the United States. Best known is Saul Alinsky's model of public confrontation between organized "have-nots" and powerful, more advantaged "targets," whose concessions can provide solutions to local community problems. Contemporary organizing also has roots in the traditions of the Black freedom movement that extend back to before the Civil War.[23]

"Power Is Not Only What You Have, But What the Target Thinks You Have"[24]

Saul Alinsky, considered by many to be the father of community organizing in the United States, began organizing in Chicago's poor neighborhoods in the 1930s. He created the IAF in 1940 and thereafter traveled around the country helping ordinary people organize to solve local community problems. Over the course of his career, Alinsky trained hundreds of other organizers, including Cesar Chavez.

Self-interest, collective power, and relationships were central to Alinsky's organizing approach, and these core ideas remain in much organizing today.[25] Alinsky saw "self-interest" as the fundamental impetus for organizing. Distinguishing self-interest from selfishness, Alinsky argued that organizations and movements could only be strong and sustained if they worked on behalf of the class interests of their members. Today, the Midwest Academy teaches organizers that "all organizing is based on relationships and self-interest, broadly defined."[26] The Academy's manual argues that economic position is at the core of self-interest:

> Self-interest is often class interest. Self-interest can mean the good feeling that comes from getting back at the landlord, standing up to the boss, or knocking an unaccountable politician out of office. Self-interest also applies across generational lines as people are motivated to fight for what helps their children and grandchildren.[27]

But the Midwest Academy also broadens the notion of self-interest far beyond material needs.

> Self-interest applies to what makes people feel good about themselves, as well as to what materially benefits them. More broadly still, many people feel a need to take on the responsibilities of citizenship and to play a role in shaping public affairs. People want interaction with the larger community and often enjoy working collectively for the common good. Sometimes self-interest is a desire to work with people of a different race or culture in order to broaden one's own perspective or to combat prejudice. Other people may be drawn to an international project, such as fighting foreign sweatshops, because they want to make a global difference.[28]

Influenced by labor organizing movements, Alinsky taught ordinary people to identify problems in their communities and use confrontational tactics such as sit-ins and boycotts to improve their lives. Only by exercise of collective power, Alinsky believed, could poor people wrest concessions from rich people, who skillfully used the power of wealth and political position to maintain social and economic advantages.

> Power must be understood for what it is, for the part it plays in every area of our life, if we are to understand it and thereby grasp the essentials of relationships and functions between groups and organizations, particularly in a pluralistic society. To know power and not fear it is essential to its constructive use and control.[29]

Just as Alinsky believed that power could be exercised by mass mobilization and direct actions, today's Midwest Academy teaches "direct action" organizing "based on the power of the people to take collective action on their own behalf."[30]

Alinsky viewed strategic relationships among organizing groups and between these groups and powerful elites, including the media, as critical for enacting power. Alinsky argued that groups must have no permanent friends and no permanent enemies, just permanent issues. We can see this tradition at work in the Alliance Schools Project in Texas. Ernesto Cortes and the IAF organizers teach the groups to develop "fear and loathing relationships" with elected officials. These relationships allow the groups to hold elected officials accountable—judging them by actions and results (rather than promises), giving them credit when they have advanced the group's agenda, and criticizing them loudly when they do not.[31]

Alinsky and his organizing methods have not been without detractors. Criticisms have focused primarily on Alinsky's emphasis on conflict and confrontation, and on his eschewing of "ideological issues" such as structural racism or the inherent inequalities of capitalism, in favor of winning more concrete victories in "the world as it is, not as it ought to be" (taken from a German proverb often quoted in IAF training). Alinsky's approach has also been faulted for the disproportionate number of White organizers and institutional leaders and, on occasion, for racist and sexist practices. In particular, feminists have criticized Alinsky's approach for drawing artificial boundaries between public and private issues (disregarding many women's concerns), placing emphasis on narrow self-interest (denying altruistic motivations), and focusing pragmatically on "wins" (neglecting the important processes of learning and building relationships).[32]

These criticisms have spawned the development of new organizations focused on racial issues and engaging communities of color. Such groups have broadened Alinsky's approach beyond narrow economic issues to include such problems as police brutality, school inequalities, and environmental justice. Many, such as the Alliance Schools project, have also augmented their repertoire of strategies beyond direct confrontation to include mutually supportive relationships between communities and local schools.[33]

"Organizing in the Spirit of Ella"[34]

Organizing also has roots in African American women's collective efforts to preserve home and community during slavery. As the institution of slavery placed Black bodies and Black families under constant threat, enslaved women banded together to protect children and one another, create and preserve traditions, and assert power where possible. This activism continued throughout the Jim Crow era. Particularly notable was the organizing of Mary McCleod Bethune, Ida B. Wells, and Mary Church Terrell, and the development of the National Association for Colored Women and the National Council for Negro Women. Throughout the first half of the 20th century these women engaged in nonviolent resistance to segregation laws, organized to develop schools for girls, advocated for union representation and economic protections for domestic workers, and battled discrimination in the defense industries in World War II.[35]

Similarly, at the end of the 19th and beginning of the 20th century, progressive White women such as Jane Addams created community-based settlement houses that sought to extend the protections afforded by homes and families to working-class, immigrant neighborhoods by improving social networks and enriching community life, as well as providing access to needed social services.[36]

The idea that powerful knowledge and solutions to problems reside in communities themselves was also at the core of the training offered to community leaders by the Highlander Folk School (now the Highlander Center) in Tennessee beginning in 1932. Highlander's founder Myles Horton argued, "the answers to the problems facing society lie in the experiences of ordinary people. Those experiences, so often belittled and denigrated in our society, are the keys to grassroots power."[37] Accordingly, Highlander sought to develop community leaders, rather than professional organizers, so that those who participated could go on to share with others and to multiply what they had learned.

In the 1940s and 1950s, Highlander provided training to community leaders and organizers such as Rosa Parks, Fannie Lou Hamer, and Ella Baker, who went on to transform existing local networks into a political force for social change during the Civil Rights Movement of the 1960s.[38] Baker was a pivotal force. Working alongside, yet very differently from, Rev. Martin Luther King, Jr., Ella Baker's approach to organizing focused on "quiet places" and working with "organizers who liked to work them" rather than on mobilizing large public protests.[39] In collaboration with Highlander leader Septima Clark, Baker established a program to train community people. Proceeding from the observation that "no one has ever taken the time to explain to the masses of society how politics determines the course of their lives,"[40] Clark's Citizen Education Program employed a pedagogy of dialogue that combined literacy teaching, personal empowerment, and political activism.

Focused on inquiry and engagement, rather than indoctrination, Clark's teaching and Baker's grassroots organizing laid the groundwork for the Mississippi Freedom Summer in 1964 and for the eventual passage of the Voting Rights Act of 1965.[41] Baker supported students who participated in the sit-ins throughout the South as they established the Student Nonviolent Coordinating Committee (SNCC). In the words of Robert Moses, one of those young people, Baker always emphasized the

> centrality of families to the work of organizing; the empowerment of grassroots people and their recruitment for leadership; and the principle of "casting down your bucket where you are," or organizing in the context in which one lives and works, and working the issues found in that context.[42]

Baker is perhaps best known for her insistence that leadership should be decentralized and should come from ordinary people rather than from professional organizers. She is often quoted as saying, "Strong people don't need strong leaders."[43] In contrast to Alinsky and the labor movement tradition where professional organizers were "outside agitators," Ella Baker's organizers worked from inside the community and adapted organizing to the community's way of life. Their task was to transform the community's everyday concerns into broad, significant political issues. As we describe below, inquiry was also at the heart of this tradition.

Notably, Baker's approach is different from Alinsky's emphasis on narrowly defined class interest as the motivator for engagement in social change activities. Baker attended to issues that cut across different sectors of the Black community (even as she brought special sensitivity to the needs of the poor). Rather than appealing to a rational weighing of the costs and benefits of action, this approach to organizing called on a sense of outrage, an appeal to the dignity of the community, and a sense of solidarity and shared identity of community members.

This more community-driven and more feminist organizing tradition can also be found in some contemporary community mobilization.[44] Many groups today share the perspective that power for change exists within networks of ordinary people who engage in collective action based on what they learn from one another. These groups rely heavily on developing indigenous leadership, even when they are supported by professional organizers. They often reject the distinction between the methods they use and the goals they seek to achieve; rather they seek both tangible "wins" and to create a space where members can experience "on a small scale the type of world they are struggling for."[45]

PARTICIPATORY SOCIAL INQUIRY AND ORGANIZING

The dynamic process of community organizing, particularly organizing in the tradition of the Highlander School and Ella Baker, has much in common with Dewey's conception of transformative participatory social inquiry. Indeed, both Myles Horton and Ella Baker developed their commitments in New York City during the 1930s while studying and working within labor, political, and educational circles that overlapped those frequented by John Dewey. Horton and Baker, however, were much more *of* the grassroots than Dewey, and this difference is reflected in their embrace of organizing alongside inquiry. Rather than relying on the transformative potential of inquiry alone, organizing connects knowledge building with power building (strategy and action) to advance education reform.

A Commitment to Inquiry

Inquiry and learning are central to the Highlander approach to organizing. Like Dewey, Myles Horton and his colleagues believed that power was created by bringing community leaders together in inquiry. Highlander always has used "participatory research" to generate knowledge and understanding. Like Dewey's inquiry, Highlander's strategy begins by documenting the knowledge, concerns, and struggles of the people engaged in its training. For example, Highlander's Web site asserts:

> By sharing experience, we realize that we are not alone. We face common problems caused by injustice. By affirming our cultural and racial diversity, we overcome differences that divide us. Together we develop the resources for collective action. By connecting communities and groups regionally, we are working to change unjust structures and to build a genuine political and economic democracy.[46]

Participatory research helps Highlander participants become more effective community educators and organizers by building their understanding of the political, social, and economic factors underlying community issues. The Highlander Center's "Grassroots Think Tank" brings organized community people together with progressive academics and promising community leaders to address the problems communities face and to explore strategies for organizing and movement building.[47]

Baker, too, believed that learning about the issues at hand was as essential to building power as mounting collective "action." She envisioned ordinary people linking their problems to broader social, cultural, and political contexts and ideologies. Ella Baker's biographer, Barbara Ransby notes:

> Radical change for Ella Baker was about a persistent and protracted process of discourse, debate, consensus, reflection, and struggle. If larger and larger numbers of communities were engaged in such a process, she reasoned, day in and day out, year after year, the revolution would be well under way. Ella Baker understood that laws, structures, and institutions had to change in order to correct injustice and oppression, but part of the process had to involve oppressed people, ordi-

nary people, infusing new meanings into the concept of democracy and finding their own individual and collective power to determine their lives and shape the direction of history.[48]

Inquiry into Action

Scholars have generally associated organizing with strategies for building institutional and political power. Yet, more recent scholarship has addressed organizing as community learning, based on a "curriculum" of common interests. This is the point of intersection between contemporary social movements and Dewey's conception of social inquiry.[49] As we discussed earlier, Ganz identifies three concurrent processes of organizing: building relationships, developing common understandings, and taking action.[50] Together, these processes build identity and power through educative inquiry and action. Certainly, they require the sort of experimentalism and broad participation described by Dewey. But they also include a political way of being in the world that action brings—sensitivity to inequality, commitment to support the interests of the group, and belief in the power of joint action to alter existing circumstances.

LESSONS FOR SCHOOL REFORM

In Chapter 3, we offered a set of four principles drawn from Dewey's work on participatory social inquiry that we believe provide useful guidance for those seeking equity-minded school reform. These principles include connecting those most affected by inequality with "experts" in egalitarian, knowledge-generating relationships; employing a stance that looks with a critical eye at "common sense" explanations of the world; generating knowledge in participatory social inquiry; and directing this knowledge toward a transformative goal. Together, the principles suggest that the creation and flow of "disruptive knowledge" promises to revitalize public life through the participation of those previously marginalized by society.

Our experiences with the Futures and Teaching to Change LA Projects (Chapters 4 and 5) illustrate how Dewey's principles came to life in the activities of students, educators, and researchers seeking more equitable schooling. The achievements of these social design experiments led us to believe that Dewey's work provides a sound basis for transformative experiences for small "protected" and scaffolded cohorts. In particular, we got to see firsthand (and we have documented), the amazing consequences of giving students and teachers the tools for systematically acquiring and making sense of new knowledge: data about schools, demographic data, and tools for rigorous analysis. We opened doors to other researchers, eased connections to like-minded allies, and provided state-of-the-art technical scaffolding so they could present their work in the most compelling ways to a variety of audiences. However, the groups in our design experiments were no match for the entrenched social norms and structures that were well insulated against transformation.

If democratic- and equity-minded educators and students have too little clout and too few resources when acting alone to make much of a dent in the structures and norms that uphold inequality, who might be their most "natural" allies to help tip the balance of knowledge and power? That question led us to grassroots groups that are using the strategies of social movement organizing. These groups had plenty of potential power, and they were clearly, if not consciously or formally, in sympathy with Dewey's principles of participatory social inquiry. Where they seemed to fall short was in just that area in which the Futures and Teaching to Change LA Projects were strongest. The grassroots groups, particularly those that were smaller and less well resourced, did not have the research and data analysis capacities that could both address their immediate local concerns and bind them in common cause with other groups battling against systemic deficiencies in schooling policy and resources.

Our analysis of social movement organizing, then, led us to add to our list of Deweyan principles for investigating and guiding efforts to make schooling more equitable. The three principles below, derived from movement-organizing strategies, are fundamentally compatible with the theory and practice of participatory social inquiry, but they also foreground what much equity-minded school reform fails to address—*power*.

- *Use Social Movement Organizing as a Site for Inquiry.* Local grassroots community groups, networks, and the coalitions such groups forge with advocacy organizations are already promising sites for inquiry. They are spaces for joint public work that centrally involve those most affected by inequality in correcting that inequality. They draw on knowledge from members' life experiences. They challenge prevailing understandings of social problems—particularly those put forth through media—with critical perspectives that locate their current "troubles" in structural and historical inequalities rather than in deficits in individuals and communities. Social movement organizations offer members a powerful collective identity as family and community, and, as such, they can raise equitable education to the highest and most passionate priority. Social movement groups seek social transformation through both correcting immediate injustices and disrupting social norms and structures that stand in the way of resolving other present and future injustices. All of these characteristics evoke, yet stretch beyond, Dewey's conception of participatory inquiry. Consequently, social movement organizations and networks seem to be particularly hospitable sites for those students, parents, and community members most negatively affected by stratified and unequal schooling to fuse their knowledge, experience, and relationships with the specialized knowledge and tools of "experts." In so doing, they can gain leverage, identify key but less obvious elements of the problems they hope to correct, and stand on an equal footing with elites who would maintain the status quo.

- *Build Relational Power.* Social movement organizations understand and expect that their efforts to change stratifying social policies will generate conflict with those who have disproportionate influence over the conduct of social policy and the flow of information. They expect that elites will use their influence to resist change, including selectively gathering data to frame arguments that give them even further advantage. Therefore, although social activists are eager for knowledge that reflects the actual distribution of resources and suggests plain solutions to inequality, they also understand that it is naive to behave as if once knowledge is made known, it will easily win support. Such change requires power. People in underserved communities typically lack "conventional" resources for developing or buying power—access to leadership positions, research, media, and networking expertise. Movement organizing strategies counter these putative *disadvantages* by developing collective leadership, constantly involving new people in leadership roles, convening community meetings that involve as many people as possible in decision-making, and creating a collective vision. They build their collective power through their relationships with one another and through strategic alliances with those whose expertise, resources, and access to power can provide them with the political clout to advance their goals.

- *Use Collective Action to Press for Change.* In contrast to Dewey, who was largely silent about how participatory social inquiry prompts social change, movement organizations see direct, collective action as an indispensable tool. Such groups not only create "disruptive knowledge" but also act on it, revitalizing public life through the civic participation and political power of groups previously marginalized by society. Organizing groups ask at every turn of their developing understanding, "What are we going to do about it together?" They use a repertoire of actions, each supported by a logic of numbers, of material damage, of bearing witness. These actions insert, figuratively and literally, the bodies of their members into the public sphere—using this presence to assert pressure for change. Linking knowledge, relationships, and action, they mobilize and deploy resources at the most advantageous moment to achieve a transformative goal.

ALLIANCES FOR EQUITY

In the two chapters that follow, we provide examples of our work in which we have sought to merge principles drawn from Deweyan participatory social inquiry with those drawn from social movement organizing. Unlike the Futures and Teaching to Change LA Projects described in Chapters 4 and 5, the two projects described in Chapters 7 and 8—Parent-U-Turn and the Educational Justice Collaborative—are as much alliances as social design experiments. The groups described in these chapters are grassroots organizations that would have existed without the participation of IDEA researchers. However, our relationship with these two groups provided them with a connection to "experts" that led to the merging of knowledge creation and power. Far from asserting the common and disparaging sense of all-knowing researchers, we have adopted a more limited role as we participate with these groups. We do bring "special skill or knowledge derived from training,"[51] but that distinctive role only partly fills a small niche in the educational justice movement. This two-way relationship has prompted learning and action and has provided us with an opportunity to investigate how this combination might advance efforts to make schools serving low-income students of color more equitable.

7

Parent-U-Turn

Parents Organized for Inquiry and Action

Mary Johnson and Justina Paque protesting overcrowded schools in South Gate.

MARY JOHNSON'S WORK as a parent activist began at home. As a young mother, she lived in an apartment complex on the border of South Gate and Lynwood, two cities on the southeastern edge of Los Angeles. "Pendleton," as the complex was known on the streets because of the plaid shirts many residents wore, included 950 low-cost housing units. Almost all of Pendleton's residents were African American or Latino. Mary moved there with her three boys and daughter after her divorce in 1989.[1]

Although Mary felt a deep sense of connection to many Pendleton families, she constantly worried that it was an unsafe place for her children. "Decent people lived there," notes Mary, but over time, the complex had deteriorated due to the building manager's neglect. The interior walls of many buildings were covered in mildew. Apartment roofs were pocked with holes. Rats and other pests infested many units. And although there were hundreds of young people living in Pendleton, there was no playground for the children or organized space for youth to congregate. Instead, the corridors and stairwells became sites of late-hour dice games, drug dealing, and prostitution. Mary remembers, "You couldn't get a pizza man to deliver to Pendleton because they got robbed so many times."

Most Pendleton residents resented this criminal activity, but they did not trust the police to improve the situation. In the early 1990s, the South Gate Police Department had a reputation for harassing local youth and disrespecting Pendleton residents. Police–community relations also were colored by tensions in neighboring Watts that had led to the community uprising after the Rodney King verdict in 1993. When South Gate police began a sweep of Pendleton's apartments in 1994, many residents reacted with anger. "They were pulling people out and taking them to jail," recalls Mary. "They asked who lived in my apartment, and I told them it was my first amendment right not to tell them." One of Mary's friends began videotaping the police, but then she became afraid and passed the camera to Mary's 11-year-old daughter. When the police spotted the camera, they began to question Mary's daughter and threatened to arrest her. Mary tearfully pleaded with the officers, who eventually released her daughter but confiscated the camera.

The incident terrified Mary, but she was not one to back down. She contacted the American Civil Liberties Union (ACLU), the National Association for the Advancement of Colored People (NAACP), and a reporter at the local paper. After the reporter inquired about the harassment and camera incident, a South Gate police sergeant called Mary to apologize for his officers' actions. Mary thanked the sergeant for his concern, but informed him that an apology was not enough. She wanted change.

The next morning, Mary started organizing. Along with her Spanish-speaking neighbor, Dora Long, Mary began knocking on the doors of Pendleton apartments, asking residents to sign a petition criticizing the South Gate Police

Department for violating the rights of Pendleton community members. In a week, Mary and Dora collected over 900 signatures. They took the petition to City Hall and presented it to the police chief, who, impressed by the numbers, made a personal commitment to build a new relationship with the Pendleton community. The chief worked with Mary and other community leaders to arrange a town hall meeting at Pendleton. Mary made flyers publicizing the meeting and distributed them to all her neighbors. The police chief brought representatives from the City Council, the Public Works Department, the Public Health Department, and the Building and Safety Department. Pendleton's owner came as well. Pendleton residents believed it was the "first time [many of these city leaders] stepped foot in [their] neighborhood."

The town hall meeting initiated a series of community gatherings. So many residents attended that the meetings were moved to a local park. After health and safety inspectors cited the Pendleton owner for several violations, actions were taken to fix the complex. A standing committee of residents gathered every Friday to talk about general concerns with upkeep and to create a list of conditions needing repair. The police began to work with community leaders to reduce crime. The department assigned new officers to Pendleton who took steps to earn the respect of community members. "They talked to us like we were human beings, not like we were animals." Remembering this change, Mary Johnson smiles and adds: "And they say you can't take on city hall."

The Pendleton community's effort showed Mary and her neighbors the potential power of people sharing concerns, developing relationships that hold officials accountable, and taking collective action for change. Using grassroots organizing strategies, they had demanded and won real improvements in the conditions of their community. The success of the Pendleton campaign encouraged community members to take action on other issues affecting their families. And the primary concern of most Pendleton families was the quality of their local schools.

In the remainder of this chapter, we trace the educational activism of Johnson, her neighbor Valerie Muñoz, and the grassroots organization of parents they founded and continue to lead—Parent-U-Turn. Our UCLA research group first met them in 1997, and we have followed their work ever since. Over the years, their inquiry and collective action have added to their community presence and power. Winning successive concrete changes in low-income community schools has been accompanied by dramatic shifts in their relationships with pubic officials. For much of that time, our UCLA group has provided Parent-U-Turn with "on-demand" research as a community public service. In the process of performing this "expert" role, our model was that of *inquiry* rather than client–provider *service*. The story we tell here focuses on how these parents fused inquiry and action as they sought to secure better schooling.

ORGANIZED PARENTS AS A SITE FOR PARTICIPATORY SOCIAL INQUIRY

Mary Johnson and Valerie Muñoz were angry about the poor quality of their local schools. Pendleton lay on the border of South Gate schools, which belonged to the larger Los Angeles Unified School District, and the independent (from Los Angeles) Lynwood Unified School District. Neither school system could promise a high-quality education. Johnson's older children went to school in South Gate, and her younger two attended Lynwood schools with Muñoz's four children. The children frequently came home with stories about unprepared or uncaring teachers, unhealthful cafeteria food, and unfair discipline policies. Mary and Valerie found a resource for understanding and addressing these problems when they met the director of UCLA Center X's Parent Curriculum Project in 1997.

Connecting with Experts

Center X (the precursor of the Institute for Democracy, Education, and Access [IDEA]) created the Parent Curriculum Project in 1995. Directed by Laila Hasan, a graduate student and mathematics education instructor for Center X, the Parent Curriculum Project set out to inform low-income parents about school reform and encourage them to become school and community leaders who would advocate on behalf of all children.[2] Hasan understood firsthand that not all communities have adequate access to knowledge about how schools work. Neither Hasan nor her mother had been privy to the rules when her South Los Angeles high school pushed her out when she was a teen. Now, having worked for years as a math teacher, she used her remarkable inquiry skills to bring her knowledge of the system to parents. "If [you] don't know what's going on," Hasan notes, you "don't know what to fight for."

Hasan invited Mary Johnson, Mary's friend Emma Street, and Valerie Muñoz to join the Parent Curriculum Project's 13-week institute in Lynwood. For 2 days a week, Johnson, Street, and Muñoz gathered with neighbors to learn "what good teaching and learning looks like." They studied the state content standards in each subject area. But, as important as *what* they learned, was *how* they learned. Hasan began the institute by asking the parents to share their educational autobiographies—their own schooling histories.

The relationship between these parents and our UCLA group grew as their work as activists expanded. Johnson, Street, and Muñoz, and then later Guadalupe ("Lupe") Aguiar, Justina Paque, Mary Galvan, and a growing number of parents who joined forces with them, increasingly asked us for help understanding the problems in their local schools, identifying potential solutions, and making sense of education policy and the policymaking process. As they increased their knowledge and influence, they became more sophisticated about what they needed generally and what they could ask for and get from researchers.

Accessing and Constructing Knowledge

The "lessons" in the Parent Curriculum Project introduced Johnson, Muñoz, and the other participants to the official, "elite" knowledge that they heard from educators in their communities. Maybe more important, they also learned the language and knowledge that was not—but should have been—used in public discussions of education quality. For example, they learned about the state's content standards, the pedagogies most likely to help students meet those standards, assessment and the web of reporting and rhetoric around accountability, and the myriad education policies associated with standards-based reform.

The Parent Curriculum Project also provided parents with new understandings about the process of learning. Laila Hasan embraced the Deweyan principle that "the only way to prepare for social life is to engage in social life."[3] The project's parent institutes modeled constructivist classrooms, involving parents in activities that called on them to discover, interpret, and make meaning through critical questioning. For many parents, the contrast between this new pedagogy and the education they had experienced came as a revelation. Justina Paque, who attended schools in Mexico and Los Angeles as a youth, commented: "I started going to those classes, and I thought, 'Is this really possible?' 'Can we really do this?' 'Do we have a right to be taught this way?'"

Paque and the other parents affirmatively sought answers to these and other "parents' rights" questions through a series of guided tours, or "learning walks," through Lynwood's classrooms. During these walks, the parents took notes on what they observed and asked students questions about what they were learning and why they thought it was important. The parents then held this evidence up to the standard of high-quality learning they had experienced at the institute. Participatory dialogue helped the parents connect their school observations, their personal experiences, and research-based knowledge to construct complex understandings of their children's schooling:

PARENT 1: Well, the classroom looks like the teacher is trying to do what the principal was talking about with the writing. She has a lot of student work all over the walls.

PARENT 2: The teacher had over half of the students in that group she was working with.

PARENT 3: She seemed to be doing most of the talk . . . why?

PARENT 4: The rest of the class was too much by themselves. I think those students need more help.

Understanding of standards, pedagogy, assessment, and education policy helped the parents develop new identities in relationship to their children's schools. Instead of asking, "Is *my* grandchild doing well," Emma Street asked teachers at Back to School Night if *all* students were receiving standards-based instruction. As Valerie Muñoz recalls, the Parent Curriculum Project helped parents realize "we had a right to come on the school campus without an appointment." With this sense of entitlement came a modest shift in how the educators viewed parents. "The teachers," noted one parent, "almost acted like it was OK for us to be there."

Most Lynwood officials hoped that the Parent Curriculum Project would increase parent volunteerism and commitment, but they were unwelcoming to parents who wanted to change the balance of power between school and community. The superintendent spoke enthusiastically about the prospects of 150 parent participants becoming "300 more hands" to help the district while warning against parents becoming "complainers." Tensions frequently accompanied parents' requests for information about school programs or finances. One parent remembers that her principal set up "roadblock after roadblock" to prevent parents from getting a copy of the school's Title 1 budget. Similarly, Valerie Muñoz received a barrage of critical questions—"Who sent you here?" "Why do you need this information?"—when she and some other parents asked to observe how students used computers at her child's school.[4]

Valerie and other parents also began to question whether they were looking for the right information to effect change. They had learned that their children's school did not provide opportunities for students to conduct online research (as is specified in the state learning standards). But, as long as the principal reasoned, "computers are not necessary . . . for children's learning," such information provided little hope for school improvement.[5] Parents needed some leverage to get the schools to do what was right—to hold school leaders accountable for their leadership decisions. In the summer of 2001, Valerie Muñoz, Mary Johnson, Emma Street, and several of their allies in Lynwood and South Gate created Parent-U-Turn, an organization dedicated to giving parents a more powerful role in educational decision making.

At about this time, UCLA's IDEA was extending its exploration of critical participation to include parents. We created a new parent leadership seminar to help parent activists access information on the distribution of educational opportunities across schools in greater Los Angeles. Parent-U-Turn's first official action was to enroll in the IDEA seminar.

Led by John Rogers, the seminar met once a month, with each meeting focused on a different schooling opportunity—access to quality teachers, safe and uncrowded schools, sufficient learning materials, and more. Every seminar session began with information from publicly accessible databases that report on conditions in Los Angeles schools. By walking step-by-step through the process, the parents learned how to access data on their own schools. As they practiced downloading and examining data, members of Parent-U-Turn

Mapping locations where parents and students can access the Internet in Parent-U-Turn neighborhoods.

were surprised to learn that Lynwood Unified had higher rates of uncredentialed teachers than all but one other district in California, and in many of the schools more than half of the teachers lacked a full credential. They learned that South Gate Middle School was the most overcrowded middle school in the country, with more than five times as many students per acre as the state of California recommends. Valerie Muñoz recalls being shocked by these statistics: "We knew the situation was bad, but we didn't know how bad."

Members of Parent-U-Turn began to imagine how the information could stimulate new ideas for change and be leverage for change. Many came to the seminar believing that the problems in their schools were idiosyncratic, likely the cause of school leaders who did not know better. While the seminar pointed to the acute problems in South Gate and Lynwood, it also highlighted broader patterns of racial inequality that suggested the need for wide-scale policy reform. Lupe Aguiar recalls:

> After I went to the IDEA seminar, I found out it wasn't just my school doing bad, it was the whole state, it was how minority groups were treated in many places. It is sad to see that. . . . Most of the parents don't know, and

they trust the teacher. When their children don't graduate from high school or can't go to the university, that is the first time they learn that the schools have problems. They assume their children are receiving everything. If I didn't realize that things were like this everywhere, I'd be much more frustrated.

Lupe and other members of Parent-U-Turn began to ask policymakers about racial inequality. As Mary Johnson said, "[we were] thirsty for knowledge [and began] asking questions and probing for answers and solutions." Members of Parent-U-Turn interviewed county officials, state assembly members, and a congresswoman about what could be done to ensure quality education for the children of South Gate and Lynwood.[6] They then met with district officials and school board members to press for particular policy solutions.

Acquiring Scientific Tools

Parent-U-Turn's thirst for knowledge led them to pressure us to include them in our summer youth seminar on the sociology of education (described in Chapter 4). This seminar began in the summer of 1999 as an extension of the Futures project. Each summer thereafter, we brought together 25–30 high school students from across Los Angeles to study social theory and conduct equity-focused research in schools and communities.[7] The seminar was an official UCLA course, with a 3-inch-thick reader filled with graduate-level texts. The parents had learned about the seminar while reading past issues of our online journal *Teaching to Change LA*. They were attracted to the idea that young people—some from their community—had produced research that documented and challenged the inequalities their communities experienced. Parent-U-Turn members believed that they too must develop these skills. That the seminar was designed for high school students did not matter to them. They needed the knowledge and they planned to attend.

In July 2002, six members of Parent-U-Turn joined 25 high school seniors at UCLA. The seminar began by looking at past efforts to address unequal education through the courts, legislation, and grassroots activism. Participants studied parents who became plaintiffs in *Brown v. Board of Education* and young people who led a mass walkout from East Los Angeles schools in 1968. They found that both groups were motivated to take action by a common set of troubling conditions: dilapidated and overcrowded facilities, inadequate learning materials, undertrained and culturally insensitive teachers, and so on.

During the seminar, members of Parent-U-Turn developed and tested several strategies for gathering information about the conditions in local schools. Their emphasis was on creating tools that parents, generally, could use to hold educational officials accountable. Many of these strategies came from seminar readings and lessons on qualitative research methods, though the parents invariably adapted the methods to match their own experience in schools.[8] For example, the parents tried out several strategies for writing up "field notes" to record their observations during school visits. After realizing that an open-ended approach did not provide enough guidance or clarity, members of the parent research team created a three-page "Parent Observation Check-List" that addressed issues ranging from bathroom cleanliness, to the attitude of office staff, to the availability of computers for "project-based learning." Similarly, parents developed a protocol to interview principals of three local high schools. The questions reveal that the parents understood that access to official knowledge requires clear "rules of engagement." "Will you let a parent observe her child's classroom without 24 hours notice?" "Would you allow parents to bring cameras on your campus?" "Will you hold monthly town hall meetings for parents and teachers to address their concerns for school improvement?"

The parents also surveyed other parents about school conditions. They imagined the parent survey as both a source of information and a strategy for reaching out to not-yet-organized parents. Members of the parent research team traveled to local stores to "catch" parents in the course of their daily activities. After their first day of surveying parents at a local shopping center, they expressed unease with their methodology. Some of their concerns echoed issues faced by many professional researchers—Mary worried that "many of the parents do not understand the terms we use in the survey." Some of the questions were revised, and in the process the team members themselves obtained a more nuanced understanding of the issues that lay behind the questions.

Parents also raised other issues that reflected their special sensitivity to the "subjects" of their research.

> **JUSTINA:** I don't think a lot of Latino families like strangers asking them personal questions about their children's school. Especially, [if] they say something negative because they fear the school will find out and hurt their children.

> **MARY:** But the surveys do not have names on them. How would the schools know even if they got their hands on these surveys somehow?

> **JUSTINA:** The fear is not logical because it does not make sense. Sometimes you see so many people getting hurt and no one has power or money to help and that is not logical either.

> **VALERIE:** Well, I am going to give them the survey and when they finish and give it back to me I will ask them to just talk freely about . . . their children's school . . . [whether this school provides] a quality education, and what that means to them.

Taking a Critical Stance

The students' and parents' research revealed conditions disturbingly similar to those they had read about in their study of *Brown* and the East L.A. walkouts. These similarities led participants to ask several critical questions: Why do these patterns of inequality persist? Why don't schools teach parents and students this history of inequality? If parents and students understand these patterns, can they challenge and overcome them? Together these questions comprise a critical stance, combining historical perspective, the needs and experiences of the people most affected, and a space in which dialogue can take place.

The seminar turned to social theory to address the parents' questions. We acknowledged the difficulty and power of engaging theoretical texts while reading Paulo Freire's letter on "Reading the Word/Reading the World."[9] Using "read arounds" and small group discussions, we grappled collectively with dense texts, often dissecting meaning line by line. In this manner, seminar participants read Jay MacLeod's chapter on social reproduction theory and Patrick Finn's very helpful summary of MacLeod's argument.[10] The idea that schools as institutions tend to reproduce inequalities in the broader political economy resonated with many parents and students. "It is very funny that I am learning about [the] reproduction cycle," wrote Mary Johnson during the seminar. "As a child, I used to hear my grandmother talking about the circle, and now I am reading about the circle theory in books."

While finding the idea of social reproduction useful, Mary and the other participants from Parent-U-Turn refused to adopt a pessimistic view about educational change. "I guess my grandmother knew about the circle, but didn't know how to change it. Just maybe, my grandmother was telling the story so one day, I just might be the one that would help to change the cycle."[11] Similarly, at the seminar's close, Valerie Muñoz spoke of her sense of agency and urgency in overcoming the social reproduction of inequality: "I still have children of my own going to public school, and it worries me that they won't be prepared for their future, but I will fight to the end and won't quit until I see changes done. The changes I am talking about would break the social reproduction cycle . . . so this motivates me a lot."

Muñoz, Johnson, and their colleagues embraced critical research as a tool for breaking the cycle. Critical research refers to a commitment to the experimental method to gather, create, or discover information that challenges prevailing inequalities. "Parents," Mary Johnson argued, "have the right to experiment . . . so we won't be oppressed and chained in bonds." Critical research also entails what Freire calls "reading the world" and "reading the word"—analyzing social life and written texts with skepticism and an eye to issues of power and inequality.[12] This means questioning all information—especially that which is provided by those who have a stake in the status quo. The seminar participants took to heart Freire's call for looking beneath surface meanings. Reading Freire, notes Mary Johnson, led her to not "just accept what I read or what people say is the truth."

Transformation Through the Creation and Flow of Disruptive Knowledge

The parents gained research skills compatible with a critical perspective. These immediately became practical tools to advance their community work. They envisioned their primary responsibility to the community as "procuring and gathering information on quality schooling"[13] One of their first actions after the seminar was to conduct a student survey on the availability of textbooks. Many parents had begun to question the truthfulness of South Gate High School's public claim that there were "sufficient numbers of textbooks to support the school's instructional program."[14] Parent-U-Turn members distributed over 100 surveys to students as they passed through the gates of South Gate High School. Seven of every 10 South Gate High School students reported that they did not have a set of textbooks in their classes, and they did not have textbooks they could take home.[15]

The parents published their findings in IDEA's online journal, *Teaching to Change LA*. Editors from the *Los Angeles Times* read the piece and cited the parents' research in a lead editorial as evidence of unequal opportunities in Los Angeles schools.[16] Members of Parent-U-Turn then met with South Gate High School's principal, who provided assurances that all students would receive a textbook in the coming school year. As Valerie Muñoz notes, Parent-U-Turn's research method played a key role in securing this change:

> If you go to a meeting and you want to express the conditions and the problems you are living in your community, [the] first thing they want to know is where is the proof. With this training we have received, we know how to gather data and research it and prepare it to the point where there is no question about is this true or not.

POWER TO HOLD THE POWERFUL ACCOUNTABLE

The force of compelling evidence alone did not always prevail when Parent-U-Turn sought policy changes in Lynwood. Parent-U-Turn began the 2002–2003 school year with two central goals:

1. The district should take aggressive action to address its extreme shortage of qualified teachers;
2. Parents should help set policies for parent involvement in creating the budget for Title 1 programs.

Presenting Parent-
U-Turn research at
a public forum.

Why Should Parents Investigate and Report on School Conditions???

Members of Parent-U-Turn met with district officials to share data about the high rates of uncredentialed teachers and to ask officials about their plans for hiring qualified teachers. The district officials disregarded the parents' information and ignored their entreaties.

When parents tried to shape the federally mandated Local Educational Association improvement plan, the district strategically avoided the parents' input by holding "public" meetings without informing the community. "They failed to notify the parents," reported Emma Street, "which is a violation of the Brown Act and No Child Left Behind."[17] At other times, school officials provided notification but publicized the wrong date. Such was the case when the middle school sent out a flyer inviting parents to elect the school site council—days after the election took place. Parent-U-Turn member Mary Galvan attended the next meeting of the council and discovered that none of the parents present had voted for the new council officers. Galvan protested, noting that parents had a right to determine who would represent their interests. The principal threatened to put Galvan out of the meeting.

shortened school year caused by the year-round schedule meant more disruption and less instruction.[24] But they knew that the recent passage of school facility bonds at the state and district level held the promise of new schools coming to relieve the overcrowding within a few years. Parent-U-Turn looked forward to participating in finding sites for the new schools and helping to create powerful parent organizations at each new campus. What they did not know was that the Los Angeles Unified School District had other plans for the transition from three-track to traditional calendar schools. With no warning or community outreach, the district sent home notices in March stating that, as of July 1, Stanford Elementary would shift from a three-track year-round school (two tracks on, one off) to a four-track school (three tracks on, one off).

Although the district imagined this change as neutral reform, teachers and community members immediately expressed frustration and anger. Initially, parents focused on the logistical challenges posed by the new plan. Families with more than one child at Stanford might end up with children enrolled in different tracks with different vacation schedules—an eventuality that would make child care more difficult and costly.

Members of Parent-U-Turn recognized the importance of this issue, but they also sought to broaden the terms of debate. They convened a meeting at Justina Paque's house and hashed out several key arguments against the district's plan. The group worried that the shift to four tracks might delay their long-awaited return to the traditional school calendar. "We thought," recalls Lupe, "that if they are going to put in a new system, how long is it going to be here?" Parents also took offense at *how* the district enacted its policies. Mary Johnson reported, "most parents and teachers feel that LAUSD has excluded their voices by not consulting with them." Finally, the parents looked on the district's decision as continuing a long history of discrimination and neglect. Why, wondered Lupe, is this new schedule "only happening in minority areas"? These parents had studied the history of South Gate schools as part of IDEA's public history project during the 2003–2004 school year, and they decried the fact that overcrowding would continue in South Gate while no such crowding problems were likely at schools in the more White and middle-class west side of Los Angeles.

Parent-U-Turn members initiated a set of direct actions with the long-term goal of returning South Gate schools to a traditional calendar and short-term goals of (1) preventing the district from implementing the shift to a four-track schedule and (2) serving notice that the district could not be so cavalier and heavy-handed about making decisions without involving the community. Wanting a sizable community presence, several members of Parent-U-Turn gathered outside Stanford every morning to pass out flyers as parents brought their children to school. They made posters saying, "No More Track Schedule," and hung them around the school and in the local park. On the weekends, Justina drove slowly along each block, using her bullhorn to call on parents to refuse the district's mandate. Justina admits that many of her neighbors "looked at

Posting signs that urge Parent-U-Turn's neighbors to boycott Stanford Elementary.

me like I was crazy" because they did not believe anyone could change what the district had decreed. Other community members shared Justina's goals but expressed fear that if they took any action, there would be reprisals against them or their children. Lupe found that the community, generally, rallied behind her once they knew the facts.

> We told the parents the whole history [of] how long we had the three tracks and how this doesn't happen in other areas. . . . A lot of this information came from UCLA. We felt confident to talk to the people because we had the information. . . . [And we received] a lot of support from the community.

This support became critical when Parent-U-Turn called a one-day boycott to disrupt business as usual at Stanford Elementary. The boycott activated a number of different organizing strategies. It inflicted material damage by reducing the funds the state sends the district for each student's daily attendance. It demonstrated the logic of numbers by bringing out the community in force. Finally, parents could bear witness to the media about their grievances.

"I never have seen a community come together like they did" on the day of the boycott, reports Mary Johnson. By 8 a.m., some 200 parents gathered in the park across from Stanford Elementary, picket signs in hand. They looked across at an empty playground. Half of all parents kept their children out of school. As the protestors began to march, mothers in aprons came out of their houses with trays of food. Justina, who was charged with keeping up the group's spirits, distributed old pots and pans and spoons and created an informal band among the marchers. Even with her bullhorn, she shouted so loud that her throat was sore for 3 days. Mary's long-standing relationship with the South Gate police department and city council also proved invaluable. The police department sent a patrol car to make sure that no one would harass the protestors. The city delivered portable toilets. Some parents called radio and television stations, and the boycott ran that evening on two Spanish-language news programs. "It was such a moving thing," remembers Mary.

A few days later, Parent-U-Turn brought four buses of parents to the Los Angeles Unified School Board meeting. Justina, Lupe, and Mary all spoke. Lupe

Marching outside of Stanford Elementary to protest the district's proposed shift to a four-track calendar.

thanked the board members for giving them a hearing, but told them, "We are tired of being experimented on with new systems." Mary Johnson demonstrated the growth of enrollment in South Gate schools based on publicly available data they had requested from IDEA.[25] She argued: "We want a solution that provides our students with decent schools, schools that are no more overcrowded than the west side of town. May 17 will be the 50th anniversary of *Brown v. Board of Education,* and still the students of color schools aren't on equal terms with our White schools." Within a few days, the district sent a letter to members of Parent-U-Turn saying that they would delay implementation of a four-track schedule. Mary pointed out that this was a small step in addressing the core problem, and she resolved that Parent-U-Turn would "continue to put the pressure on the board."

WHAT HAS PARENT-U-TURN ACCOMPLISHED?

We argued in Chapter 6 that participatory social inquiry, in the context of social movement organizing by grassroots groups, would be far more likely than inquiry strategies located inside the educational system (i.e., student and teacher inquiry) to move the educational system toward more equitable policies and practices. Our confidence came from the potential for such groups to augment the inquiry processes that we had found to be transforming for students and teachers with social movement organizing strategies that focused on relational power and direct action aimed at transforming institutions. Our relationship with Parent-U-Turn gave us our first opportunity to observe, study, and contribute to that potential. In some ways, it was a difficult test case in that Parent-U-Turn did not come to this work as an experienced grassroots group with a well-honed repertoire of social movement strategies and tactics. Nevertheless, we find the experiences of Parent-U-Turn instructive. Over time, the parents not only won concrete improvements in their local schools, they developed a collective identity as researchers and activists that enables them to tackle increasingly difficult challenges. They have developed social capital in their work together that has made them a force to be reckoned with in local education politics. Finally, they have created a structure and a process that has expanded the number of parents in their communities who, through the creation and flow of disruptive knowledge, are continuing to make a difference in the quality of schooling for the children in their communities.

Participation Fostered a Sense of Collective Identity

Mary Johnson sees herself as a different person than the young mother who took on the police department at Pendleton. "In 1994, I didn't have skills. I just was afraid. Now I have the skills to be strategic. I work off of information. . . . I have facts for my arguments to back them up. No one can deny the information I have." Mary notes that these skills have been distributed across Parent-U-Turn's leadership. "Justina, Lupe, they talk, the things that come out of their mouths amaze me. They can quote research and law and policy. I was just in a meeting, and I didn't have to say anything—they are the ones." Many members of Parent-U-Turn speak about their shared identity as change agents. Most invoke the promise of this work for their children. But they also articulate a vision of the power that this identity embodies. When you begin to participate in a campaign, remarks Emma Street, "you feel that you have that right that you have always had, but didn't know you had, and once you break that barrier, you are gone."

Developed Social Capital from Existing and Emerging Knowledge

The skills and identities embodied by Parent-U-Turn members represent a form of capital. This capital leads educators, reporters, and politicians to grant the parents greater access, privilege, or respect. "I can go to a meeting with teachers,"

Leading a workshop for principals-in-training about how low-income parents can contribute to high-quality schools.

remarks Mary Johnson, "and I can sit down at a round table and hold my own in a conversation. . . . [They] respect your knowledge and you respect them . . . it has been a long time since parents have had that arena." Parent-U-Turn members have discovered that their past work brings recognition from unexpected quarters. "Since I've been with IDEA and the online journal," remarks Mary, "wherever I go, people don't know me, but they know my name." But the most important site of capital exchange for Parent-U-Turn lies closer to home. Their work and identity provide a model for the next generation in South Gate and Lynwood. Emma Street notes: "As my children and grandchildren look up on life and see how I have struggled, and come a long ways and still struggle, it helps them as well. They can say: 'This is what my mother does. Why can't I do this?' "

Supported the Flow of Disruptive Knowledge

Parent-U-Turn forges new power by educating parents in their community. They convene and direct a series of 13-week parent institutes throughout the year. The institutes follow the model of Laila Hasan's Parent Curriculum Project. The parents study the state standards and learn about high-quality teaching and learning through practice in constructivist seminars. Parent-U-Turn has infused state and federal policy into the seminars, and they also introduce parents to the decades-long struggle for educational opportunity in African American and Latino communities. This broadened curriculum reflects Parent-U-Turn's sense that parents need to be able, as Dewey said, to "locate the source" of their problems within structures of inequality. The "more leaders that . . . have these skills," argues Mary Johnson, "the better we can analyze our conditions." Valerie Muñoz believes that Parent-U-Turn must teach these skills because district officials "have no interest in teaching parents what they need to know." In contrast, "what we give the parents," says Emma Street, "is what [the districts] don't want us to give."

Parent-U-Turn members also distinguish themselves as parent educators by building meaningful, sustained relationships. "What I like in our group," notes Mary, "is that we see everyone willing to help each other. We are willing to sacrifice ourselves. . . . We are available 7 days a week. People call us all times of night, all times of day. We don't ever turn them away. I think that is where the trust comes in." And beneath the trust lies what Cornel West refers to as a powerful "ethic of love."[26] Emma Street gets the final word: "We like to let other parents know that there is a certain amount of care and love that we must render to each student that we have in each school. We have to show this by showing love ourselves. In order to do that, we have to get out there as leaders and show them how it is done."

The Educational Justice Collaborative

Activist Groups Working Together for Equitable Schools

Rallying for educational justice on the 49th anniversary of *Brown v. Board of Education*.

Los Angeles Times

Friday, April 14, 2005

Parents Use Newfound Clout to Demand School Improvements

Aided by a new state law, mothers and fathers join in a caravan and file complaints at several South Los Angeles campuses.

By Duke Helfand,
Times Staff Writer

Two dozen South Los Angeles parents, armed with new legal powers, converged on their children's public schools Wednesday to demand more textbooks, qualified teachers and safer campuses.

Because of a new state law giving parents more clout when they address deficiencies in their schools, administrators were required not only to listen but to respond.

The mothers and fathers, some of whom took the day off from work, joined in a midday caravan to file complaints at several campuses.

But they also were savoring a more personal and subtle victory: They had challenged the powers that be and gotten answers from those in charge.

"Oh, this is a great day. This is a great day," said Naomi Haywood after she delivered her complaints about insufficient textbooks and teachers to an assistant principal at Fremont High School.

The parents' actions were among the first tests of a new complaint system that grew out of a class-action lawsuit brought by the American Civil Liberties Union.

In the case, known as *Williams vs. California*, the ACLU alleged that the state denied tens of thousands of minority children an adequate education in schools that lack adequate books and other resources.

Gov. Arnold Schwarzenegger, acknowledging that the allegations had merit, settled the case last year. The agreement gave

parents new rights to file written complaints about deficiencies in textbooks, teachers and facilities, and required schools or districts to respond and remedy those problems within 30 days.

Schools are required to post notices in classrooms, informing parents about the complaint procedure. Complaint forms also must be made available in school offices.

The new complaint system took effect in January. Since then, the school district has received about 40 complaints, including those filed Wednesday at Fremont and Locke high schools.

District officials said they were taking the parents' complaints seriously and would investigate each one.

The parents, brought together by a grass-roots group called Community Asset Development Re-defining Education, started their day with a pep rally and news conference on a street behind the Locke High School football field.

"It's time for schools to work with parents as equals," said Kenneth Hill, whose son attends Audubon Middle School in the Crenshaw district. "It's time for schools to ensure that they are a place of dignity, respect and integrity."

The parents cheered and marched with signs that read "Keep faith in our kids," and they chanted, "Parent power."

Then, with complaint forms in hand, they headed to Fremont High, the first campus on their list.

There, with the media in tow, the parents appeared to startle security aides watching Fremont's front door. The aides tried to stop a radio reporter from recording the scene and a *Times* photographer from shooting pictures.

After a few minutes of confusion, Assistant Principal Jack Baroutjian emerged and escorted the group into a conference room near the main office.

There, the parents politely but firmly made their case. Haywood complained about a lack of textbooks in her son's ninth-grade classes and said he had endured a series of substitute teachers in a course he took during his vacation time—a special program aimed at boosting student achievement.

"That's unfortunate to hear. I was not aware of that," Baroutjian said of the substitute teacher problem in the after-school program run by the district. But he reassured Haywood that the school of 5,000 students had a full complement of permanent instructors.

He also said that textbooks were available for anyone who needed them. Then it was on to 107th Street Elementary, where parent Roslyn Broadnax stepped forward.

"We're coming on behalf of parents for the *Williams* [lawsuit]," she told an administrator who seemed a little bewildered.

"So what do you want to do?" the administrator asked.

"Turn in complaint forms," Broadnax responded.

Assistant Principal Carolin McKie took over and patiently listened to worries about a shortage of textbooks. McKie said the school had taken steps to correct any deficiencies.

"We had a shortage at one point," she told the parents. "There should be enough textbooks now."

Later, Broadnax said, "I feel like I accomplished more today than I have in a lifetime. It was a day well spent."[1]

IN CHAPTERS 4 AND 5, we described how the Futures and Teaching to Change LA "design experiments" embodied the principles of participatory social inquiry that we drew from our reading of Dewey. Unfortunately, these projects, for all their considerable benefits to the participants, did not bring significant institutional change. Neither did they affect the broader political and normative environment around schooling for low-income students and students of color. In Chapter 7, we described how Parent-U-Turn drew from our work with students and schools and embraced inquiry as central to its grassroots ethos. We, and they, learned quite a lot about how inquiry and activism could be powerful for groups seeking concrete changes in their schools.

In this chapter, we cast Dewey's net wider still—beyond single groups and single neighborhoods to look at how groups such as Parent-U-Turn and Community Asset Development Re-defining Education (CADRE) can engage in participatory social inquiry within a coalition of social movement organizations. As participants in the Educational Justice Collaborative, groups across California combine knowledge construction with power building in their campaigns for state and local policies that will bring high-quality and equitable education to students that have neither.

The events that *Los Angeles Times* reporter Duke Helfand described above were part of a carefully planned "day of action" mounted by CADRE, a grassroots organization of African American and Latino parents. CADRE was begun in

2001 by Maisie Chin, an experienced community organizer, and parent Rosalinda Hill. Much like Parent-U-Turn, CADRE is a grassroots organization whose mission is to "solidify and advance parent leadership to ensure that all children are rightfully educated, regardless of where they live."[2] CADRE focuses on parent organizing in the South Los Angeles region of the Los Angeles Unified School District. Filing complaints, confronting school administrators, and demanding responses from officials were the fruition of the CADRE parents' study of education policy, review of schooling data, and understanding of how the education system treated their own children compared with children in other communities. This knowledge gave them the confidence to expect changed relational power with school officials and to take direct action to achieve improvements in their children's schools.

CADRE's activities took place in an equity-reform context that was influenced by the Educational Justice Collaborative (EJC)—a loose coalition of nearly 30 activist organizations in California that support one another's efforts to attain high-quality education for low-income children and children of color. *Williams v. California,* the lawsuit we described in Chapter 1, served as a symbolic, substantive, and strategic impetus for the formation of the EJC, which became a site where groups such as CADRE to access the highly relevant data and arguments on the inadequacy and inequality within California's educational system that we and other experts marshaled for *Williams.* The American Civil Liberties Union (ACLU) chapters from Northern and Southern California, Public Advocates, and the Mexican American Legal Defense and Educational Fund (MALDEF) were on the litigation team representing the *Williams* plaintiffs, and they too participated in the EJC. One of the EJC's main activities was to pursue a two-way flow of information between the grassroots groups that understood and experienced the conditions in their schools and the *Williams* legal and policy experts who were working to fashion arguments to gain the reforms that would address the substandard school conditions for children in low-income communities of color. *Williams* was like a keystone that allowed groups such as CADRE to understand seemingly disconnected "complaints" as part of a more powerful and coherent strategy for affecting school change.

THE DEVELOPMENT OF THE EDUCATIONAL JUSTICE COLLABORATIVE

It was not surprising that the *Williams* case caught the attention of grassroots and advocacy groups that had been active in California around "noneducational" issues such as living wage, affordable housing policies, immigrant rights, and affirmative action. They saw *Williams* as an opportunity to press Califor-

cadre (kăd′re, kä′drā) n. 1. An organization arising from a group of strong leaders. 2. A unified group of parent leaders in South Los Angeles striving for dignity and respect our schools. 3. A parent leader with the power and tools to work towards justice for our children. 1. Una organización que proviene de un grupo de lideres fuertes. 2. Un grupo unificado de padres lideres en el sur de Los Angeles trabajando para obtener dignidad y respeto en nuestras escuelas. 3. Un padre lider con el conocimiento y poder para luchar por la justicia para nuestros niños.

Wearing on his back a strong commitment to parent leadership for educational justice.

nia toward providing students in low-income communities of color with the essential conditions for high achievement and college access. They saw the possibility for building a powerful base of organized communities comprised, at least in part, of students and families who qualified as *Williams* plaintiffs.

Several groups proposed successfully to philanthropic foundations that, whatever the court decided in *Williams,* community organizing and widespread public engagement were necessary to call attention to the educational crises facing California and to garner widespread political commitment to reform. These foundations knew from the troubled history of court and legislative victories around equity, that such "wins" are not enough to ensure that court orders or new laws will be enacted or sustained in ways that match the intentions of those who fought for them. They agreed that it was worth trying to sustain potential court victories with broad-based public support built through grassroots activism.

We first encountered these grassroots advocacy groups through our colleague, Gary Blasi, a professor in the UCLA Law School's Public Interest Law and Policy program and a consultant to the *Williams* plaintiffs' litigation team. Gary asked us to share our *Williams* research with some leaders of community organizations who were eager to learn more about the case. With Gary, we convened a meeting on the UCLA campus that included professional organizers and community leaders of grassroots groups, education reform advocates, some progressive teachers, and civil rights lawyers and activists. We spent a Saturday talking about the evidence around the *Williams* issues. The participants were especially taken with the fact that in California, education is a constitutional right. Several groups proposed developing a students' "Bill of Rights" that could frame the issues in the *Williams* case proactively and be used as a tool to educate communities. At the end of the day, the groups agreed to stay connected with one another. And they expressed interest in continuing their relationship with us. They saw us as a resource for understanding and holding the system accountable. Apparently, they appreciated our capacity to provide certain empirical data about the conditions in schools, our ability to scaffold their own data-gathering and analyses, and our willingness to facilitate, convene, and ask tough generative questions that would push their thinking.

The groups impressed us with their collective potential for providing accountability from the bottom up. The legislature, the governor, the court, and the schools themselves could not be counted on to provide the daily monitoring of school conditions or to hold themselves or one another accountable. They were not likely to monitor conditions across the statewide system that would, in the words of the *Williams* judge, "prevent or detect and correct" future problems. We also saw the groups' collaborative work as an opportunity to investigate further the impact of fusing participatory social inquiry and social movement organizing. Given the groups' intention to mount campaigns in support of *Williams*, their actions might actually move inquiry about educational opportunity toward concrete changes in state policy and local practice.

Some groups remained suspicious of university researchers. One leader insisted on a one-on-one meeting with us before going any further, an organizing strategy we now recognize as standard. However, after a trial period of a couple of months, including several meetings in the neighborhoods where the groups worked, about half a dozen groups agreed to continue as an Educational Justice Collaborative. We secured funding to serve as a convener of the collaborative and to provide research support, updates about education policy, and capacity building related to the groups' independent advocacy efforts.

At the time of this writing, the EJC, now nearly 30 organizations strong, has served for 4 years as a "site" for participatory social inquiry.[3] This inquiry occurs as the groups exchange ideas and strategies; engage in activities that build their capacity to work with policymakers and the media; and collaborate voluntarily and opportunistically on one another's campaigns. The principles we draw from both Dewey and from the literature on social movement organizing come to life in this work. Together they prove to be a compelling approach to equitable school reform.

ORGANIZING AS A SITE FOR
PARTICIPATORY SOCIAL INQUIRY

The EJC's first inquiry project was developing the "Educational Bill of Rights" (see Figure 8.1). After several meetings spent reviewing academic research, examining data about the state's schools, and exploring the experiences of parent and student members, the groups produced a document that specified what every student deserved. Both inspirational and daunting, the Bill of Rights focused on the most basic resources and conditions, and thus called attention to the tremendous gap between what one should find in every public school and what California's children actually got. Although most California students and families might take these basics for granted, the EJC groups knew that securing them would require concerted action.

Producing the Educational Bill of Rights helped establish common ground across the groups and created a tool for action. Two EJC participant groups, the California affiliate of Association of Community Organizations for Reform Now (ACORN) and MALDEF, launched a campaign to have the Bill of Rights adopted by the California legislature. Their goal was to draw attention to *Williams* and advance the argument that the state is responsible for providing all students with basic schooling conditions and opportunities. At the urging of ACORN and MALDEF, Judy Chu, a member of the California Assembly, introduced a bill that would guarantee adequate instructional materials, safe school facilities, qualified teachers, and reasonable class sizes. After approval by the Assembly Education Committee, the Appropriations Committee determined that the legislation would cost "in excess of a billion dollars." The bill went no further. Although not a "win," the EJC's inquiry and action had produced a policy proposal that garnered serious discussion and considerable support. It advanced awareness of and support for *Williams*. It forced the state to place a dollar figure on the extent to which California had failed to provide basic educational opportunities to all students. Statewide collaboration in inquiry around the Bill of Rights and the grassroots and advocacy work of ACORN and MALDEF had the exhilarating effect of penetrating the Capitol walls.

Engaging Those Most Impacted

Without question, the EJC participants foreground civic participation of the young people, families, and communities most affected by unequal schools and social policy. This diverse collection of organizations is guided by the belief that the public—particularly communities historically excluded from policymaking—should be engaged in seeking solutions to these pressing problems.

Several of the EJC groups are local multiracial grassroots groups that organize low-income communities of color. The members of Californians for Justice are high school students in five cities; CADRE and Parent-U-Turn bring

AN EDUCATIONAL BILL OF RIGHTS FOR CALIFORNIA'S STUDENTS

Every student in California has a fundamental constitutional right to an adequate education that prepares him or her to graduate from high school qualified for a 4-year state university, a living wage job, and active participation in civic life. Every student has a further right to educational opportunities equal to those provided to most of the students in the State. Students, parents and members of the community at large have a right to know what they may expect California's system of public education to provide for each student in California, in accord with these fundamental constitutional principles. These abstract rights must be understood as giving to every student in any public elementary or secondary school in California a right of access to each of the following:

1) A clear statement of the academic standards that both define what students are expected to know and be able to do at every educational level and specify the basic conditions for learning that students and families can expect from the educational system.

2) Adequate learning materials and resources.

3) A suitable learning environment and school classrooms, buildings, and facilities that enable learning and health.

4) High quality teachers and counselors.

5) A course of instruction that will enable all students who wish to do so to compete for admission to any public university in the state and participate actively in California's civic life.

6) Fair and authentic assessment that is used to measure and improve the quality of education students receive and supplementary educational services that respond to identified student needs.

7) Instruction which incorporates students' home language so as to provide all students with equal opportunity to access curriculum and develop and maintain proficiency in their native language.

8) A safe and supportive school environment.

9) Easily understood, current, reliable information on the performance of every California public school in delivering each of the rights herein listed.

10) Regular public forums that allow students and parents to communicate their experiences relative to these rights to local and state elected officials responsible for insuring these rights.

FIGURE 8.1. An educational Bill of Rights for California's students.

together South and Southeast Los Angeles parents; the Community Coalition and InnerCity Struggle organize both adults and young people; the Coalition for Educational Justice connects progressive teachers with parents and students. Other grassroots groups are state affiliates of large national networks, including ACORN with 24,000 member families in neighborhood groups in 19 cities across the state, and the Pacific Institute for Community Organization (PICO), a faith-based network of 350 member congregations statewide representing 400,000 families. Although most of the grassroots groups are staffed by professional organizers, the issues the groups identify and the strategies they employ always reflect members' concerns and preferences.

Other EJC groups are advocacy or research organizations that view themselves as allies and resources to grassroots groups and to low-income communities. For example, the Advancement Project Los Angeles is a nonprofit "policy and legal action organization working to solve public sector problems," and the Justice Matters Institute is a San Francisco–based organization that seeks to "develop visionary solutions" and "develop people with the capacity to carry out these solutions." Still other participants are nonpartisan groups, such as the California Budget Project and PolicyLink, research organizations seeking fiscal and policy reforms, and citizen groups such as California's League of Women Voters, promoting informed, active participation of citizens in government.

Sustaining Meaningful Relationships

The EJC groups might be seen as occupying three spheres. Grassroots activists occupy one sphere. A second is home to the collection of allied groups that, although they do not have their own membership base, engage in legal and political advocacy on behalf of low-income communities and communities of color. We at UCLA's Institute for Democracy, Education, and Access (IDEA) occupy a third sphere of participation. We are principally researchers, or "experts" in Dewey's framing. As such, we ask generative questions and identify opportunities to provide empirical answers. Our major tasks have been "discovering and making known facts."

Within the EJC, each of the spheres seeks to support and learn from the others. For example, as we provide research products useful to the other spheres, we also scaffold the development of their research skills. At the same time, as grassroots organizations make known their questions and needs, we develop a greater understanding of the nature and meaning of their work. By providing a site for reflexive dialogue among groups, the EJC enables participating members to learn about the relational dynamics of disparate groups pursuing common goals. In sum, through the EJC, each of the "spheres" can move toward, but not become, a collective center. The partners discover overlapping interests and common struggles, and we explore the potential for learning, for shared goals, and for common work. We have joined in dialogue about the problems, potential solutions, and strategies for achieving those solutions, but decisions about action remain with individual groups or emerging coalitions.

As in our relationships with the Futures students, the teachers engaged in Teaching to Change LA, and Parent-U-Turn, to call ourselves the EJC "experts" does not imply a directionality for all knowledge transfer or construction—from researcher to activist. Indeed, all members of the coalition supply information, ask generative questions, and correct errors. In more than one instance, the knowledge of EJC members was essential to our getting the facts straight. This knowledge included, but was not limited to, their lived experience and the experiences of their families. Californians for Justice's former Executive Director Abdi Soltani explained the relationship this way:

> Relationships with researchers are always built on a common agreement to value community participation. Researchers that are hostile to community participation, or ambivalent towards it, are not the ones we end up working with. We may read their reports, and they may see us on the news. . . . The researchers that do engage with us are usually interested in what we can offer—a base of people that are engaged, the ability to engage community members in research, and the ability to apply the research findings to campaigns.

Moreover, as one of our graduate students put it, race, class, and power differences between researchers and low-income communities of color must be attended to. These differences have tremendous potential to inform inquiry and action, but they can also be a source of misunderstanding and error:

> I think respect is first and foremost in these relationships. The organizers are the experts, I am just the person who knows how to take information and process it into data. I also have to always be aware of my White privilege and my class privilege as an academic who has had a high quality [public] education. . . . I can share outrage, and I can share data, but I will never know just how upsetting it is to hear that my school is the most overcrowded in the state, or that my children won't go to college because they simply didn't have enough teachers or classrooms to help all students complete college preparatory coursework.

Accessing Knowledge and Its Construction

As we noted above, in our role as researchers, we have provided access to research knowledge about the educational problems of most interest to the groups, helped them to develop their research capacity and tools, and convened meetings in which the groups integrate their knowledge and experiences into collective understandings. Over time, the various forms of inquiry have shaped the groups' understanding and framing of problems and altered the solutions they sought. Importantly, this has not resulted primarily from community members and advocates being enlightened by academic research. Rather, new understandings have come from the juxtaposition of multiple sources of knowledge, including academic research; locally generated data; and compelling stories of students, teachers, parents, and community members.

Research Translation. Beginning with the issues in *Williams,* our UCLA team produced "translations" of academic research for EJC groups to use as inquiry and organizing tools. These consisted of brief, accessible pamphlets in English and Spanish documenting problems, summarizing the evidence related to them, and providing a quick overview of solutions as discussed in the research and policy literature. Our initial pamphlets focused on shortages of qualified teachers, inadequate instructional materials, facilities problems, overcrowding, limited accountability, the failure to serve English learners well, and disparities in the funding provided students in more and less advantaged communities.

We have also produced summaries and interpretations of student achievement data. Using California's publicly available databases, for example, we tracked the relationships of schools' achievement scores, pass rates on the high school exit exam, college-eligibility rates, and other outcomes to school characteristics such as teacher quality, provision of college preparatory curriculum, and school overcrowding. We have linked all of these to the racial and social class composition of schools. Our Web-based vehicle (www.justschoolscalifornia.org) makes it easier for groups to access this research and connect with researchers.

Research on Demand. In response to specific requests from EJC groups, we have conducted "research on demand," using existing research and data to inform specific campaigns. The questions have ranged from straightforward, factual ones (How many students disappear from California high schools without graduating? How many college preparatory courses are offered in high schools in different neighborhoods? How large are the funding disparities between schools in wealthy and poor communities?), to knotty, interpretive ones (What is the relationship between teacher certification and teaching quality? Does funding make a difference in students' achievement?).

The EJC groups recognize the power that comes from the knowledge and the clout that academic research can bring. As InnerCity Struggle Executive Director Luis Sanchez explained:

> Researchers bring a wealth of information to the partnership. They're always finding new research that helps support the work that we are doing. IDEA can give us the answer to questions within a day that would take us two weeks to figure out. It matters, on some level, that we're working collaboratively with UCLA. When you're trying to move an equity focused

policy agenda with parents and students, a lot of them ask where this information came from. It helps to tell them that we've been working with professors at UCLA to show that it is something we haven't made up.

Acquiring and Using Research Tools. Many EJC groups are eager to build their research skills and want to use research tools independently. As Sanchez continued,

> We have the people that are most impacted by the system. Our parents and students attend schools that are underserved. When our members do research, they think through what questions would be key. In the end they are the ones that are going to have to push the agenda. It should be them because they are the people most impacted by policy.

Our role, in this case, is to provide technical tools, one-on-one coaching, and training workshops. One series of workshops attracted members of 18 organizations ranging from youth-based and parent-based organizing groups to advocates and educator reform groups. Participants practiced accessing publicly available databases and conducting basic analyses of schools. They learned the rudiments of Geographic Information Systems (GIS) technology, which is useful for mapping the distribution of educational resources and conditions across communities. To ensure that the learning did not end when the workshops did, we developed a training manual with print and online resource materials and learning exercises. We also remain on call to assist with participants' research and technology projects.

Locally generated data from surveys and focus groups are powerful both as the basis of inquiry and dialogue within the groups and as tools for organizing and direct action. As Abdi Soltani explained,

> Action research bridges the space between students' knowledge of schools and where decisions are made about education. Youth have a wealth of information about the true nature of schools; action research helps young people define issues for education reform and brings those issues to education policy-makers.

Educational Exchanges. EJC convenes "education exchanges" in which members examine research on critical issues in education policy from their own perspectives. These exchanges have focused on teacher quality, school finance, and accountability. In these exchanges, there is a great deal of storytelling as participants press one another for explanations and findings that are expressed in plain and compelling language.

The impetus for the exchange on teacher quality was a difficult question ACORN raised in the context of its campaign to halt teacher layoffs in Oakland

Learning how to access online educational data about neighborhood schools.

schools. Our analysis of data about the districts had revealed stark disparities in teacher qualifications and experience between schools in the "Flatlands" (the city's low-income communities of color) and those in the hills (Whiter and wealthier neighborhoods). It also showed that, if teachers were laid off in the usual ways—according to qualifications and experience—the low-income communities would be most severely affected. The teachers most at risk for losing their jobs were younger teachers without full credentials or experience. However, several of these teachers were also young people of color who shared their students' culture and language, and some had shown a deep commitment to Flatlands students and communities. From the perspectives of many ACORN members', these teachers were far "better" than some of the fully credentialed, experienced teachers who were not likely to be laid off.

ACORN's questions about the relationship between credentialing and teacher quality were shared by other ECJ groups, and the exchange drew participants from 15 groups. For 2 days, community members, organizers, and advocates engaged in lively and intense dialogue with Professors Ken Futernick, Patricia

Gandara, and Bill Koski. All three had conducted research on the intersections of teacher quality, student achievement, standards, and accountability. They were also willing to open their work up to the scrutiny of the EJC groups.

Nothing was "resolved," in part because of the enormity of the issue. However, everybody, including the experts, learned a great deal about teacher quality in the context of low-income communities. The ACORN group resumed their campaign with a far better sense of how a statewide shortage of qualified teachers presented them with few options, none of which was likely to bring their children high-quality teaching. They could grapple in a more informed way about whether or not to fight to preserve the jobs of unqualified teachers.

Working-Group Calls. EJC participants integrate firsthand experiences, research data, and other knowledge during regular working group conference calls. Organized around policy issues of interest, these ad hoc groups have investigated some concerns raised in *Williams*, such as how to estimate the actual costs of providing high-quality education to all students. Another working group inves-

Parents sharing ideas about the qualities they look for in their children's teachers.

tigated ways to ensure that the state's high-stakes exit exam does not deny diplomas to students who have attended substandard schools.

Using multiple sources of knowledge is both an epistemological stance and a political necessity in the EJC. Organizing groups deliberate constantly about the lived experiences and perspectives of those most affected by inequality— deliberations that ground their relationships and guide their actions. Less often do these groups turn to academic research. Often they are rightfully suspicious that academics represent the class interests and racial standpoints of dominant groups. For both substantive and political reasons, then, our engagement in the production, distribution, and use of knowledge in the EJC has been anything but a one-way process in which knowledge is produced by the university, disseminated to the groups, and then used by them.

Substantively, the opportunity to use research, experience, and knowledge constructed on-the-spot is an asset that is often lost in settings where experts control the agenda. EJC's trust and knowledge ethos encourages a nimble, reflexive, and opportunistic setting where hunches can be explored and creative responses set in action. In one particularly powerful instance, UCLA postdoctoral fellow Joanna Goode was leading a workshop in which members of InnerCity Struggle were exploring a data site she had recommended. The youth discovered the Junior Reserve Officer Training Corps (JROTC) enrollment figures for their school. This was a stunning find for them, because the large presence of military recruiters at East Los Angeles high schools had been a concern of InnerCity Struggle. Now they had the data to analyze the scope of the problem. After they showed Goode the data set, and she understood their concerns, she produced a JROTC enrollment map to display the concentration of military programs in schools located in communities of color. InnerCity Struggle used this map to argue for a decreased JROTC presence in East L.A. schools.

ADOPTING A CRITICAL STANCE

In the 21st century, education policymaking elites increasingly use sophisticated communications and marketing strategies to frame problems and solutions, and to publicize "facts" that justify them. Now, every bit as much as in Dewey's 1930s, the dominant spin on social problems generally, and on schooling problems in particular, "rationaliz[es] . . . the misery and cultural degradation of others. . . . These are asserted to be the fault of those who suffer; to be the consequence of their own improvidence, lack of industry, wilful [sic] ignorance, etc."[4] Today, for example, we hear experts argue repeatedly that the "achievement gap" stems either from low-income parents' failure to be involved sufficiently in their children's schooling or from their inability to pressure their neighborhood schools to improve, as middle- and upper-class parents do, by threatening to take their children elsewhere. The solution most often proffered, including in the federal No Child Left Behind policy, is to permit those parents who care enough to send their children to better schools.

To counter this dominant frame—to even recognize that it is a frame, and neither objective truth nor common sense—the EJC's participatory social inquiry helps place knowledge and experience in larger social, economic, historical, and political contexts. Participants' critical understanding comes from the fusion of local knowledge with facts and broader social theories that help activists see their own particular circumstances in the larger contexts. Their critical questions are probing, often uncomfortable, but also open to dispute and empirical study: Who makes decisions and who is left out? Who benefits and who suffers? Why is a given practice fair or unfair? What are its origins? What alternatives can we imagine? What is required to create change?[5]

The dialogue that follows questions such as these challenges the ideas that dominate public discourse, serve the interests of elite cultural groups, and shift the blame for social misery onto those who suffer from it most. A critical stance is compatible with social movement organizing because it asks people to identify the conditions of their lives, relate them to conditions experienced by others, and determine how they came to be. As we noted in Chapter 6, scholars of social movements like Ganz and Polletta find that organizing nearly always engages participants in seeing their immediate problems as reflective of larger social, economic, historical, and political dynamics.[6]

CONSTRUCTING A TRANSFORMATIVE GOAL

The EJC seeks to revitalize public life through the civic participation of members in previously marginalized groups. This revitalization occurs, as Dewey suggested, when community members cultivate a new "public intelligence" about social problems, challenging conventional wisdom and stereotypes about low-income communities of color.[7]

As we noted above, however, in the 21st century, cultivating a new public intelligence requires more than transformative dialogue about social problems. It also demands a sophisticated framing of issues that employ communication and media strategies to advance those frames. Energized by their initial success with the Education Bill of Rights, the groups sought other ways to increase the public's recognition of, and anger about, the *Williams* conditions. After considerable inquiry and testing the research literature against their own experiences, they began to frame the conditions in the *Williams* schools as denying students "opportunities to learn." Such a framing, they believed, would both have "common sense" appeal and tap into the public's value for basic fairness, thereby advancing their agenda of remedying the *Williams* issues.

"Opportunity to learn" calls attention to concrete, policy-alterable conditions, and offers a clear alternative to prevailing frames for understanding schooling. First, it counters the familiar "blame the victim" reasoning that locates the cause of low achievement in students, families, and communities. Instead, the "opportunity to learn" frame asserts that the responsibility for good education belongs to those who would or would not provide opportunities. Second, "opportunity to learn" becomes an appealing and intuitively sound premise on which to base reform: improve education by increasing opportunities. Finally, "opportunity to learn" rests on a solid research and policy base. In research circles, "opportunity to learn" emerged from studies seeking explanations for why some countries do better than others on international tests of academic achievement.[8] In policy circles, debates have focused on whether and how to account for "opportunity to learn" in standards-based school reform.

For the EJC, the Education Bill of Rights, "opportunities to learn," and the arguments in the *Williams* case formed a nexus of philosophical, practical, and legal authority that could be embraced by each of the groups. The commonsense nature of these arguments made it hard for mainstream politicians to dismiss the EJC groups as fringe or radical. And the bold nature of these arguments meant that the groups did not feel pressured to give up any of their core "disruptive" beliefs.

The EJC groups have been extraordinarily resourceful in developing strategies for sharing their "disruptive knowledge." It has found its way into community forums, formal reports, newspaper stories, and testimony before policymakers, and on to T-shirts, banners, and placards at public demonstrations. Artfully combining compelling stories, statistics, photographs, and GIS maps showing correlations between poverty, race, and students' opportunities to learn, the groups have generated multiple representations of problems and possibilities for change. The map included in Chapter 1 depicting "opportunity to learn problems" in Los Angeles is one example. Supported by EJC's communication resources, the groups increasingly use press releases, editorial board meetings, OpEd pieces, talk show interviews, and ongoing relationships with reporters as vehicles for cultivating a new public intelligence.

BUILDING RELATIONAL POWER AND IDENTITY

As we noted in Chapter 6, social movement organizing assumes that efforts to make society more equitable will be contested. The groups know from experience that those who benefit from the status quo will resist the redistribution of resources and opportunities. Therefore, grassroots and advocacy groups proceed knowing that transformative knowledge must be used in the context of collective power, built through relationships with one another and through strategic alliances with those who have the expertise, resources, and access to power required to advance their goals.

The paid organizers of the EJC groups are intent on developing local leaders. They constantly bring new people into leadership roles and convene community meetings that engage members in making decisions and creating a collective vision. For example, the organizers at InnerCity Struggle say that when a young person walks through their doors, he or she must be treated as if he or she will become the organization's executive director some day. Every participant in the community is seen as a potential leader, and everyone on the margin is expected to one day define the core. Participants are constantly learning, constantly developing. Generating knowledge for campaigns is part of a broader process of building the capacity of members.

Along with collectively held ideas and collective power, the dialogue among members of the EJC groups also fosters a sense of collective identity. Members see their organizations as part of a statewide collective of families and communities who want and deserve high-quality education. The advocacy groups—several with expertise, resources, power, and access to power—share an understanding of the power landscape around education equity. It makes sense to them to help other groups, community members, and students develop the relationships and skills to advocate for themselves, because the victories and influence they gain are shared by all those who share the values of equitable education. The League of Women Voters—perhaps the most mainstream of the EJC groups—sees its EJC work as fulfilling its organizational mission of ensuring "informed and active participation" in government and "the citizen's right to know."[9]

Public Advocate's Liz Guillen, an attorney and legislative advocate, explained how these relationships can work to create a distributed network of powerful skills and connections:

> Each of us has different strengths and roles to play. Our contact contributes to our growing mutual respect and admiration for each other's special expertise. . . . Our community-based allies know that I am invoking their work and efforts in my advocacy in Sacramento. Therefore, I am always checking in with them about how best to characterize their efforts, whether it's the number of various groups that are part of their network or the specific issues they're focusing on. I know that they are using the information I share with them about policymakers and process when they make their long-range plans and when they make their pitch in reaching out to others to join our movement, so I have an obligation to provide current and accurate information to them. For example, if some Republicans begin showing support for the idea that taxes might be an unavoidable reality, that is something I think they should know, as that changes the landscape that they will be navigating when they come to Sacramento or when they visit their elected representatives.

Coordinating ACORN's, Californians for Justice's, and InnerCity Struggle's strategies for presenting information on the opportunities to learn in their local schools.

I have tried to make opportunities for my partners to see the arena in which I work; e.g., to invite them to meetings with legislators so they can try out their concepts and arguments and see for themselves the reactions. Sometimes I am confronted by community and grassroots advocates who are frustrated by what appears to them to be a very small or meaningless change in law. The idea of "baby steps" is hard to sell as a victory sometimes! However, experience has shown that baby steps can lead to larger steps and that any steps at all are often the result of converging forces over which we have absolutely no control.

TAKING COLLECTIVE ACTION

For social movement organizations, the power of disruptive knowledge is established by the action that follows. At every turn, the EJC groups have combined knowledge and actions, relying on their strategic relationships to maximize the power of both. In the words of InnerCity Struggle's Luis Sanchez:

> Historically, [academic] research never really trickles down to create real policy. Organized research is not powerful if it is not connected to organized people. I believe that movements, not research, create change. When you put them together it can be really powerful. . . . As we advance an agenda around education justice, we want school officials and elected leaders to understand that we know the data, we have access to it, and we'll hold them accountable.

And, as we would expect from our reading of the social movement literature, the EJC groups fuse knowledge and action in ways that evoke the power of numbers, of material damage, and of bearing witness.

For example, Californians for Justice (CFJ) has led a coalition of groups in a campaign to halt the "diploma penalty" associated with California's High School Exit Exam. Using the slogan, "First Things First," they argued the unfairness of making students pay such a high price for their schools' failure to provide adequate opportunities to learn. CFJ's Abdi Soltani described the campaign as a seamless synthesis of inquiry, disruptive knowledge, and action that, in this case, employed the logic of numbers:

> We framed the campaign on the theme of opportunity to learn, putting a spotlight on unequal resources in schools, resulting in an unfair punishment of students. We combined research on what was happening in the schools with a spirited campaign of youth and parents demanding an equal opportunity to learn.

In May 2003, CFJ's California Bus Tour for Quality Education traveled the state, making 12 stops, raising the voices of students and parents in communities of color and low-income communities, attracting strong media coverage, and gaining the attention of the State Board of Education. At the end of the tour, hundreds of students converged on the Board's meeting in Sacramento. Soltani recalled:

> State board members referred to newspaper headlines about school inequalities as they met and deliberated the exit exam. Ultimately, when they met to vote on whether to delay the exam, youth and parents from around the state packed their meeting and delivered testimony that the board president called the most powerful he had heard in his years on the board. . . . One great highlight of the action was that when we arrived en masse to enter the state board's hearing room, an hour before the hearing was set to start, the guard tried to deny us seats. Anticipating this, we had brought an attorney with us, who cited the code that allowed us to all sit, first come, first serve. An hour later, as the meeting was set to start, several

dozen professional lobbyists in suits had to stand outside, much to their chagrin, because the seats were filled with youth and parents.

They won a 2-year delay.

Similarly, CADRE's "day of action," which opened this chapter, inflicted "material damage." They called attention to textbook shortages and classes taught by substitutes instead of regular teachers, and they required school officials to stop business as usual and spend their days responding to complaints. EJC colleague Liz Guillen trained CADRE organizers in the complaint process, and they conducted workshops over 2 months to assist members as they prepared complaints. CADRE issued a press release alerting the media about the dozens of complaints they would be filing at Los Angeles schools. They began the day with a press conference followed by a caravan of parents urging school officials to fulfill the promise of the *Williams* settlement. Duke Helfand, a senior education writer at the *Los Angeles Times*, rode along on the caravan, and it is his story that we quote at the opening of this chapter.

Finally, CFJ organizer Yvonne Paul explains how the high school students used the results of their inquiry in actions that bore witness to the terrible conditions under which they were expected to learn. The problems were soon fixed:

In Long Beach, we did a local campaign around school facilities, specifically the bathroom conditions. Students took photos and did action research with surveys documenting the conditions—everything from bathroom doors that didn't work, to locked bathrooms, broken plumbing, the over-spilling sewage, the lack of soap, paper towels, toilet paper, or just basic supplies that students need. . . . We planned an event at the district, where we invited the media, and we displayed the photos. By publicly exposing the problem, students were able to get the district to address it. The district implemented policies such as daily checks to ensure that bathrooms had sufficient supplies that students need. They invited the health department to come in and conduct random inspections. And they increased the custodial staff so bathrooms could be open, accessible, and stocked with the needed supplies.

WHAT HAS THE EDUCATIONAL JUSTICE COLLABORATIVE ACHIEVED?

In August 2004, the state of California agreed to settle the *Williams* case. Newly elected Governor Arnold Schwarzenegger asked the state attorney general to negotiate with the plaintiffs, and in June 2004 Schwarzenegger articulated the state's new position:

It's terrible. It should never have happened. Every child is guaranteed to get equal education, equal quality teachers, equal textbooks, homework materials, all of this stuff ought to be equal, but it hasn't been. And this is why the State was sued. And it was crazy for the State to then go out and hire an outside firm and to fight the lawsuit. Fight what? To say this is not true what the ACLU is saying, that they actually got equal education? All anyone has to do is to just go to those schools, and I've gone to those schools because of my after-school programs. I've seen how inner city schools are falling behind because they're not getting the equal teaching and the equal books, equal learning material. So, of course, we are settling that lawsuit. We are very close in settling that, and it is part of the budget negotiation, because we've got to give every child in this state equal opportunities, equal education, equal learning materials, equal books, everything equal.[10]

The settlement included significant changes to California's education laws. The state agreed to adopt new standards and new accountability mechanisms to ensure qualified teachers, decent school buildings, and sufficient instructional materials for all students. Parents, students, teachers, and community members were given the right to complain if the standards weren't met, and schools and the state agreed to firm timelines for taking corrective action. A new monitoring system was put into place that includes regular, but unannounced, school inspections. The settlement also committed nearly a billion dollars to fix the terrible conditions the plaintiffs identified.

It is impossible to know the precise extent to which the EJC groups influenced the outcome of *Williams*, although there is no doubt that they did. Throughout the case, the groups used their organizing and media strategies to raise public awareness of the horrendous conditions in California schools that gave rise to the case. Their specific campaigns exposed facts about California schools and demanded relief from the inequalities that left low-income children of color with the fewest qualified teachers, with the least textbooks and instructional materials, and with the most dilapidated and overcrowded school buildings. They served as a reference group for the litigation team as it framed possible remedies and considered which proposals were most likely to bring meaningful improvements to the plaintiffs' schools. Together the grassroots and advocacy groups built relationships and took direct action to persuade the state to respond to the case—from behind-the-scenes legislative advocacy, to confrontations at public meetings, to garnering media attention, to mobilizing members for mass actions, to research in schools and communities, and more. That their "opportunity to learn" framing of the problems penetrated the deliberations in the case and, ultimately, the settlement is evident in Governor Schwarzenegger's own words: "I've seen how inner city schools are falling behind because they're not getting the equal teaching and the equal books, equal learning material."[11]

BEYOND *WILLIAMS*

As helpful as the *Williams* settlement may be, the EJC groups knew as well as anyone in the state that it was only a first step toward adequate and equitable schools. California's precipitous funding decline in the 25 years since the *Serrano* decision and the Proposition 13 taxpayers' revolt has left deficits in resources and learning opportunities that are extraordinarily difficult to correct and will continue to limit students' ability to meet the state standards. The burdens of underfunding have been borne most heavily in high-poverty schools, disproportionately attended by children of color and immigrants still learning English. And, although a billion dollars of relief is not inconsequential, the settlement allocation was not "new" money. Rather, it was to be drawn from the existing and already strapped pot of educational funds.

Other serious obstacles to high-quality and equitable schooling were left untouched. Unfathomable complexities in the state's education code and an accountability system that focuses only on test scores limit the information that policymakers and parents have to diagnose problems and monitor the conditions in the future. Nothing in the settlement solved that problem. California's pervasive teacher recruitment and retention problems in low-income communities were not addressed in a systematic way. No provision was made for changes in the tax and public finance policies to generate new funds if the billion dollars promised by the settlement turned out to be insufficient. The Governor did appoint a new commission to put a price tag on high-quality schooling and to recommend changes in the state's funding system. But no action was required. Even with the considerable positive outcomes of *Williams*, there was much work left to be done.

Perhaps one of the greatest strengths of the EJC is that it does not see itself as a campaign or even as a single issue collaborative. Although the *Williams* case has been a focal event, and the settlement a significant win, the groups' fundamental commitments are to creating a structure and culture of California schooling that serves all students well. The *Williams* settlement is a useful tool toward that end, but not the end in itself.

In the year following the *Williams* settlement, the EJC has continued its work with increased vigor. The groups' specific campaign goals range from altering California's school finance system, to expanding the state's school accountability system to hold state and local school officials accountable, to reforming the state's data system so that the public can monitor the quality of schools, and more. Increasingly, the EJC groups are challenging within-school disparities that have been impervious to traditional school reforms.

In spring 2005, several EJC groups piloted a process for accessing and reporting about school conditions. They wanted to know about their schools, inform the *Williams* monitoring and implementation process, and help their members

Introducing a public forum on the School Quality Report Card.

develop collaborative relationships with local education officials. Each group focused attention on one local school. They examined the school's existing "School *Accountability* Report Card (required by the state as an official means of communicating how schools and students are doing), conducted surveys of youth and parents, interviewed school leaders, tracked complaints, and accessed state data. With all of this information gathered by the groups, we developed a "School *Quality* Report Card" for each pilot school. These new report cards served as the foundation for school-based public forums, where the groups made the information public and engaged with school officials about solving problems. The project fostered a different climate for public accountability by showing that organized youth and parents can prompt education officials to improve school conditions. It also provided a tool that can be used to inform statewide policies on how to improve the current School Accountability Report Card.

Californians for Justice's statewide coalition is continuing its campaign to make California's high school graduation requirement fair and to ensure that all students have a meaningful opportunity to meet it. With the return of the California Exit Exam's diploma penalty looming for the class of 2006, the coalition continues to insist that the state fix the "real problems" (including the lack of textbooks, overcrowding, and lack of qualified teachers), instead of taking diplomas away from students who are doing their best under terrible conditions. It also has pressed for two policy options that could offset, at least in part, what are sure to be disproportionately negative effects of the exit exam on low-income students and students of color. One would require monitoring and intervention to support students in high schools that lack the resources and conditions that a meaningful opportunity to learn requires. The second authorizes local districts to develop performance assessments to use alongside the state's paper-and-pencil test as they decide who should earn diplomas. At this writing, both ideas have made their way through important state legislative committees, and, perhaps most important, the idea that students should have both opportunities to learn and alternative assessments has become part of the mainstream policy discourse.

Finally, some of the groups have turned their attention to the pervasive inequalities in students' access to college—the very problem we struggled with at Wilson High and that was the focus of our Futures project. InnerCity Struggle's campus-based clubs in East Los Angeles public high schools have turned their attention toward increasing college access for low-income Latino students. Their specific campaign goal is to make sure that the students in East Los Angeles high schools have the same courses available to them as students in the city's wealthier neighborhoods. They also want the schools to provide the counseling and extra support students need to take advantage of, and succeed in, college preparatory courses.

In the course of their campaign, InnerCity Struggle youth collected surveys from hundreds of their peers. Conducting the survey enabled them to act as political agents as well as researchers. They asserted their right to gather information. The questions and format of the survey communicated powerful ideas to other students about what issues deserve attention and how youth can take action when they become dissatisfied. And they forced school officials to take them seriously. Their demands resulted in more college preparatory courses, including ethnic studies classes, as well as more counselors and discipline policies that do not automatically suspend students from class (and, as a result, cause students to miss important instruction) over such relatively minor infractions as tardiness.

InnerCity Struggle has also joined forces with the Community Coalition, Alliance for Better Communities, and other Los Angeles–based grassroots and advocacy organizations in a campaign to convince the Los Angeles Unified School District that all of the district's students should graduate from high school able to choose college if they wish. We had helped the groups analyze data about the district's high schools that revealed the striking differences in college preparatory course offerings in schools across the city. Together, we had constructed maps, much like the one included in Chapter 1, that provided powerful visual images of the relationship between students' opportunities to prepare for college and the wealth and racial composition of their neighborhoods. These analyses, together with our summary of the strong research evidence on the benefits to high school students of taking challenging academic courses, became important tools in the campaign. In spring 2005, the Los Angeles Unified School District Board of Education responded to the campaign by voting to make California's required college preparatory courses the "default" curriculum for all high school students. The groups will now participate in the implementation of the new policy that aims to prepare all students for the state's 4-year colleges. A broader goal is to take Los Angeles's new college preparation policy statewide.

In all this work, the groups' "successes" are difficult to characterize or compare in any conventional sense. Surely, they have altered the course of state legislation and local policies. They have acted as advocates for individuals and groups in schools. They have increased the number of people who participate in public engagement. Even when they have gained no tangible "win," they have altered the terms of public, community, and political debate. Perhaps most significant, they have forced educational policymaking to account for and legitimize their movement-organizing strategies as a proper, even necessary, form of public engagement.

9

Making Schools and Society Just

The Power of Inquiry and Organizing

FIFTY YEARS AGO, W. E. B. Du Bois anticipated that "many and long steps along Freedom Road lie ahead" before *Brown*'s promise of education "on equal terms" would be achieved. Du Bois understood that Jim Crow was not an American anomaly that could be rooted out by a Supreme Court decision.[1] He knew that the principle of "equal terms" conflicted deeply with a long history of White supremacy and the fundamental norms and power distribution of democratic capitalism. Conditions in American schools today confirm the endurance of those pre-*Brown* norms and politics. Decades of court cases and reform since *Brown* have altered some of the policies, structures, and practices of schooling that underlay *de jure* segregation. But the courts have barely dented the normative fortress that protects school segregation and the unequal distribution of learning opportunities.

We have argued throughout this book that taking those "many and long steps" requires the participation of an activist public that has itself experienced social and educational inequality. We have highlighted students, teachers, parents, and community members who have constructed transformative knowledge through social inquiry, and we have revealed some of their steps toward political power. Inquiry combined with movement organizing, we suggest, has given these groups a presence that makes policymakers pay attention and school officials respond.

This engagement points toward a democracy in which people of all races and social classes engage "on equal terms" to learn from one another as they make decisions about how to live and work together. Back in 1871, Walt Whitman noted that the history of such a robust democracy "remains unwritten, because that history has yet to be enacted."[2] Much the same could be said today. Yet, the great social movements of the 20th century created profound, if short-lived, demonstrations of radical democracy in which working people and people of color built power and challenged the norms and structures of social inequality.

In this final chapter, we argue that movement organizing informed by public inquiry provides our best hope for disrupting the logic of schooling that creates and sustains inequality. We hold further that our social design experiments suggest provocative and promising directions for pursuing this strategy. We close by exploring two essential questions that remain:

- Is it likely that organizing and inquiry can take hold as an equity reform strategy?
- If it does take hold, how will we know that we are moving toward the salutary changes we seek?

INEQUALITY AND THE LOGIC OF SCHOOLING

Creating equitable schools requires challenging and disrupting the social norms that hold inequality in place. Yet, technical school reforms alone do not do this. Unaware of, or unwilling to confront, the entrenched interests that shape education, policymakers and education professionals typically limit their reforms to redesigning structures, increasing professional knowledge, and improving practice. These technical reforms leave the prevailing norms and politics of social inequality untouched.

This characterization is not a wholesale indictment of passionate and committed individuals seeking equity reform from within schools and the policy arena. Quite simply, they often put up a "good fight" only to be overrun by greater power, mobilized and waiting on the sidelines. Equity reformers typically do not anticipate, nor are they able to counter, responses such as the statewide backlash to school finance litigation that had ordered equal spending between wealthy and poor California schools. Efforts to equalize resources among schools and school systems, local fights over racial desegregation plans, and within-school battles over tracking all illustrate how efforts at school reform get caught up in, and overwhelmed by, larger social struggles.

Powerful cultural narratives or "logics" frame these social struggles and give shape to how people make sense of schooling: the logic of merit, the logic of deficits, and the logic of scarcity. The first assumes that young people compete for schooling advantages with their talents and effort in a context of equal opportunity. The second presumes that low-income children, children of color, and their families are limited by cultural, situational, and individual deficits that schools cannot affect. That they systematically get fewer education and social advantages is a result of these deficits and not of structural problems in the educational system. The combined effect of these narratives is compounded today by a logic of scarcity—the belief that our society can afford only limited investment in public life and public education. Hence, the supply of "quality" schooling is shrinking at the same time that good jobs (and middle-class lives) demand more and better education. Together, these narratives, or logics, make it difficult for Americans to see that inequality is the result of flawed policies and structures that undermine democracy.

The Logic of Merit

As an instrument of democracy, the American public school has been expected to bring together all of the community's children to experience a core of civic education, respectful social relations, and solidarity as a community of equal citizens. However, for at least the past century, American schools have also been asked to prepare students for a highly differentiated workforce. That means schools are expected to sort students into different programs, providing different learning experiences in preparation for very different and unequal places in the nation's economy. These contradictory purposes of schooling cohere with the contradictions of democratic capitalism: Americans expect their schools to balance the political equality required for democracy with the economic inequality required by capitalism.[3]

Schools have reconciled these potentially conflicting values for commonness and differentiation through a strong ideology of meritocracy—the belief that everyone has an equal chance to rise to the distinction that his or her unique talent merits. In this logic, students are not sorted capriciously; rather they are placed in programs that suit them best according to supposedly objective measures of ability. By treating students differently, schools prepare young people for their "rightful" places in an unequal economy. That is, although Americans may end up with unequal amounts of education and social privilege, these outcomes are justified because the system provides all an "equal opportunity," and success comes in proportion to talent and hard work.

The Logic of Deficits

Meritocratic sorting is not neutral in its effect on race and social class stratification. Because the definitions and measures of merit and ability are closely aligned with race and social class, the distribution of schooling advantages mirrors inequalities outside of school. A prevailing logic of deficit justifies this outcome. Americans hold deep-seated views about what poor children and children of color are capable of, what their families want, what their cultural backgrounds permit, what type of schooling best suits them, and what their futures are likely to be.[4] These beliefs are rooted in pre-*Brown* conceptions of intelligence and ability, racial differences, and the intrinsic values of curricula tightly linked to Western traditions and religions.

The persistence of the "achievement gap," as reified by politicians and media, can be seen as the inevitable conclusion to the narrative that begins with the beliefs just noted. The combined logics of merit and deficits tell schools to sort deserving from undeserving and expect low-income students of color to fall disproportionately into the latter category. The "fact" that African American, Latino, and low-income students score lower than their middle-class White and Asian peers is not only expected, it completes the story. No other information is needed. In this manner, most Americans view racial gaps in resources and opportunities as normal and expected, even if it is increasingly unacceptable to say so. Many mistrust evidence that low-income students of color can routinely achieve well. Recall the famous example of the College Board's assumption that Jaime Escalante's Latino Advanced Placement students in East Los Angeles must have cheated to do so well on their tests. In both blatant and subtle ways, such outrages occur daily in American schooling.[5]

Normalizing the achievement gap (even as we charge ourselves with eliminating it) simply completes one cycle of an iterative process that returns to and makes sense of factors thought to cause that gap, including low expectations and lack of motivation on the part of children and the adults associated with them. Identifying the achievement gap as natural, reasonable, and normal, leads to the next step—viewing unequal resources and unsuitable structures and practices as conditions that do not matter, given the intractable nature of the "problem." Within this frame, the only thing that can close the gap is changing the beliefs and values of the people on the wrong side of the gap. This is why No Child Left Behind seeks to increase adult expectations, motivation, and effort—it assumes that inequality is the result of a lack of commitment by the people who live or work in low-income communities of color. Thus, the key policy lever to promote educational equity is not better resources more fairly distributed, but rather behavioral prompts in the form of public exposure followed by incentives or (more likely) punishments.

Instead of casting doubt on the fairness of social and educational policies, the logic of deficits focuses all attention on the "failings" of students and their families. In so doing, it legitimizes the fewer schooling advantages for low-income children and children of color. The logic of deficits also blunts moral concerns that arise when advantaged families use their considerable resources to ensure that their own children get the "best" schooling. In a world of scarcity, where everyone is vulnerable, families that scramble for advantage feel they are acting out of self-protection rather than selfishness.

The Logic of Scarcity

The logic of merit has always implied a competition for advantages that not everyone could obtain. The slots in the best high school programs and the best universities have always been limited to those who outshine their peers through their ability and hard work. This competition for relative advantage has been widely perceived as the engine that powers national prosperity and individual worth.

Today, however, the unequal consequences of the logics of merit and deficit are compounded by a powerful logic of scarcity. The scarcity narrative has heightened the competition for advantage in schools and further undermined prospects for equity. It emerges from the very real and quite substantial pressures that global capitalism is placing on the economy to reduce the cost of labor and shrink investment in the public sector. Lower wages, reduced benefits, and lower taxes are thought to create a more favorable "business climate" and help keep the United States competitive in the face of opportunities for outsourcing. The systematic slashing of investments in the nation's social infrastructure has been justified on moral as well as economic grounds. In this view, society is weakened if government stifles innovation by regulating the conditions in public or private institutions or by providing individuals with supports that diminish their motivation to work hard and excel.

An Internet search shows over 200,000 entries for the expression "starving the beast." These words, uttered by high-profile politicians and political activists, have become deeply engrained in mainstream political ideology. The "beast" here is government, and the political strategy is "starving" the government of resources so it can no longer provide services perceived as wasteful at best, but also weakening the nation's initiative and resolve for hard, productive work. Rather, this view holds that the keys to social creativity and productivity lie in deregulation and policies that create the right incentives (rewards and sanctions) for individuals to work hard and use their capacities to the fullest. It leads to pronouncements that "money doesn't matter" for educational quality and to policies that hold schools accountable only for test score performance.

Over the past decades, scarcity has not so much altered the dynamics of schooling as it has raised the stakes. In the global economy, "knowledge-sector" jobs require much higher levels of education than was the case in the industrial past. Federal and state policies set very high academic standards for all students. Yet, the rhetoric of a "world class" education for all belies the reality of a labor market bifurcated into highly valued knowledge workers and low-wage service workers.[6] The structure of this labor market means that only some students need to attain the highest standards, and so the stakes are very high for students who do or do not make the cut for the limited highly valued slots in the new economy.

Scarcity is not the inevitable outcome of circumstances beyond public control; scarcity is an instrument of public policy, carefully cultivated for political and economic ends. This is borne out by conditions revealed in cases such as *Williams v. California* in which lack of qualified teachers and inadequate space cannot be attributed to the overall limited resources in a state with among the highest per capita income rates in the nation. Similarly, California and other states have made a political decision *not* to expand the seats in higher educa-tion in response to the increased demand for and worth of a college education. Such choices dramatically raise the stakes for gaining the highest quality learn-ing opportunities.

As Barbara Ehrenreich has observed, upper-middle-class Americans, fearing their children will not attain their affluence, have been plagued with social and economic anxieties that contribute to their becoming politically conservative.[7] Doctors, lawyers, college professors, business executives, and other privileged Americans see elite education as the only hope for not sliding down econom-ically. Their competition for increasingly scarce, high-quality public school opportunities is fiercer than ever, both aided by and reflected in policies encour-aging parental choice. Thus, parents use whatever capital they have at hand—economic, social, and cultural—to move away from the neighborhoods and schools of greatest vulnerability. Yet public schools value these high-capacity and influential families, and retaining their children becomes one of schools' highest priorities.

Satisfying and holding on to middle-class parents leads well-meaning edu-cators and policymakers to adopt triage strategies that salvage a few out of many. Tracking and targeted support programs make some sense within a logic of scarcity. Magnet or charter schools that may (but likely do not) provide mar-ginally better opportunities for a few become the best schooling hope for the future. But, by ignoring the vast majority of underserved students, triage poli-cies simply encourage parents and students to develop an array of escape strate-gies—strategies that erode the capacity of the institutions left behind. Without determined efforts to correct scarcity and disrupt the perception that it is inevitable, triage practices and stark inequalities are bound to continue in schools.[8]

The Failure of Equity Reform to Confront the Logics of Merit, Deficit, and Scarcity

These are the cultural norms and politics that conventional reform cannot begin to dent. Because equity reformers seek to create (at a minimum) parity of tangible services and entitlements, their appeal is not attractive to those who read "equitable distribution" as undermining the advantages that "meritori-ous" students deserve. Even though equity reforms rarely reduce the material or nonmaterial opportunities of more advantaged students, inherent in them is the goal for low-income students and students of color to gain the advan-tages and life outcomes that are currently held by White higher income stu-dents. In a context of scarcity, this goal of social equalizing threatens the ten-uous status of the privileged.

Schools serving poor children and children of color are often beset with challenges that professional educators cannot begin to understand, let alone resolve. Lacking a social or political critique of the logic of schooling, they have little to go on except to assign problems to whatever deficit seems most closely attached to a problem. Terrible facilities? The kids do not take care of them. Lack of qualified teachers? The kids are not rewarding to teach. Low scores and behavior problems? Parents do not care. Even those who acknowledge the importance of school conditions to student achievement are not likely to look to macropolitical and economic influences.

The existing public sphere does not enable educators and community members to make sense of the causes and consequences of educational inequality, let alone to recognize that they can take action to effect change. The logic of scarcity, especially the supposition that scarcity is inevitable, undermines investment in the public spaces that support and sustain public dialogue. This weakness, perceived and actual, makes calls for public participation unpersuasive—both to elites who control public investment and to the communities who cannot imagine the forms that their collective power might take. The project of revitalizing public life is thus bound up with the struggle to overturn the logics of merit, deficit, and scarcity. A robust public sphere in which citizens come together to identify their common interests and deliberate about how to serve them can begin to shift the norms and politics that advantage the few at the great expense of the many. This is the hard work that the Educational Justice Collaborative groups described in Chapter 8 are attempting.

REVITALIZING THE PUBLIC'S DEMOCRATIC IMAGINATION

A vital public life is the foundation of our democratic society, and education plays a central role in shaping the public sphere. The fact that civil rights leaders in the 1950s decided to target the education system as opposed to any other public institution was no accident. Education has the potential to broaden the pool of future citizens who have access to the knowledge and tools needed for a diverse, healthy democracy. And organizing for educational equity engages parents and community members as active participants in democratic life.

As a number of scholars have argued recently, the need for revitalizing democracy is particularly acute today, as public spaces are shrinking and, along with them, opportunities for public deliberation about public policies.[9] Like us, some of these scholars also hearken to John Dewey for understanding the demise of the public sphere as well as the promise of democratic deliberation for public action. Following Dewey's concern over the "eclipse of the public," scholar Archon Fung observes that today, as in Dewey's time, most social and political institutions inhibit citizens from coming together as "publics" in ways that allow them to understand and influence public policymaking. The result, he argues, is government disconnected from "democratic guidance."[10] Fung also notes, and we concur, that the problem has grown more intractable since Dewey's time, as evidenced by record lows in voter turnout, pervasive distrust of government, and cynicism about whether politics simply masks the control of government by "special interests."

Fung critiques current reform debates as skirting

> the problem of constituting pragmatic publics. Improving governance, for example, has largely focused on administration rather than democracy; in many modern treatments, this in turn means increasing the satisfaction of clients as consumers of government largess.[11]

The antidotes, Fung notes, are new institutions that make possible the deliberative, democratic publics that Dewey envisioned:

> Effective democratic publics consist of citizens who feel the actions of government on them, understand the relationship of polities to these effects, discuss the connections between these ends and means, and in turn are connected through democratic arrangements to a state that respected their discussions.[12]

Similarly, Harry Boyte laments that the American culture over the past generation has become "dominated by values of savage competition, consumerism, and 'get rich quick'." At the same time, politics has become "structured by a thin conception of citizenship," consisting of voting and individual volunteerism. Boyte seeks to reclaim the notion of a "citizen as a creative, intelligent, and, above all, 'political' agent in the deepest meaning of the word, political—someone able to negotiate diverse views and interests for the sake of accomplishing some public task."[13] However, Boyte eschews narrow confrontational protests focused on grievances. Rather, he looks to Dewey to infuse organizing with social intelligence to provide "a democratic vision of the meaning of democracy and abundance."[14] Boyte seeks to connect "ordinary citizens" with "experts," as long as expertise does not take precedence over "civic intelligence" to impose professional solutions on communities and their families.

This contemporary theorizing about constituting a deliberative democracy through organizing and inquiry clearly echoes the works of Myles Horton, Septima Clark, and Ella Baker at the Highlander School and in backwater communities in the South. As we described in Chapter 6, their "participatory research" was a primary strategy for generating knowledge and understanding that grounded their organizing and actions. Horton's, Clark's, and Baker's work was characterized by elements that have been not fully considered by contemporary scholars. In particular, these earlier movement organizers emphasized the public inquiry and activism of the most marginalized groups, finding essential their inclusion as full participants in public discourse.

By foregrounding the participation of those directly impacted by inequality, Horton, Baker, and Clark constructed a public sphere particularly well suited to challenging inequality. They offered a vision of radical inclusion that pressed for universalizing the rights of some, rather than asserting marginal privilege over those with even less power. At Highlander, inquiry assumed that all people could learn and "act to shape their own lives," and that meant "all people everywhere, not just your family or your own countrymen or your color."[15] These democratic commitments were sustained by social interaction as well as words. Horton remembered, "We made our speech about social equality without saying anything, but by *doing* it."[16] The learning at issue here was not received ideologies from a radical leadership, but an arduous process through which participants made sense of their own experience, the historical context in which they lived, and the potential pathways for having their own voices determining their futures. The critical focus of this work challenged the inevitability of conditions that affected the participants' lives by looking at the power that held those conditions in place. In Francesca Polletta's terms, participants in the Highlander School conversations "prefigured" the radical democratic practices they sought to create in the broader society.

As we described earlier, we similarly have concluded that advancing equity requires the legitimate participation and leadership of those most negatively affected by inequality. Such engagement includes the Dewey-like construction of new understandings that allow students, families, and communities to see their individual and local troubles in larger cultural, structural, and political contexts. At that point they begin to imagine themselves as efficacious participants in a just society that offers both relief from oppression and access to benefits. Our work with the Futures students and the teachers and students in the Teaching to Change LA Project allowed us to witness the interplay between transforming identities and transformative actions. As these young people and teachers shared the knowledge they constructed with differently situated audiences—including those with sophisticated academic expertise, those with professional education experience, and those with little formal knowledge—they came to see themselves as change agents with powerful voices and with relevant substance to convey.

But still, neither the new identities and understandings nor the vital teaching and learning forged through these two projects compelled powerful actors to rethink prevailing assumptions or refashion restrictive policies. In contrast, the inquiry of Parent-U-Turn and the Educational Justice Collaborative has a much greater reach. These groups have become a steadfast counterforce to the logic of merit, deficit, and scarcity. Like the students and teachers, few of the individuals in these groups began their activism with a strongly developed identity as transformative actors. Even fewer started out with a developed capacity to bring transformative knowledge to a broader social agenda. Yet, before long, these groups could stand on equal footing with those who would preserve the status quo; indeed, one might say that they were "more than equal" given their often superior data, knowledge of law, arguments, and compelling stories.

Through their public engagement with allies, public officials, and experts, these low-income people and people of color took on new identities as powerful social activists as they saw their local actions find currency beyond their communities. As their stories took hold in the public consciousness through vehicles such as media features, scholarly publications, public meetings, political lobbying, engaging with teachers, and ceaseless schmoozing, many of the understandings that used to reside only in their private lives and local experiences became "common knowledge." In spite of a steady and successful commitment to "stay local," their inquiry in public spaces multiplied their public power beyond their neighborhoods.

We also saw a powerful transformation among those of us at UCLA's Institute for Democracy, Education, and Access (IDEA). We learned how to support students, teachers, parents, and activists to make presentations instead of just presenting data ourselves. When we were called on to share data, we were pushed to think of new formats to present numbers that were clear and rigorous. We learned that our legitimacy is earned not just by publishing articles but also by meeting our partners on their terms and in their communities.

Together, we learned that the tools and methods of inquiry interrogate the origins and legitimacy of power as they challenge the particular conditions under scrutiny. This characteristic of inquiry gives grassroots activists generic skills and dispositions to address multiple and usually related conditions. Rather than sticking exclusively with a demand *du jour*, inquiry builds knowledge of local power and develops a cumulative understanding of many conditions that comprise the status quo—allowing groups to work on multiple "fronts," including actions in which they are not the principal actors. For example, a grassroots group that understands a range of education equity issues as well as the power dynamics at a school does not have to be the sole agent for equity reform. It can provide both support and a buffer for equity-minded teachers struggling to dismantle tracking or install a culturally sensitive curriculum without tracking. Such actions not only address inequitable practices but also enhance the group's position for future disputes and alliances.

Finally, organizers have taught us that any one domain of inequality, such as schools, is unlikely to be isolated from other domains such as affordable housing, available health care, safe neighborhoods, and good jobs. For members of grassroots groups, the question of whether school inadequacies *or* community problems limit their children's achievements must seem out-of-touch with the reality of their lives. Professional educators and academics may debate such a question, but community activists rarely do. Both matter, and they are inseparable. Further, although the specific issues and the technical knowledge bases required to understand them are very different, the dynamics for accessing and persuading relevant power holders may be more similar. Surely, groups that organize specifically around education do so because they seek particular changes in education policy and local schools. But they also see the community power that is built in the context of education organizing as transferable to other essential social goods. And, they recognize that organizing for better public schools marks out a new relationship between their members and the public sphere.

How Likely Are Public Inquiry and Organizing to Achieve Educational Justice?

The examples of inquiry and organizing we have shared come from a set of "social design experiments"—two that we initiated, and two that we joined as research partners. The four partnerships provided alternate sites for young people, educators, parents, community members, activists, and researchers to merge academic research, everyday experience, and a press for racial and educational justice. In each case we positioned IDEA as a partner whose particular contribution would be to provide research relevant to the groups' diverse actions, to scaffold the other partners' doing and analyzing their own research, to facilitate inquiry within and among groups, and to disseminate through scholarly channels the substance and meaning of the groups' efforts. This role for IDEA and its resulting relationships did not begin with a self-aware intention of becoming "movement-like." However, it was soon evident that the richest and most relevant source of insights for the groups' work and our own understanding was the literature on (and some of the groups' current involvement with) social movement organizing.

How likely is such inquiry-based, social movement organizing to make a real difference in schooling for low-income communities and communities of color? Our cautious optimism is based on two very different types of evidence and reasoning. One is the growing use of organizing for school reform across the country and the increasing interest among researchers in being connected with this work. The second cause for optimism is an analysis of the conditions that give rise to social movements. Included here is the likelihood that the current frame for American education—embodied in No Child Left Behind—cannot be sustained, because of the strong contradiction between its expansive goals and its reliance on the logic of scarcity.

Increase in Organizing for Educational Reform Nationwide

Across the country, hundreds of other groups in low-income communities and communities of color have had remarkable success with campaigns for racial and economic justice as applied to a number of social issues. Increasingly, these organizations are adding to their agendas campaigns for higher quality and more equitable schools. Large networks like the Association of Community Organizations for Reform Now (ACORN), the Pacific Institute for Community Organization (PICO), and the Industrial Areas Foundation (IAF), as well as many "unaffiliated" groups, are bringing to education the experience and political power they have developed in campaigns for living wage jobs, affordable housing, health care, and other social goods. A study in 2001 identified more than 200 groups engaged in campaigns for educational justice,[17] and far more groups are organizing today. A survey we conducted in 2005 located 65 such groups in California alone.[18] In many instances, these groups are joining forces with researchers to inform their activism with inquiry.

One well-studied example, which we mentioned in Chapter 6, is the IAF Alliance Schools Project in low-income communities across Texas, led in the 1980s and 1990s by Ernesto Cortes. IAF rejects the idea that schools can improve on their own. Given schools' entanglement with powerful political, social, and historical factors, solutions to school problems can only be accomplished by linking school reform to community empowerment. Dennis Shirley, a researcher who has studied the Alliance Schools, notes,

> Educators must be bold enough to conceptualize the school as *the center of the community*—as a vital geographical nexus in which friends and neighbors convene to identify, debate, and correct the exasperating proliferation of social problems which have accompanied the economic and social dislocations of the last quarter century.[19]

Although the IAF activities were often resisted at first, the organizing produced concrete improvements and state funding, as well as increased social and political capital for community members, and more racially inclusive and effective politics.[20]

Another example comes from New York City, where ACORN, a group representing 20,000 mostly low-income New Yorkers, took action against tracking when a 1995 report showed that African Americans and Latinos were heavily underrepresented in the crown jewels of the New York City Public Schools: Stuyvesant and Bronx Science high schools. Knowing that enriched academic experiences early on were required to qualify for these selective schools, White and non-White ACORN parent "testers" visited about 50 New York City elementary schools to inquire about programs available to their young children. Finding that White parents were told more often about gifted programs than parents of color, ACORN called for a moratorium on gifted programs until the school's chancellor could verify citywide that the programs were not substantially segregated and that they were open to any children who could meet reasonable admission policies. ACORN also demanded that the chancellor evaluate the programs' content and approach. Of particular interest was to determine what gifted programs do differently than regular schools and why the approaches used in gifted programs could not be extended to all students. Such activism on the part of community groups can pave the way for tracking reform.

Growing Relationships Between Researchers and Activists

UCLA IDEA's role in the Futures Project, Teaching to Change LA, Parent-U-Turn, and the Educational Justice Collaborative follows from the historic mission of higher education, and particularly of "land grant" universities, to serve the public good—a mission that is currently enjoying a widespread revival. Although the language is a bit dated, Daniel Coit's 1876 inaugural address as the first president of Johns Hopkins University expressed the public mission of higher education well: The university should "make for less misery among the poor, less ignorance in the schools, less bigotry in the temple, less suffering in the hospital, less fraud in business, less folly in politics."[21]

Today, a growing community of scholars and policymakers is calling for an "engaged university"—one that is connected and activist in making research a tool for solving public problems. "Since democratic schooling is essential for a democratic society,"[22] notes higher education scholar Ira Harkavy,

> We need to take a democratic great leap forward—a leap propelled by what Martin Luther King termed "the fierce urgency of now." Pleased with our accomplishments, dissatisfied and impatient with the present state of affairs, motivated by a bold, inclusive democratic vision, we (democratic-minded academics) need to do the hard, sustained work that builds democracy and a movement.[23]

Boyte also argues that the university has a special obligation to acknowledge its responsibility for the weak public sphere and to engage in developing a new "everyday politics." He writes:

> Today, much of our research culture is detached from the problems and currents of the larger society.
> Democratizing education—in the sense of its reconnection with the political life of communities, and in the sense of educational and learning activities as sites for democratizing the larger society—is key to changing this phenomenology of powerlessness and innocence.
> This means schools, universities, and other educational sites becoming public and political spaces, as well as John Dewey's social ones.[24]

A growing number of groups of researchers, like IDEA, are resources for organizing groups and advocates working on equity school reform. Harry Boyte's Center for Democracy and Citizenship at the Hubert H. Humphrey Institute of Public Affairs at the University of Minnesota is a national leader in helping higher education institutions recast themselves in ways that strengthen civic capacities and democratize professional (expert) interaction with citizens and communities.[25] Ira Harkavy's Center for Community Partnerships at the University of Pennsylvania is developing partnerships among higher education, communities, and schools to develop "community schools" that educate, engage, activate, and serve all members of the community.[26]

Several university groups like IDEA conduct research that supports organizing for school reform. For example, Fordham University's National Center for Schools and Communities provides policy analysis, data, and technical assistance to groups in cities across the United States[27] and was the research partner in ACORN's work described above. The Institute for Education and Social Policy at New York University works with about 13 organizations that are organizing around education in New York City and in major northeastern cities.[28] The NYU Institute conducts research on community organizing for school reform. This research involves community members in research design, data collection, analyses, and reporting.[29] In Washington, DC, the Community Research and Learning Network (CoRAL) serves as a consortium of community-based organizations and seven universities. CoRAL helps community groups access research design and data analysis resources to advance their social justice missions, while simultaneously learning from the community.[30]

Many individual faculty members work with community groups engaged in educational justice struggles. For example, Pauline Lipman, professor of education at DePaul University in Chicago, has not only studied and written extensively about race and class power relations on urban schools, she is also a founding member and active participant in Chicago Teachers for Social Justice. Further, many ethnic studies programs, created out of movement action in another era, continue to place a strong value on such connections. Places like the Cesar Chavez Center at San Francisco State University offer a strong institutional base for this sort of work.

A number of nonprofit research and policy groups support community-organizing campaigns that focus on education. Foremost among these independent groups is Research for Action (RFA) in Philadelphia.[31] RFA staff work with educators, parents, and students to teach them research skills and engage them in action research. RFA emphasizes research as a tool for increased democratic participation and enriched public dialogue about schooling.

The Right Conditions for Activism

But how likely is it that enough people would participate in public inquiry and movement organizing to actually make a difference? Education scholar Jean Anyon asks this question in *Radical Possibilities: Public Policy, Urban Education, and a New Social Movement*.[32] Anyon combines McAdam, Tarrow, and Tilly's analyses with her own considerable scholarship, experience, and insights about the political economy of urban education to identify conditions that could prompt individuals to participate in social movements for educational change.[33]

First, Anyon argues that people become motivated to organize around education when changes in social conditions provide new opportunities to push effectively against the status quo. Anyon gives, as one example, the increase in poor people moving to the suburbs, which creates an opening to organize metropolitan alliances for better schools. Second, powerful inducements for activism occur when events bring contradictions between political rhetoric and social reality into sharp relief. Here, Anyon gives the historical example of the outbreaks of urban violence in the 1960s when the "dashed expectations of millions of Southern Blacks who had fled Jim Crow hoping to find freedom and jobs in the North . . . were clearly disappointed by what they encountered."[34] Third, social movements take hold when the media and government bestow legitimacy on them by recognizing the moral force of their claims and by "certifying" their goals as part of the official government agenda. Anyon's prime historical example here is the national consensus (built initially from televised brutality against protesters) about the goodness of the Civil Rights Movement's objectives. She also notes the legitimacy accorded specific goals, as civil rights measures became part of presidential legislative agendas, culminating in the Civil Rights Act of 1964, the Voting Rights Act of 1965, and the 1968 Fair Housing Act.

Anyon's analyses are particularly useful for understanding why *now* could be a promising time for movement organizing for educational justice to emerge. In what follows, we move beyond Anyon to describe other changes in the political economy that could be recognized as opportunities, contradictions between political rhetoric of equity and the reality of inequality, and the increasing perception that demands for equity are legitimate. All of these suggest that the conditions for increased activism are emerging.

Recognition of Opportunities to Push Against the Status Quo. The visible presence of an educational system that is increasingly racially separate and materially unequal provides an opportunity to challenge the prevailing rationale that merit explains why the "best" schooling outcomes and life chances remain disproportionately the purview of the nation's White and privileged students. Public awareness of this inequality has grown alongside the growth of the Latino population. This growth in California and elsewhere has brought the national non-White K–12 enrollment to almost 40%.[35] At the same time, racial segregation has also increased, as has the gap between affluent and poor Americans. In both schools and neighborhoods, the relative resources and opportunities for low-income communities of color have declined sharply.[36]

These demographic and economic shifts have changed both the perception and politics around the schooling opportunities of these young people. The education of "poor" and "minority" students in schools has moved from being a marginal problem in an overwhelmingly White educational system to being the most significant educational problem of the period, and one that threatens society as a whole. For many, the steady dismantling of desegregation orders over the past 30 years has diminished hopes that that the courts will serve as the primary agent of education reform. Alongside a profound disappointment with this trend, many activists recognize it as an opportunity to demand that that racially and economically segregated schools provide equal resources and opportunities.

Another opportunity to push against the status quo lies in the renewed focus on organizing within certain sectors of the labor movement—particularly among low-wage workers. Increased union activism may spread as unions of low-wage workers devote increasing resources to organizing and activist strategies.[37] This labor organizing may also trigger new organizing around education, because it is occurring in communities where children attend the most segregated and underresourced schools. Over the past 10 years, for example, the Service Employees International Union (SEIU) has organized close to 1 million service workers who are largely people of color, immigrants, and working women, providing an avenue for low-income people to enter into a public. Together, the changing demographics and increased union organizing in states like California have contributed to Latinos' substantial gains in political power and corresponding opportunity for movement organizing.

Social Contradictions That Provide Impetus for Action. Today, many low-income students of color, parents, community members, and teachers are increasingly disappointed by the apparent contradictions between the much-touted promises of No Child Left Behind and the failure of the law to provide funding to close the huge gaps among racial groups in basic school resources. It is becoming increasingly obvious that the law's most potent provision is high-stakes accountability tests that further disadvantage students in severely underresourced schools who have limited opportunity to learn the material on which they are tested. Similarly, oft-repeated pronouncements that 21st century jobs will require a much more highly educated workforce contradict the apparent unwillingness of business leaders and policymakers to provide the resources to prepare low-income students for these jobs.

Legitimization of Concerns and Demands. Today, the success of school adequacy cases in states around the country and the settlement of the *Williams* case in California have initiated legal sanctions and moral outrage. In California, media coverage of the school conditions that led to *Williams,* Governor Schwarzenegger's outrage at the inadequacies that the plaintiffs suffered, and legislation enacting the terms of the settlement, provide legitimacy to activists' demands for meaningful "opportunities to learn" for every child. And, despite the contradiction in No Child Left Behind, noted above, its compelling rhetoric voiced by its most prominent spokesperson, the President of the United States, is likely to strengthen activists' conviction and the public's perception that their cause is righteous.

This legitimizing, in turn, has fueled further struggles for equal and adequate resources and opportunities. For example, in California, groups are demanding that the state's college preparatory courses become the "default curriculum" for all high school students. They also seek to modify the state's accountability policies so that communities can hold district and state officials accountable for providing high-quality resources and opportunities. They are campaigning for a rigorous "costing out" study that would specify the costs of educating all students in the state to meet the standards (including the cost differentials for students and communities where the needs are greatest) and that could become the basis of a restructured school finance system.

Influential media are beginning to cover grassroots groups' education "actions" in ways that portray the groups and their goals sympathetically—a strong departure from previous media policies of ignoring the groups or framing them in a negative light. Spanish-language media are enthusiastic consumers of data and news releases that the groups bring to them, as are the increasing numbers of legislators of color in California and the nation.

In sum, our own analyses are consistent with Anyon's. The conditions seem to be in place for social movement organizing around educational justice. Shifts in the political economy giving greater visibility and clout to communities of color, the obvious contradictions between the promises of No Child Left Behind and the huge disparities in educational resources and opportunities, and the legitimacy being given to the outrage of these disparities by the courts and the media all set the stage for activism for more equitable schools.

WHAT CONSTITUTES EVIDENCE OF SUCCESSFUL INQUIRY AND ORGANIZING?

If inquiry and organizing strategies gain wide currency in communities and become a salient force in the reform of education policy and practice, what would that look like? What changes might we expect in schools and in society? What would constitute success or meaningful progress toward it? We must concede that these questions are at least partly rhetorical. Is equitable schooling a cause or an effect of a good society? Is "public participation" a means or an end? On the other hand, some answers to the questions above are substantially empirical. Being the researchers that we are, we close this book by reviewing what a vibrant public can know and suggesting how better data and framing could help us know and communicate more effectively.

Our vision of success is a public education system from which American young people graduate well prepared for college, meaningful work, and active

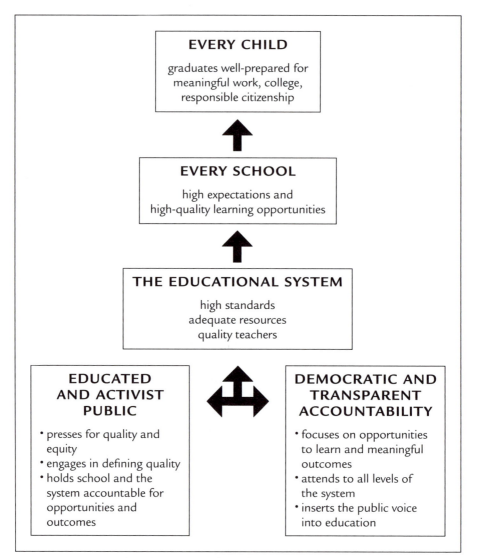

FIGURE 9.1. An education system of an educated, activist public.

citizenship. Such a system would be characterized by the engagement of an educated, activist public that, armed with research, defines, presses for, and holds educational officials accountable for adequate and equitable education. In Figure 9.1, we illustrate how such a system can and should work.

Several indicators could reveal progress toward such a system and the social change it would foster. We should see reduced race and social class disparities in successful college-going and preparation for high-skill, high-wage work. We should see the precursors of these outcomes in academic achievement, high school graduation rates, and college eligibility rates.

Underpinning these outcomes, widespread inquiry and organizing should shift the public will. We would expect an engaged and activist public to move away from the logics of merit and deficit and reject the logic of scarcity in favor of a logic of *sufficiency.* The logic of sufficiency calls for enough resources to support quality schooling for all students in all schools. Quality schooling, in this sense, means that schools provide students with the tools necessary to attain meaningful and well-paid work and participate vigorously in public life. This shift to sufficiency would mean a broad public commitment to ensuring the most basic and tangible elements of schooling—such as clean, safe, and uncrowded school facilities; fully qualified teachers; ample and appropriate instructional materials; and access to a college preparatory curriculum. It also would mean providing equally essential but less tangible elements—caring; support; and recognition that all students can succeed academically without having to relinquish their culture, language, or commitments to family and community. We would also expect new policy structures that support a logic of sufficiency by basing education expenditures on studies that cost out the resources required to ensure that all students learn the standards.

Of course, a logic of sufficiency, as we have defined it, also paves the way for other powerful schooling logics: a logic of intelligence that says that, with sufficient resources and opportunities, all students are capable of high-level learning; a logic of valuable families and communities that sees children and the families they come from as having cultural assets that, together with sufficient schooling resources and opportunities, help them grow into strong, civic-minded people; and a logic of empowerment that says all people can play a powerful and meaningful role in governing public schools and constituting a robust public.

Shifting the logic of schooling would also mean that schools would strike a better balance between the civic role of education and the economic one—striving to produce better citizens as well as better workers. We might see this shift in new accountability frameworks at the state level that require students to demonstrate civic competence alongside proficiency in reading and math. Certainly these frameworks would call for engaging alternatives to prevailing norm-referenced standardized assessment and allow students to display a wide array of skills and knowledge in multiple and authentic ways. The shift might be revealed superficially in schools' curricula (what schools require and what they do not), but a deeper understanding of students' civic-learning opportunities could be gleaned by looking at the civic activities in which students actually participate. We could expect schools to provide low-income youth with critical research and political skills and forums to use these skills so that their voices are heard and their interests represented in public discourse. We would also be likely to see dominant deficit narratives challenged by powerful counternarratives of low-income youth of color who are intellectually engaged and civic-minded and who cannot easily be dismissed as "exceptions" to the rule.

Shifts in political participation and the distribution of power would also be likely. Access to relevant information lets students and community members compare their schools with other schools, as well as with the state's own standards. With these accessible data, they would know who to hold responsible at all levels of the system, in order to press for optimal conditions for all students. Moreover, an expanded view of who has the right and obligation to access and interpret data can build bridges between universities, community organizations, and government. And with the empowerment that comes from organizing among their own community with support of allies from other institutions and public spheres, they would feel entitled to act on this knowledge. They would know about and weigh in on state and federal policies that shape schooling in fundamental ways, such as taxation, teacher credentialing, curriculum standards, and assessment.

Such a flow of information and more even patterns of participation would generate passionate responses, some of which would surely be acrimonious, but many of which would be highly productive. Just as surely, students would gain from the passion, knowledge, action, and even anger of their parents, about whom no one would dare say, "Those parents don't care."

Further, the success of an inquiry and organizing approach to equity reform would be evident in the process itself. Inquiry is necessarily educative and capacity enhancing because new information comes only with the application of skills. The skills themselves are tools for constructing authentic information. The overall validity of the information is checked through exposure to research and experience and tested "under fire" when it is communicated to powerful institutional actors. The tangible wins achieved at first may well be small, but they will also be also significant indicators of success because they complete an inquiry cycle that orients new learning and provides the groundwork for far more significant future inquiry, action, and change.

Perhaps the most important indicator of an educated, activist public would be that millions of people would be talking with one another about how they can jointly take action to improve the quality of schooling for all children. Such a public would be eager to engage with educators in defining high-quality schools and would be ready to hold the system accountable for ensuring that quality. This is democracy in action.

OPTIMISM AND CONSIDERABLE CAUTION

It would be naive to overlook the considerable challenges to widespread public inquiry and activism for educational and social justice. We cite just a few here to temper our optimism. First, placing the onus on low-income people of color

to initiate "participatory social inquiry" and social activism calls on them to surmount the material and political asymmetries that underlie their current disadvantages. Most lack the financial resources and social capital that are major
factors in building power and mounting successful social and political campaigns (especially in today's era of sophisticated message development and
expensive media buys that shape public opinion). In response, we must hearken
again, with considerable awe, to the work of Ella Baker and Septima Clark, who
brought the satisfaction of learning and community engagement to "quiet
places" in the rural South in the 1950s. By "casting down their buckets" where
they were, participants in the Citizen Education Program of the 1940s and 1950s
became a potent political force for social change that buried Jim Crow. So, too,
are Parent-U-Turn, CADRE, Californians for Justice, ACORN, PICO, and the
many other groups like them in communities across the nation powerful agents
for social change. And this would be even truer if they had access to sustained
and predictable material support from foundations and other civic organizations.

A second hurdle is in convincing schooling professionals and researchers to
abandon their traditional relationships with community members. Within the
education enterprise, administrators and teachers have sought the mantle of
"professionalism" and, with it, near-exclusive control over educational policy
and practice. They are unlikely to willingly share their authority over schooling with activist communities, however knowledgeable the activists may be. The
teachers unions, highly protective of hard-won gains in salary and working
conditions, and routinely blamed for all that is wrong with schooling, are
unlikely to see much advantage in opening up the conditions of their work to
public deliberation.

Dewey, on the other hand, argued persuasively for teachers to cast their lot
with other working Americans:

> The cause goes back to the excessive control of legislation and administration exer-
> cised by the small and powerful class that is economically privileged. Position,
> promotion, security of the tenure of teachers has depended largely upon conform-
> ity with the desires and plans of this [elite] class.[38]

Educators, he reasoned, would be far better served by identifying their common
interests with other workers, and joining forces with them:

> If teachers are workers who are bound in common ties with all other workers, what
> action do they need to take? The answer is short and inclusive. Ally themselves
> with their friends against their common foe, the privileged class, and in the
> alliance develop the character, skill, and intelligence that are necessary to make a
> democratic social order a fact. . . . In union is strength, and without the strength
> of union and united effort, the state of servility, of undemocratic administration
> adherence to tradition, and unresponsiveness to the needs of the community . . .
> will persist.[39]

Following this analysis, teachers unions could seize the moral high ground in school reform and become active agents in securing their unique role as those who "produce a higher standard of intelligence in the community."[40] We are heartened to see this ideal embraced by the new insurgent leadership of the Los Angeles teachers union.

Perhaps the biggest challenge, and arguably the most important, lies in bringing people together across race and social classes to create inclusive, progressive movements.[41] Many well-meaning Whites are oblivious to the privilege and racism they bring with them to these initiatives and how these inevitably undermine the movements' goals and outcomes.[42] Additionally, as we noted in our earlier discussion, the growing income inequality and the shrinking of the middle class in the United States no doubt increase the likelihood that the "haves" will feel threatened by equity reforms.

At the same time, however, there is considerable appeal to a more egalitarian democracy as an antidote to the fierce, often losing, battle to maintain advantage in a world where the logic of scarcity extends far beyond school. Success comes at the price of hurried lives, where the joys of family and community fade next to the glare of acquisition, status, and fear of being the target of downsizing and outsourcing. We believe that middle-class Americans value democratic, neighborly communities and that they know, at some level, that such communities cannot be recreated behind community gates or in privatized schools.

Most Americans respond with considerable outrage to evidence of the multiple forms of inequality related to race and poverty in education and across other public institutions. They feel the unfairness of families' unequal opportunities, related to their race and income, to accumulate and pass on to their children the private resources that determine the next generation's access to high-quality schooling. To transform such sentiments into action, however, requires narratives that allow Americans to imagine how their common interests will be served by more equitable social policy.[43] Such narratives must counter those of individual merit, deficits, and scarcity.

Critical public dialogue is not likely to happen without significant trauma and confrontation. Moreover, we step into utopian realms gingerly, knowing that social movements have the power for good and ill associated with all utopian projects. We are also well aware that some social movement scholars caution that such efforts rarely achieve the virtuous ends they seek.[44] Nevertheless, we believe that, given the current threats to our democracy, these risks are all worth taking.

TAKING "MANY AND LONG STEPS"

Every day, as we navigate the streets of Los Angeles, we see the wreckage of a society that has abandoned its schools to the logics of merit, deficit, and scarcity in an economy where many must fail. This, in a city with more millionaires than any other and in a state whose economic prowess rivals most nations.[45] Low-income African American and Latino children bring to school with them their families' hope that education will bring a better life. Some of their families—like those of immigrants Nina Melendez and Arturo Alvarez in Chapter 4—have risked everything to realize the promise of American schooling. Few do. For the most part, these young people get overcrowded, woefully ill-equipped, and shamefully understaffed schools. More than half never graduate. Based on prior trends, they face a life of poverty-wage work, unaffordable housing costs, little access to health services or child care, inadequate public transportation, and dangerous neighborhoods with few parks, libraries, or other spaces for communities to come together. This, of course, is based on *what we know*. What we do not know is how much worse these conditions can get in the ensuing 20 or 40 years.

In the course of our work, we have also met many young people and families who have gone to enormous lengths and broken many rules to get their children into "good" schools like Wilson High, only to find that the fine resources and opportunities the school provides to some children are closed off to their own. Here, too, is deeply disturbing evidence of the logics of merit, deficit, and scarcity.

Over the past few years, we have also seen stunning evidence that citizens can join together across race and social class in public inquiry and powerful actions to achieve high-quality education for some portion of poor children—African Americans, Latinos, and other children of color. To make these successes commonplace, we all must learn more power.

> We are going to have to learn to think in radical terms. I use the term *radical* in its original meaning—getting down to and understanding the root cause. It means facing a system that does not lend itself to your needs and devising means by which you change that system. That is easier said than done. But one of the things that has to be faced is, in the process of wanting to change that system, how much have we got to do to find out who we are, where we have come from and where we are going.
>
> Ella Baker, 1969

Notes

Note: Frequent reference is made to portions of the 37-volume compilation of John Dewey's complete writings (edited by Jo Ann Boydston and published by Southern Illinois University Press, Carbondale, 1969–1991), *The Collected Works of John Dewey, 1882–1953*. The work was published in three series, referenced herein in shorthand form by series and volume number, as follows: *EW, The Early Works, 1882–1898* (Vols. 1–5); *MW, The Middle Works, 1899–1924* (Vols. 1–15); and *LW, The Later Works, 1925–1953* (Vols. 1–17).

PROLOGUE

1. Hayasaki, 2003.
2. Pittman, 2002.
3. Núñez, 2005.

CHAPTER 1

1. Cremin, 1961, pp. 9–10.
2. Mann, 1848.
3. *Brown v. Board of Education*, 1954.
4. Du Bois, 1954, p. 5.
5. Orfield, 2001.
6. Hoffman and Sable, 2006, pp. 11–16.
7. The findings on Washington Middle School come from a 2002 report from the Social Policy Research Associates of a set of case studies they conducted at California schools experiencing shortages of qualified teachers. The researchers began their study knowing that the schools had problems attracting and keeping qualified teachers, but they were quite unprepared for the seriousness of problems and the compound impact of multiple problems on students' chances for a good education. Friedlaender and Frankel, 2002.
8. Fewer than two thirds was selected as the threshold for a serious curriculum problem because California requires that students seeking to prepare for 4-year colleges must take two thirds of their classes from a set of approved college-preparatory courses.
9. *Williams v. State of California*, 2000; *Williams v. State of California*, 2005.
10. The team included, in addition to the two of us, Linda Darling-Hammond, Michelle Fine, William Koski, Norton Grubb, Patricia Gándara, Russell Rumberger, Kenji Hakuta, Heinrich Mintrop, Gary Orfield, Michael Russell, Valerie Lee, and Kevin Welner, among several others. Reports of this research are published in a special double issue of *Teachers College Record, 106*, 10 and 11 (see Oakes, 2004).

11. Du Bois, 1954, p. 5.
12. Du Bois, 1954, p. 5.
13. Dewey, 1937, "Democracy Is Radical," *LW*, *11*, 299.
14. Throughout this book, we follow Dewey in his use of the term "citizen" when speaking of members of the broader body politic. We use "citizen" to refer to *all* community residents, including immigrants who lack legal documentation.
15. Dewey, 1935, *Liberalism and Social Action*, *LW*, *11*, 64.

CHAPTER 2

1. Woodrow Wilson High School and the Wilson community are pseudonyms.
2. For further elaboration of this argument, see Oakes and Wells, 2004.
3. Many scholars have explained the failure of American society to realize the promise of *Brown* by focusing on political resistance to legal change. Far less attention has been paid to political resistance to educational change. Yet, that is the dominant story of the last 35 years. After legal resistance to integration broke down in the late 1960s, cultural and political barriers to equitable education have persisted and in some ways strengthened the hold of unequal educational practices. See, for example, Welner, 2001.
4. Our prior research has shown that "bimodal" Wilson is not unique. Many such schools provide one trajectory of access for a wealthy (largely White and increasingly Asian) population and quite another trajectory for poorer (predominantly African American and Latino) students. These schools exist throughout the nation, and not a few of them are in liberal university towns. See, for example, Oakes, Wells, Yonezawa, and Ray, 2000.
5. See, for example, Guba and Clark, 1978; see also Hargreaves, Lieberman, Fullan, and Hopkins, 1998.
6. For a review of the research on tracking and detracking that is summarized in this chapter, see Oakes, 2005.
7. Oakes, 2005.
8. Oakes, 2005.
9. For a compelling elaboration of this argument regarding merit and competition, see Lemann, 1998.
10. See, for example, Brantlinger, 2003; Horvat, Lareau, and Weininger, 2002; Lipman, 1998; Sapon-Shevin, 1994; Staiger, 2004; Useem, 1992.
11. Oakes, Welner, Yonezawa, and Allen, 1998.
12. For more elaborated discussions of this point, see Brantlinger, 2003; Oakes, Wells, Datnow, and Jones, 1997; Staiger, 2004.
13. Hargreaves, Lieberman, Fullan, and Hopkins, 1998.
14. See, for example, Blase, 1998.
15. As we noted at the outset, conventional strategies are based on knowledge diffusion and planned educational change theory mostly borrowed from the business world. They typically separate the substance of the reform (teaching methods, school reorganization, etc.) from the processes by which educators learn about the reform and believe in it ("buy-in" or "organizational learning").
16. Hargreaves, 2001. For a discussion of the prevailing culture of school reform as a "reform mill," see Oakes, Quartz, Ryan, and Lipton, 2000.
17. Welner, 2001.
18. Datnow, 1997; Wells and Serna, 1996; Welner, 2001.
19. Although we refer broadly to "middle-class" parents, we are mindful of the breadth of self and social identities that that label may encompass or exclude. For

example, many of Wilson's students come from families of extraordinary wealth, yet they typically do not refer to themselves as "upper class" or "wealthy." Similarly, White "working-class" or "poor" families would find those labels embarrassing or pejorative. It may be that when White families send their children to a multiracial public, community school, they are solidifying their middle-class identity, regardless of other class factors.

20. Another way that equity reforms have been thwarted is by declaring victory over the problem. For example, most high schools now report they do not track. And, in fact, few have rigid tracking systems that lock students into the academic, general, and vocational programs that were once commonplace. Rather, as in the schools we studied, high schools today permit their students to "choose" from a menu of courses with varying levels of academic challenge. However, as sociologist Samuel Lucas's analysis concludes, these more flexible arrangements in high schools provide students with no greater opportunity and mobility than the older ones did. The culture of stratification through schooling is uncannily robust. Schools have changed the facade on their inequality structure, but behind the outer wall the rooms all look the same. See Lucas, 1999; Wells and Serna, 2002.

21. See, for example, Balkin, 2001, 2002; Bell, 1980. Jack Balkin is Knight Professor of Constitutional Law and the First Amendment at Yale Law School.

CHAPTER 3

1. West, 2000.
2. Dewey, 1918, "Philosophy and Democracy," *MW, 11,* 51.
3. Dewey, 1932, *Ethics, LW, 7,* 347–348.
4. Dewey, 1922, "Mediocrity and Individuality," *MW, 11,* 289.
5. See, generally, Rogers, 1994.
6. Dewey, 1932, *Ethics, LW, 7,* 350.
7. Dewey noted that the lack of such material conditions was a prime contributor to illiteracy. See, Dewey, 1930, "Our Illiteracy Problem," *LW, 5,* 314.
8. Dewey, 1930, "Philosophy and Education," *LW, 5,* 297; Dewey, 1938, "The Economic Basis of the New Society," *LW, 13,* 320.
9. Dewey, 1918, "Philosophy and Democracy," *MW, 11,* 53.
10. Putnam, 1992, p. 180.
11. Dewey, 1930, "Philosophy and Education," *LW, 5,* 297.
12. Dewey, 1918, "Philosophy and Democracy," *MW, 11,* 53.
13. Dewey, 1927, *The Public and Its Problems, LW, 2,* 339.
14. Dewey, 1897, "Ethical Principles Underlying Education," *EW, 5,* 59.
15. Dewey, 1903, "Emerson—The Philosopher of Democracy," *MW, 3,* 190. Dewey wrote these words in his essay on Emerson, but, as Cornel West argues, it speaks broadly to Dewey's central concern with democratizing knowledge. See West, 1989, p. 75.
16. Dewey, 1899, "The School and Society," *MW, 1,* 16.
17. Dewey, 1916, *Democracy and Education, MW, 9,* 326.
18. Dewey, 1922, "Education as Politics," *MW, 13,* 331.
19. Dewey, 1930, "Our Illiteracy Problem," *LW, 5,* 313.
20. Dewey, 1927, *The Public and Its Problems, LW, 2,* 362.
21. Dewey, 1927, *The Public and Its Problems, LW, 2,* 339.
22. Dewey, 1927, *The Public and Its Problems, LW, 2,* 364, 367.
23. Dewey, 1927, *The Public and Its Problems, LW, 2,* 364.
24. Dewey, 1927, *The Public and Its Problems, LW, 2,* 344.
25. Morris, 1999, p. 619.

26. In the inimitable words of Cornel West: "Critical intelligence is available to all peoples; it is neither the birthright of the highbrow nor the property of the professional." West, 1989, p. 97.

27. Dewey, 1927, *The Public and Its Problems, LW, 2,* 365.

28. Dewey, 1927, *The Public and Its Problems, LW, 2,* 364. This warning and the subsequent discussion on the role of experts served as a direct rebuttal to Walter Lippmann's democratic realism. In language that evokes Lippmann's 1925 text, Dewey spoke of how, in recent years, society had come to be dominated by a new class that claimed to rule "not in virtue of birth and hereditary status, but in virtue of ability in management and of the burden of social responsibilities which it carries, in virtue of the position which superior abilities have conferred upon it."

29. Dewey, 1927, *The Public and Its Problems, LW, 2,* 362–363.

30. Dewey, 1927, *The Public and Its Problems, LW, 2,* 364.

31. In his conclusion to *The Public and Its Problems,* Dewey argued that "It is outside the scope of our discussion to look into the prospects of the reconstruction" of publics. Dewey, 1927, *The Public and Its Problems, LW, 2,* 368. Similarly, he closed his other major work in political philosophy, *Liberalism and Social Action,* by noting: "It is no part of my task to outline in detail a program for renascent liberalism." Dewey, 1935, *Liberalism and Social Action, LW, 11,* 64.

32. Dewey, 1931, "Setting New Goals at 70," *LW, 6,* 407; Dewey, 1931, "Is There Hope for Politics?" *LW, 6,* 188.

33. Dewey, 1931, "Is There Hope for Politics?" *LW, 6,* 230; Dewey, 1932, "Address to the National Association for the Advancement of Colored People," *LW, 6,* 182.

34. Dewey, 1931, "Is There Hope for Politics?" *LW, 6,* 188; Dewey, 1932, "Help for Brookwood," *LW, 6,* 328.

35. Dewey, 1932, "Help for Brookwood," *LW, 6,* 328. Such political education, he argued, offered more hope than efforts of "social agencies" in "character-building" or "faith-restoring."

36. Dewey, 1931, "Is There Hope for Politics?" *LW, 6,* 188.

37. Dewey, 1931, "Is There Hope for Politics?" *LW, 6,* 188; Dewey, 1935, "United, We Shall Stand," *LW, 11,* 350.

38. Dewey, 1935, "United, We Shall Stand," *LW, 11,* 350.

39. Dewey, 1930, "Social Change and Its Human Direction," *LW, 5,* 364.

40. Dewey, 1935, "The Meaning of Liberalism," *LW, 11,* 364.

41. Dewey, 1930, "Social Change and Its Human Direction," *LW, 5,* 346.

42. Dewey, 1928, "Freedom and Workers' Education," *LW, 5,* 331.

43. Dewey, 1935, "United, We Shall Stand," *LW, 11,* 352.

44. Dewey, 1932, "The Economic Situation: A Challenge to Education," *LW, 6,* 130.

45. Dewey, 1935, "The Teacher and the Public," *LW, 11,* 161.

46. Dewey, 1935, "United, We Shall Stand," *LW, 11,* 350.

47. Dewey, 1935, "United, We Shall Stand," *LW, 11,* 350.

48. Dewey, 1927, *The Public and Its Problems, LW, 2,* 365.

49. Dewey, 1927, *The Public and Its Problems, LW, 2,* 364.

50. Dewey, 1903, "Emerson—The Philosopher of Democracy," *MW, 3,* 190.

51. Dewey, 1927, *The Public and Its Problems, LW, 2,* 340.

52. Dewey, 1927, *The Public and Its Problems, LW, 2,* 340.

53. Dewey, 1931, "Is There Hope for Politics?" *LW, 6,* 185; Dewey, 1935, "United, We Shall Stand," *LW, 11,* 350.

54. Dewey, 1932, *Ethics, LW, 7,* 347–348.

55. Dewey, 1899, "The School and Society," *MW*, *1*, 16.

56. Dewey, 1932, "Help for Brookwood," *LW*, *6*, 328.

57. Brown, 1992, pp. 141–178; Collins, 1992. See also Cobb, Confrey, diSessa, Lehrer, and Schauble, 2003, pp. 9–13.

CHAPTER 4

1. That is, Futures came to function as a site of learning and action in which students and adults worked jointly on research into Wilson's "two-school" problem.

2. Dewey, 1935, "United, We Shall Stand," *LW*, *11*, 350.

3. Yonezawa, 1997.

4. MacLeod, 1995.

5. Dewey, 1927, *The Public and Its Problems, LW*, *2*, 339.

6. Dewey, 1927, *The Public and Its Problems, LW*, *2*, 362.

7. Dewey, 1935, "United, We Shall Stand," *LW*, *11*, 350.

8. *Daniel v. California*, 1999.

9. Dewey, 1932, *Ethics, LW*, *7*, 347.

10. Giroux, 1983; Hill Collins, 1990; MacLeod, 1995; Solórzano, 1995, 1998; Solórzano and Delgado Bernal, 2001; Solórzano and Yosso, 2001.

11. Solórzano and Villalpando, 1998, p. 217.

12. Interview with Daniel Solórzano, August 28, 1999.

13. A non-Futures student was selected to serve as a match to each Futures student based on gender, ethnicity, language, limited English proficiency (LEP) status (eighth grade), free/reduced lunch status (eighth grade), special education status (eighth grade), SAT9 standardized test scores in eighth and ninth grade, eighth-grade grade point average (GPA; total, math and science), ninth-grade college prep credits (points), and ninth-grade GPA. The matched group of 60 students entered high school with a GPA of 2.61. Ninth-grade SAT9 scores were comparable between the two groups: both groups scored approximately 30 in reading, and 37 in language; in math the comparison group scored slightly higher, with 43 compared to the Futures score of 33.

14. In 1997, 802 freshmen began their high school career at Wilson High School. Four years later, approximately 60% of those students who entered as ninth graders would graduate from Wilson High School and qualify to enter California's public 4-year universities: 72% of White and Asian students would graduate and qualify. In contrast, Latino and African American students qualified to enter these institutions at almost half that rate. Of the 347 Latino and African American students who graduated 4 years later, 37% qualified to enter California's public 4-year universities (and only 15% enrolled in such institutions). These figures are inflated somewhat by the higher-than-normal rates of college eligibility of the Futures students. Of the 359 Latino and African American students who entered Wilson High School as ninth graders in 1996, 1 year earlier, only 260 (72%) graduated, only 71 (20%) were eligible for California public 4-year universities, and only 28 (8%) enrolled in a California public 4-year university 4 years later. Notably, the percentages attending selective 4-year schools and less selective 2-year schools differed significantly—53% and 26%, respectively, for the Futures students, compared with 15% and 67% for the comparison group. Moreover, only 14% of the Futures students attend college part-time, compared with 48% of their non-Futures peers.

15. National studies find that 59% of African Americans and 68% of Hispanics who enrolled in postsecondary education in 1995–1996 either attained their degree goal or persisted 3 years beyond initial enrollment (Berkner, Horn, & Clune, 2000).

CHAPTER 5

1. This account of teacher inquiry draws on Otoya, 2000, and Rogers, 1999. It also relies on a series of "Reader's Theater" presentations created and performed by teachers at the annual meetings of the American Educational Research Association in Montreal in 1999 and in Seattle in 2001. See Bueno et al., 1999; Rogers et al., 2001.
2. Dewey, 1927, *The Public and Its Problems, LW, 2,* 365.
3. Dewey, 1927, *The Public and Its Problems, LW, 2,* 238.
4. Dewey, 1927, *The Public and Its Problems, LW, 2,* 339.
5. Dewey, 1927, *The Public and Its Problems, LW, 2,* 342.
6. Darling-Hammond, 1996, pp. 5–17.
7. Dewey, 1927, *The Public and Its Problems, LW, 2,* 319.
8. Sirotnik and Oakes, 1986.
9. Transcript of *In Focus,* KLCS television program, March 21, 2001.
10. Dewey, 1927, *The Public and Its Problems, LW, 2,* 345.
11. Whitman, 1860.
12. *Teaching to Change LA* Online Journal, 2001a.
13. *Teaching to Change LA* Online Journal, 2001a.
14. Martínez, 2001.
15. *Teaching to Change LA* Online Journal, 2001a.
16. *Teaching to Change LA* Online Journal, 2001b.
17. *Teaching to Change LA* Online Journal, 2001b.
18. *Teaching to Change LA* Online Journal, 2001b.
19. Dewey, 1927, *The Public and Its Problems, LW, 2,* 368.
20. King, 2000.
21. Bass, 1941, p. 1. This article appeared in *The California Eagle,* which was an African American daily newspaper in Los Angeles.
22. Our account of the Equal Terms Project draws on teacher reflections developed as part of our teacher seminar, as well as notes from public meetings.
23. *Teaching to Change LA* Online Journal, 2004.
24. *Teaching to Change LA* Online Journal, 2004.
25. *Teaching to Change LA* Online Journal, 2004.
26. *Teaching to Change LA* Online Journal, 2004.
27. Dewey, 1927, *The Public and Its Problems, LW, 2,* 367.
28. *Teaching to Change LA* Online Journal, 2004.
29. Dewey, 1927, *The Public and Its Problems, LW, 2,* 368.

CHAPTER 6

1. West, 1993, p. 70. West contrasts Dewey's "standpoint" with that of Marx, who "theorizes from the vantage point of and in solidarity with the industrial working class of nineteenth-century Europe—an exploited, unfranchised, and downtrodden people."
2. Dewey, 1932, "The Economic Situation: A Challenge to Education," *LW, 6,* 130.
3. Our argument here follows Cornel West's sympathetic, but critical, reading of Dewey.
4. Of course, not all social movements are progressive, and nonprogressive movements use many of the same strategies as progressive ones. Our references here, however, are to examples of the literature on progressive movements. For a comprehensive review of the literature on social movements, see Della Porta and Diani, 1999.

5. Stall and Stoecker, 1998; Comm-Org, 2005.

6. Sen, 2003, p. xvii. Sen is codirector of the Center for Third World Organizing, a national network and training center for organizers. Note, also, that Randy Shaw writes in *The Activist's Handbook*, "grassroots activism is increasingly recognized as the most potent counterbalance to a political system dominated by corporations and big money" (Shaw, 2001, p. ix). Additionally, the Web site of PolicyLink, a national advocacy support organization, claims, "throughout history, progress has not spontaneously occurred; it happens because people organize for change." PolicyLink, 2005.

7. Bobo, Kendall, and Max, 2001; Midwest Academy, 2005. The Midwest Academy in Chicago "offers on site training and consulting as well as five day training sessions for leaders and staff of citizen and community groups. The Academy is one of the nation's oldest and best known schools for community organizations, citizen organizations and individuals committed to progressive social change."

8. Stall and Stoecker, 1998, p. 630.

9. Ganz, 2002; see also the many working papers on Ganz's Harvard University Web site at http://ksghome.harvard.edu/~mganz.

10. Bobo, Kendall, and Max, 2001, p. 10.

11. By 2004, ACORN had grown into a national organization of approximately 150,000 dues-paying families in a network of 80 city chapters in 31 states, supported by 720 full-time staff.

12. In 2004, the IAF had 55 affiliates in 21 states, each made up of religious congregations, labor locals, parents' associations, schools, and other community groups. IAF has approximately 150 professional organizers. PICO today claims 1,000 affiliated congregations, schools and other neighborhood institutions comprised of 1 million families in 150 locales.

13. Stoecker, 2001.

14. Bobo, Kendall, and Max, 2001, p. 12.

15. Bobo, Kendall, and Max, 2001, p. 12.

16. See, for example, Coleman, 1990; Putnam, Leonardi, and Nanetti, 1993.

17. Stoecker, 2001.

18. Ganz, 2002.

19. Polletta, 2002.

20. Ganz, 2002.

21. Della Porta and Diani, 1999, p. 178.

22. Della Porta and Diani, 1999.

23. For a more comprehensive discussion of these two traditions, see Stall and Stoecker, 1998.

24. Alinsky, 1971.

25. Alinsky, 1969, 1971; Chambers and Cowan, 2003; Cortes, 1993.

26. Bobo, Kendall, and Max, 2001.

27. Bobo, Kendall, and Max, 2001, p. 10.

28. Bobo, Kendall, and Max, 2001, p. 10.

29. Alinsky, 1971, p. 52.

30. Midwest Academy, 2000.

31. Shaw, 2001.

32. See discussion in Sen, 2003.

33. Warren, 2001.

34. This phrase is taken from the title of Robert Moses' 1989 article, "The Algebra Project: Organizing in the Spirit of Ella."

35. Robnett, 1997.
36. Addams, 1912.
37. The Highlander Center's stated goal is to "provide education and support to poor and working people fighting economic injustice, poverty, prejudice, and environmental destruction. We help grassroots leaders create the tools necessary for building broad-based movements for change." Highlander Center, 2005.
38. Collins, 1992; Dittmer, 1994; Payne, 1995.
39. Moses, Kamii, Swap, and Howard, 1989.
40. Greenberg, 1994, p. 226, as quoted by Robnett, 1997, p. 89.
41. Robnett, 1997.
42. Moses, Kamii, Swap, and Howard, 1989, p. 425.
43. See, for example, North Carolina State University, 2000.
44. Stall and Stoecker, 1998.
45. Stall and Stoecker, 1998, p. 635.
46. Highlander Center, 2005.
47. Highlander Center, 2005.
48. Ransby, 2003, p. 1.
49. Additionally, there is also a growing interest and a much broader range of organizations seeking to engage citizens across race and social class more actively and directly in democratic deliberations about the central political issues of civil society, culture, and democracy—what Benjamin Barber, 1998, has called "strong democracy."
50. Ganz, 2002.
51. Merriam-Webster OnLine, 2005, defines "expert" as "having, involving, or displaying special skill or knowledge derived from training or experience."

CHAPTER 7

1. This account of Parent-U-Turn draws on interviews and correspondence with Parent-U-Turn members. It also relies on Hasan, 2004; Rogers, 2004; Wilson Cooper, 2001.
2. Laila Hasan came to the Parent Curriculum Project in its second year. The project was created by Lois Andre-Bechely with the support of Rae Jeane Williams and Jeannie Oakes.
3. Dewey, 1897, "Ethical Principles Underlying Education," *EW, 5,* 62.
4. Muñoz, 2001.
5. Herrera, 2001.
6. See, for example, *Teaching to Change LA*'s special issue on teacher quality, 2001–2002.
7. Morrell, 2004.
8. See, for example, Kinchloe and McLaren, 1998; Merriam, 1998.
9. Freire, 1997.
10. Finn, 1999; MacLeod, 1995.
11. Solórzano and Delgado Bernal, 2001. Mary's comments reflect the influence of Daniel Solórzano's guest lecture (and article) on what he terms "transformational resistance."
12. Freire, 1997, p. 17.
13. *Teaching to Change LA* Online Journal, 2002–2003.
14. This claim was made in South Gate High School's 2002–2003 School Accountability Report Card.
15. *Teaching to Change LA* Online Journal, 2002–2003.
16. "Ease Up on the Exit Exams," 2003.
17. Herrera, 2003.

18. *Teaching to Change LA* Online Journal, 2002–2003.
19. Herrera, 2003.
20. Lynwood Unified School District Educational Services, 2004.
21. U.S. Census Bureau, 1970, 1980, 1990, and 2000. See also Nicolaides, 2002.
22. Comments of Mayor Henry Gonzalez during a public forum at South Gate Middle School, June 14, 2004.
23. California Basic Educational Data Systems, 2005.
24. For a discussion of the problems associated with multi-track year round schools, see Oakes, 2003.
25. Mary's oration was so impressive that an LAUSD official approached her and told her that he did not believe that the Parent-U-Turn members were "just parents." "I can tell by the way you talk," he added.
26. West, 1993, p. 19.

CHAPTER 8

1. Helfand, 2005, p. B3.
2. CADRE and JMI, 2004, p. 4.
3. We enclose the word "site" within quotation marks here because the EJC does not have a physical location. Rather, it consists of an agreement among the groups to engage in collaborative work.
4. Dewey, 1932, *Ethics, LW,* 7, 347–348.
5. The progressive education group Rethinking Schools offers these examples of critical questions that they believe should be adopted with age-appropriate modifications for classroom use. See Rethinking Schools, 2004.
6. Polletta, 2002; Ganz, 2002.
7. Dewey, 1937, "Democracy Is Radical," *LW, 11,* 298.
8. The key finding has been that variance in achievement test scores can be explained, at least in part, by whether or not students have access to the knowledge and skills that they are expected to learn and whether they have experienced instruction that makes learning possible. McDonnell, 1995.
9. League of Women Voters of California, 2005.
10. Schwarzenegger, 2004.
11. Schwarzenegger, 2004.

CHAPTER 9

1. Bell, 1994; Hochschild, 1984.
2. Whitman, [1871] 1981, p. 495.
3. For a thoughtful discussion of the relationship between schooling and work, see Grubb and Lazerson, 2004.
4. Each of these logics has a long history in American culture. For a discussion of the historical roots of deficit thinking, see Valencia, 1997.
5. See, for example, Solórzano, 1998.
6. See, for example, Reich, 1991.
7. Ehrenreich, 1989.
8. For a related analysis of "triage" in the public sphere, see Williams, 1998.
9. Scholars such as Benjamin Barber, Harry Boyte, and Archon Fung, along with civic leaders such as David Matthews (former Secretary of Health, Education, and Wel-

fare, and currently president of the Kettering Foundation) and Michael Edwards (Ford Foundation program director), among many others, have all issued strong calls for the revitalization of the public sphere. See Barber, 1998; Boyte, 2004; Edwards, 2004; Fung, 2002. Visit http://www.kettering.org for a summary of Matthews's work at the Kettering Foundation.

10. Fung, 2002, p. 67.
11. Fung, 2002, p. 67.
12. Fung, 2002, p. 67.
13. Boyte, 2002.
14. Boyte, 2002.
15. Horton and Freire, 1991, p. 177.
16. Horton and Freire, 1991, p. 164.
17. Mediratta and Fruchter, 2001.
18. Renée, Oakes, and Rogers, 2005.
19. Shirley, 1997, p. 27.
20. Shirley, 1997, 2002. See also Warren, 2001.
21. Gilman, as quoted by Harkavy, 2002, p. 6.
22. Harkavy, 2002, p. 8.
23. Harkavy, 2002, p. 9.
24. Boyte, 2002.
25. Center for Democracy and Citizenship, 2005.
26. Center for Community Partnerships, 2005.
27. National Center for Schools & Communities, 2005.
28. Institute for Education and Social Policy, 2005.
29. Mediratta and Fruchter, 2001.
30. Community Research and Learning Network, 2005.
31. Research for Action, 2005.
32. Anyon, 2005.
33. McAdam, Tarrow, and Tilly, 2001.
34. Anyon, 2005, p. 147.
35. Frankenberg, Lee, and Orfield, 2002.
36. Frankenberg, Lee, and Orfield, 2002; Orfield, Eaton, and Harvard Project on School Desegregation, 1996; Schofield, 1995.
37. For example, the new Change to Win Coalition of unions that have broken away from the AFL-CIO pledging to place greater emphasis on organizing, particularly among low-wage workers, includes the Service Employees (SEIU), Teamsters, UNITE HERE (textile and hotel workers), and UFCW (food and commercial workers). Moberg, 2005.
38. Dewey, 1935, "The Teacher and the Public," *LW, 11*, 161.
39. Dewey, 1935, "The Teacher and the Public," *LW, 11*, 161.
40. Dewey, 1935, "The Teacher and the Public," *LW, 11*, 159.
41. Rose, 2000; Stout, 1996.
42. Anner, 1996.
43. For examples of how widening inequality compromises the quality of life for all, see Kawachi and Kennedy, 2002.
44. Sabl, 2002.
45. Dreier, 2005.

References

Note: All electronic citations herein were accessible at the time of publication (February 2006).

Addams, J. (1912). *Twenty years at Hull-House.* New York: Macmillan.

Alinsky, S. D. (1969). *Reveille for radicals.* New York: Vintage Books.

Alinsky, S. D. (1971). *Rules for radicals; A practical primer for realistic radicals.* New York: Vintage Books.

Anner, J. (1996). *Beyond identity politics: Emerging social justice movements in communities of color.* Boston, MA: South End Press.

Anyon, J. (2005). *Radical possibilities: Public policy, urban education, and a new social movement.* New York: Routledge.

Balkin, J. M. (Ed.). (2001). *What "Brown v. Board of Education" should have said: The nation's top legal experts rewrite America's landmark civil rights decision.* New York: New York University Press.

Balkin, J. M. (2002). Would African-Americans have been better off without *Brown v. Board of Education? The Journal of Blacks in Higher Education, 35,* 102–106.

Barber, B. R. (1998). *A place for us: How to make society civil and democracy strong.* New York: Hill and Wang.

Bass, C. (1941, February 20). Stage mock lynchings of six at local school. *The California Eagle,* p. 1.

Bell, D. (1980). *Brown v. Board of Education* and the interest-convergence dilemma. *Harvard Law Review, 93,* 518.

Bell, D. (1994, May 23). Affirmative reaction: The Freedom of Employment Act. *The Nation, 258*(20).

Berkner, L., Horn, L., & Clune, M. (2000). *Descriptive summary of 1995–96 beginning postsecondary student: Three years later, with an essay on students who started at less-than-4 year institutions.* Washington, DC: National Center for Education Statistics.

Blase, J. (1998). The micropolitics of educational change. In A. Hargreaves, A. Lieberman, M. Fullan, & D. W. Hopkins (Eds.), *International handbook of educational change* (pp. 544–557). London: Kluwer Academic.

Bobo, K., Kendall, J., & Max, S. (2001). *Organizing for social change: Midwest Academy manual for activists* (3rd ed.). Santa Ana, CA: Seven Locks Press.

Boyte, H. C. (2002, November). *A different kind of politics: John Dewey and the meaning of citizenship in the 21st century.* Paper presented at the Dewey Lecture, University of Michigan, Ann Arbor.

Boyte, H. C. (2004). *Everyday politics: Reconnecting citizens and public life.* Philadelphia: University of Pennsylvania Press.

Brantlinger, E. (2003). *Dividing classes: How the middle class negotiates and rationalizes school advantage.* New York: RoutledgeFalmer.

Brown, A. L. (1992). Design experiments: Theoretical and methodological challenges in creating complex interventions in classroom settings. *Journal of the Learning Sciences, 2*(2), 141–178.

Brown v. Board of Education, 347 (U.S. 483 1954).

Bueno, R., Kim, L., Maresso, L., Markoe, S., Otoya, K., & Rogers, J. (1999, April). *Becoming social justice educators: Inquiry, identity, and development of first year urban teachers.* Paper presented at the American Educational Research Association Annual Conference, Montreal.

CADRE & JMI. (2004). *We interrupt this crisis with our side of the story: Relationships between South Los Angeles parents and schools.* Los Angeles: Community Asset Development Redefining Education (CADRE) and Justice Matters Institute (JMI).

California Basic Educational Data Systems. (2005). *Racial and ethnic survey: 1966 Los Angeles City Schools.* Retrieved from http://www.cde.ca.gov/ds/sd/cb/

Center for Community Partnerships. (2005). Center for Community Partnerships. Web site: http://www.upenn.edu/ccp

Center for Democracy and Citizenship. (2005). Center for Democracy and Citizenship. Web site: http://www.publicwork.org

Chambers, E. T., & Cowan, M. A. (2003). *Roots for radicals: Organizing for power, action, and justice.* New York: Continuum.

Cobb, P., Confrey, J., diSessa, A., Lehrer, R., & Schauble, L. (2003). Design experiments in educational research. *Educational Researcher, 32*(1), 9–13.

Coleman, J. S. (1990). *Foundations of social theory.* Cambridge, MA: Belknap Press of Harvard University Press.

Collins, A. (1992). Toward a design science of education. In E. Scanlon & T. O'Shea (Eds.), *New directions in educational technology.* New York: Springer-Verlag.

Comm-Org. (2005). Comm-Org: The On-Line Conference on Community Organizing and Development. Web site: http://comm-org.wisc.edu/

Community Research and Learning Network. (2005). CoRAL. Web site: http://www.coral network.org/

Cortes, E. (1993). Reweaving the fabric: The iron rule and the IAF strategy for power and politics. In H. Cisneros (Ed.), *Interwoven destinies: Cities and the nation* (pp. 294–319). New York: Norton.

Cremin, L. (1961). *The transformation of the school: Progressivism in American education.* New York: Knopf.

Daniel v. California, No. BC214156 (Cal. Super. Ct. 1999).

Darling-Hammond, L. (1996). The right to learn and the advancement of teaching: Research, policy, and practice for democratic education. *Educational Researcher, 25*(6), 5–17.

Datnow, A. (1997). *The gender politics of educational change.* New York: RoutledgeFalmer.

Della Porta, D., & Diani, M. (1999). *Social movements: An introduction.* Oxford: Blackwell.

Dewey, J. (1969–1991). *The collected works of John Dewey, 1882–1953* (37 vols.) (Series Ed. Jo Ann Boydston). Carbondale: Southern Illinois University Press. (Original works published 1882–1953) [The work was published in three series, referenced herein in shorthand form by series and volume number, as follows: *EW, The Early Works, 1882–1898* (Vols. 1–5); *MW, The Middle Works, 1899–1924* (Vols. 1–15); and *LW, The Later Works, 1925–1953* (Vols. 1–17).]

Dewey, J. (1897). Ethical principles underlying education. *EW, 5,* 54–83.

Dewey, J. (1899). The school and society. *MW, 1,* 1–112.

Dewey, J. (1903). Emerson—The philosopher of democracy. *MW, 3,* 184–192.

Dewey, J. (1916). *Democracy and education. MW, 9,* 1–370.

Dewey, J. (1918). Philosophy and democracy. *MW, 11,* 41–53.

Dewey, J. (1922). Mediocrity and individuality. *MW, 11,* 289–294.

Dewey, J. (1922). Education as politics. *MW, 13,* 329–334.

Dewey, J. (1927). *The public and its problems. LW, 2,* 235–372.

Dewey, J. (1928). Freedom and workers' education. *LW, 5,* 331–337.

Dewey, J. (1930). Our illiteracy problem. *LW, 5,* 311–318.

Dewey, J. (1930). Philosophy and education. *LW, 5,* 289–298.

Dewey, J. (1930). Social change and its human direction. *LW, 5,* 363–368.

Dewey, J. (1931). Setting new goals at 70. *LW, 6,* 403–407.

Dewey, J. (1931). Is there hope for politics? *LW, 6,* 182–189.

Dewey, J. (1932). Address to the National Association for the Advancement of Colored People. *LW, 6,* 224–230.

Dewey, J. (1932). *Ethics. LW, 7,* 1–462.

Dewey, J. (1932). Help for Brookwood. *LW, 6,* 328–329.

Dewey, J. (1932). The economic situation: A challenge to education. *LW, 6,* 123–130.

Dewey, J. (1935). *Liberalism and social action. LW, 11,* 1–66.

Dewey, J. (1935). The teacher and the public. *LW, 11,* 158–161.

Dewey, J. (1935). United, we shall stand. *LW, 11,* 348–352.

Dewey, J. (1935). The meaning of liberalism. *LW, 11,* 364–367.

Dewey, J. (1937). Democracy is radical. *LW, 11,* 296–300.

Dewey, J. (1938). The economic basis of the new society. *LW, 13,* 309–322.

Dittmer, J. (1994). *Local people: The struggle for civil rights in Mississippi.* Urbana: University of Illinois Press.

Douglass, F. [1849] (1991). Letter to an abolitionist associate. In K. Bobo, J. Kendall, & S. Max (Eds.), *Organizing for social change: A mandate for activity in the 1990s.* Washington, DC: Seven Locks Press.

Dreier, P. (2005, June 15). Can a city be progressive? *The Nation Online.* Retrieved from http://www.thenation.com/doc/20050704/dreier

Du Bois, W. E. B. (1954, May 31). We rejoice in the word . . . but we must go farther: WEB Du Bois writes on the school desegregation decision. *National Guardian, 6*(32), 5.

Ease up on the exit exams. (2003, March 8). *Los Angeles Times,* p. B24.

Edwards, M. (2004). *Civil society.* Malden, MA: Polity Press; Blackwell.

Ehrenreich, B. (1989). *Fear of falling: The inner life of the middle class.* New York: Pantheon Books.

Finn, P. (1999). *Literacy with an attitude: Educating working class children in their own self interest.* New York: SUNY Press.

Frankenberg, E., Lee, C., & Orfield, G. (2002). *A multiracial society with segregated schools: Are we losing the dream?* Cambridge, MA: Harvard Civil Rights Project.

Freire, P. (1997). *Teachers as cultural workers: Letters to those who dare teach.* Boulder, CO: Westview Press.

Friedlaender, D., & Frankel, S. (2002). *School equity study.* Oakland, CA: Social Policy Research Associates.

Fung, A. (2002). Creating deliberative publics: Governance after devolution and democratic centralism. *The Good Society, 11*(1), 67–71.

Ganz, M. (2002). What is organizing? *Social Policy, 33*(1).

Giroux, H. A. (1983). *Theory and resistance in education: A pedagogy for the opposition.* South Hadley, MA: Bergin & Garvey.

Greenberg, J. (1994). *Crusaders in the courts.* New York: Basic Books.

Grubb, N. W., & Lazerson, M. (2004). *The education gospel: The economic power of schooling.* Cambridge, MA: Harvard University Press.

Guba, E., & Clark, D. L. (1978). Levels of R & D productivity in schools of education. *Educational Researcher, 7*(5), 3–9.

Hargreaves, A. (2001). The emotional geographies of teaching. *Teachers College Record, 103*(6), 1056–1080.

Hargreaves, A., Lieberman, A., Fullan, M., & Hopkins, D. W. (Eds.). (1998). *International handbook of educational change.* London: Kluwer.

Harkavy, I. (2002). *Honoring community, honoring place: Campus Compact reader.* Retrieved from http://www.compact.org/publication/Reader/Fall_2002.PDF

Hasan, A. M. (2004). *Deconstructing and reconstructing parent involvement.* Unpublished doctoral thesis, University of California, Los Angeles, 2004.

Hayasaki, Erika. (2003, May 21). Schools see 'an awakening' of student activism. *Los Angeles Times.*

Helfand, D. (2005, April 14). Parents use newfound clout to demand school improvements. *Los Angeles Times,* p. B3.

Herrera, K. (2003, June 5). Parents say district left them behind. *Wave Newspapers,* p. A1.

Herrera, M. G. (2001). *Letters re: computer access in the Lynwood community.* Retrieved from http://tcla.gseis.ucla.edu/divide/community/lynwood/herrera.html

Highlander Center. (2005). Highlander Research and Education Center. Web site: http://www.highlandercenter.org/

Hill Collins, P. (1990). *Black feminist thought: Knowledge, consciousness, and the politics of empowerment.* Boston: Unwin Hyman.

Hochschild, J. (1984). *The new American dilemma: Liberal democracy and school desegregation.* New Haven, CT: Yale University Press.

Hoffman, L., & Sable, J. (2006). Public elementary and secondary students, staff, schools, and school districts: School year 2003–2004 (NCES 2006-307). Washington, DC: U.S. Department of Education, National Center for Education Statistics.

Horton, M., & Freire, P. (1991). *We make the road by walking: Conversations on education and social change.* Philadelphia: Temple University Press.

Horvat, E. M., Lareau, A., & Weininger, E. B. (2002, April). *From social ties to social capital: Class differences between schools and parent networks.* Paper presented at the Annual Meeting of the Educational Research Association, New Orleans.

In Focus. (2001, March 21). [Broadcast on KLCS, a noncommercial educational television station licensed to the Los Angeles Unified School District.]

Institute for Education and Social Policy. (2005). Institute for Education and Social Policy. Web site: http://www.nyu.edu/iesp/programs/community.html

Kawachi, I., & Kennedy, B. P. (2002). *The health of nations: Why inequality is harmful to your health.* New York: New Press.

Kinchloe, J. L., & McLaren, P. (1998). Rethinking critical qualitative research. In N. Denzin & Y. Lincoln (Eds.), *Handbook of qualitative research* (pp. 260–299). Thousand Oaks, CA: Sage.

King, M. L. (2000). Give us the ballot. In C. Carson, S. Carson, A. Clay, V. Shaldron & K. Taylor (Eds.), *The papers of Martin Luther King, Jr.* (Vol. 4) (pp. 208–215). Berkeley: University of California Press.

League of Women Voters of California. (2005). *Principles.* Retrieved from http://ca.lwv.org/lwvc/aboutlwvc/principles.html

Lemann, N. (1998, April 26). Rewarding the best, forgetting the rest. *New York Times*, p. A12.

Lipman, P. (1998). *Race, class, and power in school restructuring.* Albany: State University of New York Press.

Lippmann, W. (1925). *The phantom public.* New York: Harcourt, Brace.

Lucas, S. (1999). *Tracking inequality.* New York: Teachers College Press.

Lynwood Unified School District Educational Services. (2004). *Memorandum: 04-05:039 on resolution of agreement with Parent U-Turn.* Lynwood, CA: Lynwood Unified School District.

MacLeod, J. (1995). *Ain't no makin' it: Aspirations and attainment in a low-income neighborhood.* Boulder, CO: Westview Press.

Mann, H. (1848). *Twelfth annual report of Horace Mann as Secretary of Massachusetts State Board of Education.*

Martínez, R. (2001). Proposition 227, Stanford 9 and Open Court: Three strikes against English language learners. *Teaching to Change LA, 1*(1). Retrieved from http://tcla.gseis.ucla.edu/democracy/politics/prop227.html

McAdam, D., Tarrow, S. G., & Tilly, C. (2001). *Dynamics of contention.* New York: Cambridge University Press.

McDonnell, L. (1995). Opportunity to learn as a research concept and a policy instrument. *Educational Evaluation and Policy Analysis, 17*(3), 305–322.

Mediratta, K., & Fruchter, N. (2001). *Mapping the field of organizing for school improvement: A report on education organizing in Baltimore, Chicago, Los Angeles, the Mississippi Delta, New York City, Philadelphia, San Francisco and Washington D.C.* New York: Institute for Education and Social Policy, New York University; California Tomorrow; Designs for Change; Southern Echo.

Meier, D. (2000). *Will Standards Save Public Education?* Boston: Beacon Press.

Mendez v. Westminster School District, 64F. Supp. 544 (5.D. Cal. 1946).

Merriam, S. (1998). *Qualitative research and case study applications in education.* San Francisco: Jossey-Bass.

Merriam-Webster OnLine. (2005). *Expert* [Definition]. Retrieved from http://www.m-w.com

Midwest Academy. (2000). The Midwest Academy direct action organizing process. Retrieved from http://www.mindspring.com/~midwestacademy/Organize/page5.html

Midwest Academy. (2005). The Midwest Academy: Training and consulting that works for citizen organizations. Web site: http://www.midwestacademy.com

Moberg, D. (2005). Look who's walking. *The Nation Online.* Retrieved from http://www.thenation.com/doc/20050801/moberg

Morrell, E. (2004). *Becoming critical researchers: Literacy and empowerment for urban youth.* New York: P. Lang.

Morris, D. (1999). How shall we read what we call reality? John Dewey's new science of democracy. *American Journal of Political Science, 43*(2).

Moses, R. P., Kamii, M., Swap, S. M., & Howard, J. (1989). The algebra project: Organizing in the spirit of Ella. *Harvard Educational Review, 59*(4), 423–443.

Muñoz, V. (2001). *Letters re: computer access in the Lynwood community.* Retrieved from http://tcla.gseis.ucla.edu/divide/community/lynwood/vmunoz.html

National Center for Schools & Communities. (2005). National Center for Schools and Communities, Fordham University. Web site: http://www.ncscatfordham.org/pages/home.cfm

Nicolaides, B. M. (2002). *My blue heaven: Life and politics in the working-class suburbs of Los Angeles, 1920–1965.* Chicago: University of Chicago Press.

North Carolina State University. (2000). *We who believe in freedom cannot rest: Ella J. Baker ("Miss Baker") and the birth of the Student Nonviolent Coordinating Committee.* Retrieved from http://www.ncsu.edu/chass/mds/ellahome.html

Nuñez, F. (2005, October 6). Remarks at Inner City Struggle's Award Dinner. Los Angeles, CA.

Oakes, J. (2003). Educational inadequacy, inequality and failed state policy: A synthesis of expert reports prepared for *Williams v. State of California. Santa Clara Law Review, 43*(4), 1299–1398.

Oakes, J. (Ed.). (2004). *Williams v. State of California* (Special Issue). *Teachers College Record, 106*(10 and 11).

Oakes, J. (2005). *Keeping track: How schools structure inequality* (2nd ed.). New Haven, CT: Yale University Press.

Oakes, J., Quartz, K. H., Ryan, S., & Lipton, M. (2000). *Becoming good American schools: The struggle for civic virtue in education reform.* San Francisco: Jossey-Bass.

Oakes, J., & Wells, A. (2004). The comprehensive high school, detracking, and the persistence of social stratification. In F. M. Hammack (Ed.), *A future for the comprehensive high school?* New York: Teachers College Press.

Oakes, J., Wells, A., Datnow, A., & Jones, M. (1997). Detracking: The social construction of ability, cultural politics and resistance to reform. *Teachers College Record, 98*(3), 482–511.

Oakes, J., Wells, A., Yonezawa, S., & Ray, K. (2000). Change agentry and the quest for equity: Lessons from detracking schools. In N. Bascia & A. Hargreaves (Eds.), *The sharp edge of educational change.* London: RoutledgeFalmer.

Oakes, J., Welner, K., Yonezawa, S., & Allen, R. L. (1998). Norms and politics of equity-minded change: Researching the "zone of mediation." In A. Hargreaves, A. Lieberman, M. Fullan, & D. W. Hopkins (Eds.), *International handbook of educational change* (pp. 952–975). London: Kluwer.

Orfield, G. (2001). *Schools more separate: Consequences of a decade of resegregation.* Cambridge, MA: The Civil Rights Project, Harvard University.

Orfield, G., Eaton, S. E., & Harvard Project on School Desegregation. (1996). *Dismantling desegregation: The quiet reversal of* Brown v. Board of Education. New York: New Press.

Otoya, K. B. (2000). *The impact of critical inquiry in teacher development: A multiple case study of eight first-year central city teachers.* Unpublished doctoral thesis, University of California, Los Angeles, 2000.

Payne, C. M. (1995). *I've got the light of freedom: The organizing tradition and the Mississippi freedom struggle.* Berkeley: University of California Press.

Pittman, M. (2002). Commencement 2002: Of alumni and award winners. Harvard Graduate School of Education News. Retrieved from http://www.gse.harvard.edu/news/features/commencement06042002.html

PolicyLink. (2005). *Organizing and coalition building: Increasing your strength.* Retrieved from http://www.policylink.org/AdvocatingForChange/Organizing/

Polletta, F. (2002). *Freedom is an endless meeting: Democracy in American social movements.* Chicago: University of Chicago Press.

Putnam, H. (1990). A reconsideration of Deweyan democracy. *Southern California Law Review, 63*(6), 1671–1697.

Putnam, H. (1992). *Renewing philosophy.* Cambridge, MA: Harvard University Press.

Putnam, R., Leonardi, R., & Nanetti, R. (1993). *Making democracy work: Civic traditions in modern Italy.* Princeton, NJ: Princeton University Press.

Ransby, B. (2003). *Ella Baker and the Black freedom movement: A radical democratic vision.* Chapel Hill: University of North Carolina Press.

Reich, R. B. (1991). *The work of nations: Preparing ourselves for 21st-century capitalism.* New York: A. A. Knopf.

Renée, M., Oakes, J., & Rogers, J. (2005). *IDEA survey of California education organizations.* Los Angeles: UCLA Institute for Democracy Education and Access.

Research for Action. (2005). Research for Action. Web site: http://www.researchforaction .org/index.htm

Rethinking Schools. (2004). Editorial: Teaching against the lies. *Rethinking Schools Online, 18*(4). Retrieved from http://www.rethinkingschools.org/archive/18_04/edit184.shtml

Robnett, B. (1997). *How long? How long? African-American women in the struggle for civil rights.* New York: Oxford University Press.

Rogers, J. (1994). *Education as politics, politics as education: John Dewey and critical intelligence.* Unpublished doctoral thesis, Stanford University, Stanford, CA.

Rogers, J. (1999, April). *Becoming social justice educators: Teacher inquiry as a community of practice.* Paper presented at the American Educational Research Association Annual Conference, Montreal.

Rogers, J. (2004). Creating a public school accountability for California's schools. *Teachers College Record, 106*(11), 2172–2192.

Rogers, J., Goode, J., Morris, C., Herrera, W., Martinez, R., Cooper, K., et al. (2001, April). *Becoming inquirers: How early career teachers learn through inquiry.* Paper presented at the American Educational Research Association Annual Conference, Seattle.

Rose, F. (2000). *Coalitions across the class divide: Lessons from the labor, peace, and environmental movements.* Ithaca, NY: Cornell University Press.

Sabl, A. (2002). *Ruling passions: Political offices and democratic ethics.* Princeton, NJ: Princeton University Press.

Sapon-Shevin, M. (1994). *Playing favorites: Gifted education and the disruption of community.* Albany: State University of New York Press.

Schofield, J. W. (1995). Review of research on school desegregation's impact on elementary and secondary school students. In J. Banks & C. McGee Banks (Eds.), *Handbook for research on multicultural education.* New York: Simon & Schuster Macmillan.

Schwarzenegger, A. (2004). *The capitol morning report.* Sacramento: Office of the Governor of California.

Sen, R. (2003). *Stir it up: Lessons in community organizing and advocacy.* San Francisco: Jossey-Bass.

Shaw, R. (2001). *The activist's handbook: A primer for the 1990s and beyond.* Berkeley: University of California Press.

Shirley, D. (1997). *Community organizing for urban school reform.* Austin: University of Texas Press.

Shirley, D. (2002). *Valley Interfaith and school reform: Organizing for power in South Texas.* Austin: University of Texas Press.

Sirotnik, K., & Oakes, J. (1986). Critical inquiry for school renewal. In K. Sirotnik & J. Oakes (Eds.), *Critical perspectives on the organizaton and improvement of schooling* (pp. 3–94). Boston: Kluwer-Nijhoff.

Solórzano, D. G. (1995). The doctorate production and baccalaureate origins of African-Americans in the sciences and engineering. *Journal of Negro Education, 64*(1), 15–32.

Solórzano, D. G. (1998). Critical race theory, race and gender microaggressions, and the experience of Chicana and Chicano scholars. *Qualitative Studies in Education, 11*(1), 121–136.

Solórzano, D. G., & Delgado Bernal, D. (2001). Examining transformational resistance through a critical race and LatCrit theory framework: Chicana and Chicano students in an urban context. *Urban Education, 36*(3), 308–342.

Solórzano, D. G., & Villalpando, O. (1998). Critical race theory, marginality, and the experience of minority students in higher education. In C. Torres & T. Mitchell (Eds.), *Emerging issues in the sociology of education: Comparative perspectives* (pp. 211–224). Albany: State University of New York Press.

Solórzano, D. G., & Yosso, T. J. (2001). Maintaining social justice hopes within academic realities: A Freirean approach to critical race/LatCrit pedagogy. *Denver University Law Review, 78*(4), 595–621.

Staiger, A. (2004). Whiteness as giftedness: Racial formation at an urban high school. *Social Problems, 51,* 161–182.

Stall, S., & Stoecker, R. (1998). Community organizing or organizing community? Gender and the crafts of empowerment. *Gender and Society, 12*(6), 729–756.

Stoecker, R. (2001). *Report to the West Bank CDC: Primer on community organizing.* Retrieved from http://comm-org.wisc.edu/cr/crreportc.htm

Stout, L. (1996). *Bridging the class divide: And other lessons for grassroots organizing.* Boston: Beacon Press.

Teaching to Change LA Online Journal. (2001a). Democracy 2000. *Teaching to Change LA, 1*(1). Retrieved from http://www.tcla.gseis.ucla.edu/democracy/home.html

Teaching to Change LA Online Journal. (2001b). The digital divide. *Teaching to Change LA, 1*(2). Retrieved from http://www.tcla.gseis.ucla.edu/divide/index.html

Teaching to Change LA Online Journal. (2001–2002). An educational bill of rights. *Teaching to Change LA, 2*(1–7). Retrieved from http://www.tcla.gseis.ucla.edu/rights/index.html

Teaching to Change LA Online Journal. (2002–2003). TCLA's school report card. *Teaching to Change LA, 3*(1–5). Retrieved from http://www.tcla.gseis.ucla.edu/reportcard/archive/issue1_5.html

Teaching to Change LA Online Journal. (2004). Equal terms in LA: The struggle for educational justice, 1954–2004. Equal terms: Youth Summit 2004. *Teaching to Change LA, 4*(3). Retrieved from http://www.tcla.gseis.ucla.edu/equalterms/index.html

U.S. Census Bureau. (1970). *United States census.* Washington, DC: U.S. Census Bureau.

U.S. Census Bureau. (1980). *United States census.* Washington, DC: U.S. Census Bureau.

U.S. Census Bureau. (1990). *United States census.* Washington, DC: U.S. Census Bureau.

U.S. Census Bureau. (2000). *United States census.* Washington, DC: U.S. Census Bureau.

Useem, E. L. (1992). Middle schools and math groups: Parents' involvement in children's placement. *Sociology of Education, 65,* 263–279.

Valencia, R. (1997). *The evolution of deficit thinking: Educational thought and practice.* Washington, DC: Falmer Press.

Warren, M. R. (2001). *Dry bones rattling: Community building to revitalize American democracy.* Princeton, NJ: Princeton University Press.

Wells, A., & Serna, I. (1996). The politics of culture: Understanding local political resistance to detracking in racially mixed schools. *Harvard Educational Review, 66*(1), 93–118.

Wells, A., & Serna, I. (2002). Choosing tracks: How students structure inequality. *American Educational Research Journal, 39*(1), 37–68.

Welner, K. (2001). *Legal rights, local wrongs: When community control collides with educational equity.* Albany: State University of New York Press.

West, C. (1989). *The American evasion of philosophy.* Madison: University of Wisconsin Press.

West, C. (1993). *Race matters.* New York: Random House.

West, C. (2000, November). *Cornel West's opening remarks.* Speech presented at the Coalition of Essential Schools Fall Forum 2000: Essential Teaching and Learning, Providence, RI. Retrieved from http://www.essentialschools.org/pub/ces_docs/fforum/2000/speeches/west_00.html

West, C. (2004). *Democracy matters: Winning the fight against imperialism.* New York: Penguin Press.

Whitman, W. (1860). *Leaves of grass.* Boston: Thayer and Eldridge.

Whitman, W. [1871] (1981). Democratic vistas. In L. Buell (Ed.), *Leaves of grass and selected prose* (pp. 468–524). New York: Random House.

Williams v. California, No. 312236. First amended complaint for injunctive and declaratory relief (Cal. Super. Ct. 2000).

Williams v. State of California, No. 312236 (Cal. Super. Ct. 2005).

Williams, P. J. (1998). *Seeing a color-blind future: The paradox of race.* New York: Noonday Press.

Wilson Cooper, C. (2001). *Perceptions of the parent curriculum project's program goals and effectiveness in the Lynwood Unified School District* (UCLA Outreach and Evaluation Occasional Report Series No. 2). Los Angeles: UCLA Graduate School of Education and Information Studies.

Yonezawa, S. S. (1997). *Making decisions about students' lives: An interactive study of secondary school students' academic program selection.* Unpublished doctoral thesis, University of California, Los Angeles, 1997.

Index

Names of schools and individuals that appear in quotation marks are pseudonyms. Page numbers followed by an "*f*" indicate illustrative material, and those followed by an "*n*" indicate material in the Notes section of the text.

About the Authors

JEANNIE OAKES is Presidential Professor in Educational Equity and Director of UCLA's Institute for Democracy, Education, and Access. She studies and writes about schooling inequalities and the struggle for more socially just schools, including in her previous books: *Keeping Track: How Schools Structure Inequality, Becoming Good American Schools: The Struggle for Civic Virtue in Education Reform,* and *Teaching to Change the World.* Oakes has received three major awards from the American Educational Research Association. She is also the recipient of Southern Christian Leadership Conference's Ralph David Abernathy Award for Public Service and a member of the National Academy of Education.

JOHN ROGERS is the Associate Director of UCLA's Institute for Democracy, Education, and Access and the founding editor of *Teaching to Change LA,* an online journal. He studies strategies for engaging urban youth, community members, and teachers in efforts to make schools powerful and democratic sites for learning. Rogers has received awards for his work on educational equity from the American Civil Liberties Union and the Southern California Library for Social Studies and Research.

MARTIN LIPTON is Communications Analyst at UCLA's Institute for Democracy, Education, and Access. A former public high school teacher, Lipton has had a parallel career as education writer and consultant. His photographs, appearing in this book and elsewhere, portray the disappointments and possibilities for educational justice in urban schools and communities.